Microsoft Power
Performance
Best Practices

A comprehensive guide to building consistently fast
Power BI solutions

Bhavik Merchant

BIRMINGHAM—MUMBAI

Microsoft Power BI Performance Best Practices

Copyright © 2022 Packt Publishing

Publishing Product Manager: Ali Abidi
Senior Editor: David Sugarman
Content Development Editor: Priyanka Soam
Technical Editor: Devanshi Ayare
Copy Editor: Safis Editing
Project Coordinator: Aparna Ravikumar Nair
Proofreader: Safis Editing
Indexer: Rekha Nair
Production Designer: Jyoti Chauhan
Marketing Coordinator: Priyanka Mhatre

First published: April 2022

Production reference: 1240322

Published by Packt Publishing Ltd.
Livery Place
35 Livery Street
Birmingham
B3 2PB, UK.

ISBN 978-1-80107-644-9

www.packt.com

"Like so many other authors, I dedicate this book, first and foremost, to my wife and 5-year-old son. The little one especially, for being a real trooper and reluctantly allowing me many hours on weekends to write this book instead of spending time with him. I didn't realize how critical their support was until I reached the final chapters, as the long months with COVID were even more challenging for us with some personal and professional hurdles to overcome. Despite being isolated and in a new country, they kept encouraging me and celebrating my small wins each time a chapter draft or review was done. My deepest, heartfelt gratitude goes out to them both.

I also want to thank everyone I worked with during my time at Microsoft in the Power BI product team. I learned a lot from many experts, such as the CAT team, architects, engineering managers, and deep subject matter experts in areas such as reports. The list is long, and I prefer not to name anyone for fear of missing someone out! I really hope that all their knowledge, coupled with my own experiences serving innovative customers around the world, will help you take your Power BI solutions to the next level."

Foreword

Ask anyone who has ever presented at a database conference, written blog posts about databases, or recorded videos about them, what the most popular database-related topic is and they will all tell you the same thing: performance tuning. While a skilfully crafted conference presentation on database design best practices will draw a good number of attendees, a basic presentation on performance tuning will draw the crowds. Why is this? I think it's because the goal of performance tuning is so simple: you have something slow and you need to make it fast. It's the struggle that every DBA, report developer, or business analyst faces every day of their professional life. Speed represents usability, faster decisions, happy users, and, ultimately, success. Some people have gained minor celebrity status and undertaken lucrative careers by being able to make your queries and calculations go faster.

Power BI is no different from any other BI tool or database in this respect. One of the most common causes of failure, and certainly the most common cause of complaints, for any BI project is poor report performance. In general, Power BI is extremely fast, even when you're working with relatively large amounts of data, but if you make a mistake somewhere, write a complex calculation incorrectly, or fail to model your data in the right way, for example, you will end up in trouble. As a Power BI professional, it's essential that you know how to design for performance, how to troubleshoot your reports when things go wrong, and how to rectify your errors.

All of this is why Bhavik's book is so important. Even though performance tuning is such an important and popular topic, I believe this is the first book that has ever been dedicated to performance tuning Power BI. It brings together hints, tips, and best practices that have been scattered around the official documentation, blog posts, videos, and training courses and is enriched by the author's years of personal experience as a program manager on the Power BI development team working with some of the largest Power BI customers in the world. Rather than focusing on one particular aspect of performance tuning, such as DAX, it looks at the subject holistically. As a result, you're holding in your hands (or maybe viewing on your screen) an invaluable resource that could make the difference between the success or the failure of your Power BI project. Study it carefully and follow its advice!

Christopher Webb

Principal Program Manager, Power BI CAT Team; 13 year MVP and author of multiple SSAS and Power BI titles

Contributors

About the author

Bhavik Merchant has nearly 18 years of in-depth BI experience. He is a director of product analytics at Salesforce. Prior to that, he was at Microsoft, first as a cloud solution architect, and then as a product manager in the Power BI engineering team. At Power BI, he led the customer-facing insights program, being responsible for the strategy and technical framework to deliver system-wide usage and performance insights to customers. Before Microsoft, Bhavik spent years managing high-caliber consulting teams, delivering enterprise-scale BI projects. He has delivered much technical and theoretical BI training over the years, including expert Power BI performance training that he developed for top Microsoft partners globally.

About the reviewers

Suresh Datla has been in the IT Industry for over two decades and has vast experience across multiple Business and Technology domains. He is an Architect, Adviser, Evangelist, and Trainer. He has been working on Azure and Power Platform since their inception and he also works very closely with the Microsoft team developing industry vertical solutions. He is a speaker at Microsoft-sponsored events on Power Platform, Power BI, Power BI Premium, Security, and Performance. He organizes the Southern California Power Platform User Group every month and strongly believes that the success of a platform lies in the strength of the community. Suresh is the principal at Synergis Consulting and leads a group of Data Architects, Designers, Engineers, and Developers.

Vishwanath Muzumdar has more than 8 years' experience in information technology consulting, business analysis, business development, and business process management in the BI space.

He is an MS Power BI developer (champion) in the creation of powerful visual reporting for clients. His goal is to utilize his strong prioritization skills, analytical ability, team management skills, and expertise in the Microsoft Power BI reporting tool in order to achieve organizational objectives.

Table of Contents

3

DirectQuery Optimization

Part 2: Performance Analysis, Improvement, and Management

4

Analyzing Logs and Metrics

5

Desktop Performance Analyzer

6

Third-Party Utilities

7

Governing with a Performance Framework

Part 3: Fetching, Transforming, and Visualizing Data

8

Loading, Transforming, and Refreshing Data

9
Report and Dashboard Design

Part 4: Data Models, Calculations, and Large Datasets

10
Data Modeling and Row-Level Security

11
Improving DAX

12
High-Scale Patterns

Part 5: Optimizing Premium and Embedded Capacities

13
Optimizing Premium and Embedded Capacities

14

Embedding in Applications

Index

Other Books You May Enjoy

Preface

It is very easy to start building analytical solutions in Power BI. Insightful content can take on a life of its own and grow in terms of popularity and volume of data accessed. If you have not planned for this scale appropriately, you can hit performance problems in many different areas. This book can help by comprehensively covering performance optimization for every layer of Power BI, from the report canvas to data modeling, transformations, storage, and architecture.

Developers and architects working with Power BI will be able to put their knowledge to work with this practical guide to design and implement solutions at every stage of the analytics solution life cycle. This book not only is a unique collection of best practices and tips but also provides you with a structured process and hands-on approach to identifying and fixing common performance issues.

Complete with explanations of essential concepts and practical examples, you'll learn about common design choices that affect performance and consume more resources and how to avoid these problems. You'll grasp general architectural issues and settings that affect most solutions broadly. As you progress, you'll walk through each layer of a typical Power BI solution, learning how to ensure your designs can perform well and handle scale while not sacrificing usability. You'll focus on the data layer and then work your way up to report design. We will also cover Power BI Premium, including capacity planning and load testing, and the usage of Azure services for additional scale.

By the end of this Power BI book, you'll be able to confidently maintain well-performing Power BI solutions with reduced effort. You'll know how to use freely available tools and a systematic process to monitor and diagnose performance problems.

Who this book is for

This book is for data analysts, **business intelligence (BI)** developers, and other data professionals who have learned the basics of Power BI. They will find this BI book useful when they want to build solutions that will perform at their best and scale well with large data and user volumes. It will also prove useful to help diagnose and resolve existing performance issues. Familiarity with the major components of Power BI and a beginner-level understanding of their purposes and use cases are required.

What this book covers

Chapter 1, Setting Targets and Identifying Problem Areas, describes a Power BI solution as a stream of data from multiple sources reaching consumers in a consolidated fashion. We'll look at how data can be stored in Power BI and the different paths it can take before reaching a user. Many of the initial architectural design choices made in the early stages of the solution are very difficult and costly to switch later. That's why it is important to have a solid grasp of the implications of those choices and how to decide what's best at the start.

Chapter 2, Exploring Power BI Architecture and Configuration, provides general guidance to improve throughput and latency. This chapter also looks at data storage modes in Power BI and how the data reaches the data model since choices here affect dataset size and freshness. This chapter also covers how best to deploy Power BI gateways, which are commonly used to connect to external data sources. This is important because users often demand up-to-date data, historical data, and can number thousands in parallel.

Chapter 3, DirectQuery Optimization, explores DirectQuery, which relies on an external data source. It is a common storage choice in Power BI when organizations have very large datasets. These sources are often not designed for analytical queries and significantly reduce report and data refresh performance. We will cover optimizations that can be made in both Power BI and the external source to avoid hitting limits too quickly.

Chapter 4, Analyzing Logs and Metrics, describes how performance can only be improved if it can be measured objectively. Therefore, this chapter covers all the sources of performance data and how to make sense of the information provided to identify the parts of the solution that are bottlenecks. This includes useful native and third-party utilities. We also provide guidelines to help monitor and manage performance continuously.

Chapter 5, Desktop Performance Analyzer, describes the easiest way to see where time is being spent in reports. This is done using Power BI Desktop Performance Analyzer to get detailed breakdowns for every user action, on a per-visual basis. This chapter details all the features, highlights, and issues to be aware of, explains what the metrics mean, and demonstrates how to interpret and act on the data.

Chapter 6, Third-Party Utilities, describes some popular third-party utilities that are effective in performance investigation and tuning. This chapter walks through typical use cases around connecting them to Power BI, collecting metrics, and what to look for when diagnosing performance problems.

Chapter 7, Governing with a Performance Framework, describes how the metrics and tools covered in earlier chapters are essential building blocks for performance management. However, success is more likely with a structured and repeatable approach to build performance-related thinking into the entire Power BI solution life cycle. This chapter provides guidelines to set up data-driven processes to avoid sudden scale issues for new content and prevent degradations for existing content. We also discuss typical roles in analytics projects, ranging from self-service to centrally governed analytics, and we suggest what they can do to help with performance improvement efforts.

Chapter 8, Loading, Transforming, and Refreshing Data, introduces how loading data periodically is a critical part of any analytical system, and in Power BI, this applies to Import mode datasets. Data refresh operations in Import mode are some of the most CPU- and memory-intensive, which can lead to long delays or failures, especially with large datasets. This can leave users with stale data, slow down development significantly, or even overload capacities with expensive data refreshes. Therefore, data transformations should be designed with performance in mind.

Chapter 9, Report and Dashboard Design, focuses on how reports and dashboards are the "tip of the iceberg" in a Power BI solution since that's what consumers interact with regularly. Regardless of how it's exposed, this core visual layer of Power BI is a JavaScript application running in a browser. This chapter covers important considerations and practices to apply regarding visual layout, configuration, and slicing/filtering. It also looks at paginated reports, which behave differently from interactive reports and have special performance considerations.

Chapter 10, Data Modeling and Row-Level Security, describes how the Power BI dataset is where data lands after being shaped, and from where data is retrieved for analysis. Hence, it is arguably the most critical piece, at the core of a Power BI solution. Power BI's feature richness and modeling flexibility provide alternatives when modeling data. Some choices can make development easier at the expense of query performance and/or dataset size. This chapter provides guidance on model design, dataset size reduction, and faster relationships. We then cover recommended practices to optimize row-level security.

Chapter 11, Improving DAX, describes how DAX formulas allow BI developers to add a diverse range of additional functionality to the model. The same correct result can be achieved by writing different DAX formulas without realizing that one version may be significantly slower in a certain query or visual configuration. This chapter highlights common DAX issues and recommended practices to get calculations performing at their best.

Chapter 12, High-Scale Patterns, describes how the amount of data that organizations collect and process is increasing all the time, leading to challenges with big data. Even with Power BI's data compression technology, it isn't always possible to load and store massive amounts of data in an Import mode dataset in a reasonable amount of time. This problem is worse when you need to support hundreds or thousands of users in parallel. This chapter covers the options available to deal with such issues by using Power BI Premium, Azure technologies, composite models, and aggregations.

Chapter 13, Optimizing Premium and Embedded Capacities, covers how Power BI Premium offers dedicated capacity, higher limits, and many additional capabilities, such as paginated reports and AI. We cover Premium Gen2 in this chapter and explain how the system deals with excessive load and how autoscale works. We will also cover available workload settings that can affect performance. We will learn how to plan for the right capacity size and how to perform load testing. We'll also learn how to use the Capacity Metrics app to identify and troubleshoot capacity load issues.

Chapter 14, Embedding in Applications, covers how embedding Power BI content in a custom web app is a great way to expose data analytics within a completely customized UI experience, along with other non-Power BI-related content. This pattern introduces additional considerations since the Power BI application is hosted externally via API calls. This chapter looks at how to do this efficiently.

To get the most out of this book

Some chapters in this book come with sample files that you can open in Power BI Desktop to explore the concepts and enhancements we provide. The examples largely show designs before and after performance improvements have been implemented. Therefore, it is not mandatory to review these examples, but they do provide useful context and can help teach new concepts through hands-on experience.

Software/hardware covered in the book	Operating system requirements
Power BI Desktop	Windows
DAX Studio 2.17.3	
Tabular Editor 3	
Power BI Helper 12.0	

We always recommend having the latest version of Power BI Desktop available due to the monthly release cycle.

If you are using the digital version of this book, we advise you to type the code yourself or access the code from the book's GitHub repository (a link is available in the next section). Doing so will help you avoid any potential errors related to the copying and pasting of code.

Download the example code files

You can download the example code files for this book from GitHub at `https://github.com/PacktPublishing/Microsoft-Power-BI-Performance-Best-Practices`. If there's an update to the code, it will be updated in the GitHub repository.

We also have other code bundles from our rich catalog of books and videos available at `https://github.com/PacktPublishing/`. Check them out!

Download the color images

We also provide a PDF file that has color images of the screenshots and diagrams used in this book. You can download it here: `https://static.packt-cdn.com/downloads/9781801076449_ColorImages.pdf`.

Conventions used

There are a number of text conventions used throughout this book.

`Code in text`: Indicates code words in text, database table names, folder names, filenames, file extensions, pathnames, dummy URLs, user input, and Twitter handles. Here is an example: "Simply paste the following script into the tool, run it, then restart `TabularEditor` to have the rules available."

A block of code is set as follows:

```
System.Net.WebClient w = new System.Net.WebClient();
string path = System.Environment.GetFolderPath(System.Environment.SpecialFolder.LocalApplicationData);
string url = "https://raw.githubusercontent.com/microsoft/Analysis-Services/master/BestPracticeRules/BPARules.json";
string downloadLoc = path+@"\TabularEditor\BPARules.json";
w.DownloadFile(url, downloadLoc);
```

Bold: Indicates a new term, an important word, or words that you see onscreen. For instance, words in menus or dialog boxes appear in **bold**. Here is an example: "The **Workloads** section contains settings relevant to performance."

> **Tips or Important Notes**
> Appear like this.

Get in touch

Feedback from our readers is always welcome.

General feedback: If you have questions about any aspect of this book, email us at customercare@packtpub.com and mention the book title in the subject of your message.

Errata: Although we have taken every care to ensure the accuracy of our content, mistakes do happen. If you have found a mistake in this book, we would be grateful if you would report this to us. Please visit www.packtpub.com/support/errata and fill in the form.

Piracy: If you come across any illegal copies of our works in any form on the internet, we would be grateful if you would provide us with the location address or website name. Please contact us at copyright@packt.com with a link to the material.

If you are interested in becoming an author: If there is a topic that you have expertise in and you are interested in either writing or contributing to a book, please visit authors.packtpub.com.

Share Your Thoughts

Once you've read *Microsoft Power BI Performance Best Practices*, we'd love to hear your thoughts! Scan the QR code below to go straight to the Amazon review page for this book and share your feedback.

https://packt.link/r/1-801-07644-8

Your review is important to us and the tech community and will help us make sure we're delivering excellent quality content.

Part 1: Architecture, Bottlenecks, and Performance Targets

In this part, we will have a high-level review of the Power BI architecture and identify areas where performance can be affected by design choices. After this part, you will know how to define realistic performance targets.

This part comprises the following chapters:

- *Chapter 1, Setting Targets and Identifying Problem Areas*
- *Chapter 2, Exploring Power BI Architecture and Configuration*
- *Chapter 3, DirectQuery Optimization*

1
Setting Targets and Identifying Problem Areas

Many people would consider report performance as the most critical area to focus on when trying to improve the speed of an analytics solution. This is largely true, because it is the most visible part of the system used by pretty much every class of user, from administrators to business executives. However, you will learn that there are other areas of a complete solution that should be considered if performance is to be managed comprehensively. For example, achieving good performance in the reporting layer might be of no consequence if the underlying dataset that powers the report takes a long time to be refreshed or is susceptible to failures due to resource limits or system limits being reached. In this case, users may have great-looking, fast reports that do not provide value due to the data being stale.

The author of this book has experienced the effects of poor report performance firsthand. In one project, a large utility company underwent a large migration from one reporting platform to another, from a different vendor. Even though the new platform was technically and functionally superior, the developers tried to copy the old reporting functionality across exactly. This led to poor design choices and very slow report performance. Millions of dollars in licensing and consulting fees were spent, yet most users refused to adopt the new system because it slowed them down so much. While it is extreme, this example demonstrates the potential ramifications when you do not build good performance into an analytical solution.

In this chapter, you will begin your journey to achieving good and consistent performance in Microsoft Power BI. To introduce the full scope of performance management, we will describe a Power BI solution as a stream of data from multiple sources being consolidated and presented to data analysts and information workers. We look at how data can be stored in Power BI and the different paths it can take before reaching a user. Many of the initial architectural design choices made in the early stages of the solution are very difficult and costly to change later. Hence, it is important to have a solid grasp of the implications of these choices and use a data-driven approach to help us decide what is best right at the start.

An area of performance management that is easily overlooked is that of setting performance targets. How do you know whether the experience you are delivering is great, merely acceptable, or poor? We will begin by exploring this theoretical area first to define our goals before diving into technical concepts.

This chapter is broken into the following sections:

- Defining good performance
- Considering areas that can slow you down
- Which choices affect performance?

Defining good performance

With the advent of ever-faster computers and the massive scale of processing available today by way of cloud computing, business users expect and demand analytical solutions that perform well. This is essential for competitive business decision making. **Business Intelligence (BI)** software vendors echo this need and tend to promise quick results in their sales and marketing materials. These expectations mean that it is uncommon to find users getting excited about how fast reports are or how fresh data is because it is something implicit to them having a positive experience. Conversely, when users have to wait a long time for a report to load, they are quite vocal and tend to escalate such issues via multiple channels. When these problems are widespread it can damage the reputation of both a software platform such as Power BI and the teams involved in building and maintaining those solutions. In the worst possible case, users may refuse to adopt these solutions and management may begin looking for alternative platforms. It's important to think about performance from the onset because it is often very costly and time-consuming to fix performance after a solution has reached production, potentially affecting thousands of users.

Report performance goals

Today, most BI solutions are consumed via a web interface. A typical report consumption experience involves not just opening a report, but also interacting with it. In Power BI terms, this translates to opening a report and then interacting with filters, slicers, and report visuals, and navigating to other pages explicitly or via bookmarks and drilling through. With each report interaction, the user generally has a specific intention, and the goal is to not interrupt their flow. A term commonly used in the industry is *analysis at the speed of thought*. This experience and the related expectations are very similar to navigating regular web pages or interacting with a web-based software system.

Therefore, defining good performance for a BI solution can take some cues from the many studies on web and user interface performance that have been performed over the past two or three decades; it is not a complex task. Nah, F. (2004) conducted a study focusing on **tolerable wait time (TWT)** for web users. TWT was defined as how long users are willing to wait before abandoning the download of a web page. Nah reviewed many previous studies that explored the thresholds at which users' behavioral intentions get lost and also when their attitudes begin to become negative. From this research, we can derive that a well-performing Power BI report should completely load a page or the result of an interaction ideally in less than 4 seconds and in most cases not more than 12 seconds. We should always measure report performance from the user's perspective, which means we measure from the time they request the report (for example, click a report link on the Power BI web portal) until the time the last report visual finishes drawing its results on the screen.

Setting realistic performance targets

Now that we have research-based guidance to set targets, we need to apply it to real-world scenarios. A common mistake is to set a single performance target for every report in the organization and to expect it to be met every single time a user interacts. This approach is flawed because even a well-designed system with heavy optimization could be complex enough to never meet an aggressive performance target. For example, very large dataset sizes (tens of GB) combined with complex nested DAX calculations that are then displayed on multiple hierarchical levels of granularity in a **Table** visual will naturally need significant time to be processed and displayed. This would generally not be the case with a report working over a small data model (tens of MB) containing a row of simple sum totals, each displayed within a **Card** visual.

Due to the variability of the solution complexity and other factors beyond the developer's control (such as the speed of a user's computer or which web browser they use) it is recommended that you think of performance targets in terms of *typical user experience* and acknowledge that there may be exceptions and outliers. Therefore, the performance target metric should consider what the majority of users experience. We recommend report performance metrics that use the 90th percentile of the report load or interaction duration, often referred to as *P90*. Applying the research guidance on how long a user can wait before becoming frustrated, a reasonable performance target would be P90 report load duration of 10 seconds or less. This means 90% of report loads should occur in under 10 seconds.

However, a single target such as P90 is still not sufficient and we will introduce further ideas about this in *Chapter 7, Governing with a Performance Framework*. For now, we should consider that there may be different levels of complexity, so it is recommended to set up a range of targets that reflect the complexity of solutions and the tolerance levels of users and management alike. The following table presents an example of a performance target table that could be adopted in an organization:

	Typical Report	Complex Report
P90 Duration Target	Under 10 Seconds	Under 25 Seconds

Figure 1.1   Example Power BI report performance targets

Next, we will take a look at Power BI from a high level to get a broad understanding of the areas that need to be considered for performance improvement.

Considering areas that can slow you down

The next step in our performance management journey is to understand where time is spent. A Power BI solution is ultimately about exposing data to a user and can be thought of as a flow of data from source systems or data stores, through various Power BI system components, eventually reaching a user through a computer or mobile device. A simplified view of a Power BI solution is presented in *Figure 1.2*:

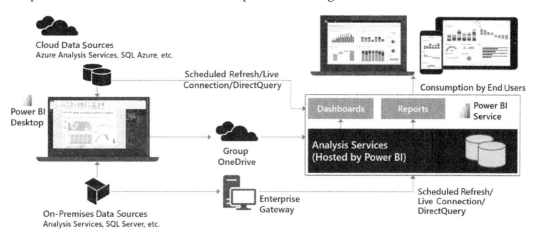

Figure 1.2 – Simplified overview of a Power BI solution

Next, we will briefly focus on the different parts of a typical solution to explain why each piece has important considerations for users and the effect poor performance can have. Some of these areas will be covered in more detail in *Chapter 2, Exploring Power BI Architecture and Configuration*.

Connecting data sources

The following diagram highlights the areas of the solution that are affected when data sources and connectivity methods do not perform well:

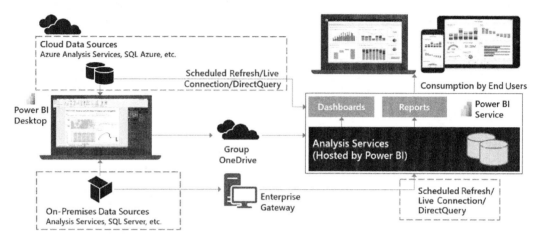

Figure 1.3 – Areas affected by data source and connectivity issues

Import mode

When using **Import mode** datasets, developers can experience sluggish user interface responsiveness when working with **Power Query** or M in Power BI Desktop. In extreme cases, this can extend data transformation development from hours to days. Once the solution is deployed, problems in this area can cause refresh times to extend or fail. The Power BI service has a refresh limit of 2 hours, while Power BI Premium extends this to 5 hours. Any refresh hitting this time limit will be canceled by the system.

DirectQuery mode

DirectQuery mode leaves the data at the source and needs to fetch data and process it within Power BI for almost every user interaction. Issues with this part of the configuration most often cause slow reports for users. Visuals will take a longer time to load, and users may get frustrated and then interrupt and interact with other views or filter conditions. This itself can issue more queries and ironically slow down the report even further by placing additional load on the external source system.

Live connection mode

Live connection mode originally referred exclusively to connections to external Analysis Services deployments, which could be cloud-native (Azure Analysis Services) or on-premises (SQL Server Analysis Services). More recently, this mode was extended to more use cases with the introduction of shared datasets and the ability to connect Power BI Desktop to build a report against a published dataset in the Power BI service. Since the underlying dataset could be Import or DirectQuery mode, the experience may vary as described in previous sections.

The Power BI enterprise gateway

The Power BI **gateway** is a middleware component used to connect to external data sources. It is usually part of the same physical or virtual network, and it establishes a secure outgoing connection to Power BI, over which it can send data to satisfy report queries and data refresh requests.

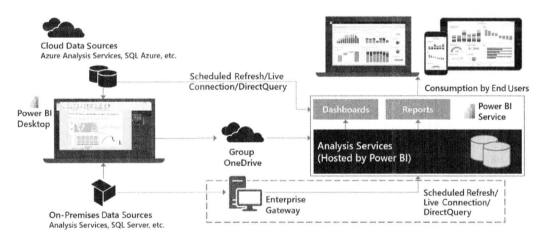

Figure 1.4 – Power BI enterprise gateway

The gateway is not just a conduit for data, which is a common misconception. In addition to providing authenticated and approved connections to data sources, it contains the mashup engine that performs data transformations and compresses data before sending it to the Power BI service. When the gateway is not optimized it can lead to long-running data refreshes, data refresh failures, slow report interactions, or visuals failing to load due to query timeouts.

Network latency

Network latency is about how long a piece of information takes to travel from one point to another in a network. Network latency is measured in milliseconds and is typically measured by performing a **ping**. A ping measures the time taken to send a small packet of information to a destination and receive a response acknowledging the message. Ping times that reach seconds can be problematic. The main drivers of network latency are geographical distance, the number of hops the information needs to take on the way, and how busy the networks are overall.

The following diagram highlights the possible paths that data takes within Power BI. It's worth noting that each individual arrow could have different latency, which means effects can be felt disproportionately by certain users or in certain parts of the solution.

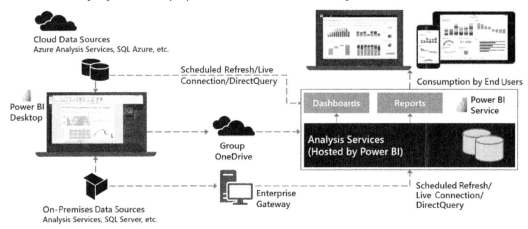

Figure 1.5 – Data movement affected by network latency

High network latency is most felt when users are interacting with reports. It is a significant contributor of slow performance primarily when there are many visuals in a report and therefore many queries to be executed. This is because such configurations require many individual pieces of information to be sent and received, and each one is affected by the latency.

The Power BI service

The Power BI service is the central part of any Power BI solution. The system components in the service are largely out of the control of developers and users. The stability and performance of these are monitored by Microsoft. The exception is Power BI Premium and Embedded, where the underlying infrastructure is still managed by Microsoft, but your administrators have many choices available on how to manage their dedicated capacity. This will be covered in detail in *Chapter 13, Optimizing Premium and Embedded Capacities.*

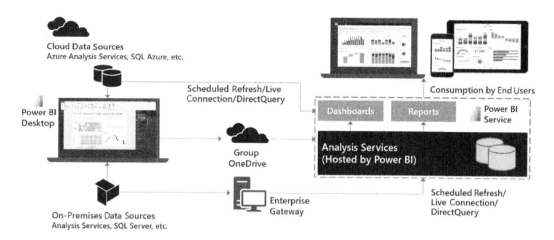

Figure 1.6 – The Power BI service

The major component of the Power BI service that *is* under your control is the Analysis Services engine, which sits at the core of any Power BI solution. Even with the Power BI service running efficiently under Microsoft's management, poor design choices related to Analysis Services data modeling and DAX calculations can lead to very large datasets, high memory usage, and slow query execution. This generally translates to slow reports. On Premium/Embedded capacities Analysis Services issues can have an exponential effect because they can affect multiple datasets on the capacity.

The final section of this chapter identifies specific areas in Power BI where you can achieve the same result with different design patterns. The choices you make here can affect performance.

Which choices affect performance?

While there are many aspects of each individual Power BI component that can be optimized for performance, the following list is a good summary that can serve as a checklist for every solution:

- **Inappropriate use of DirectQuery/Import**: Decisions here balance model size and refresh time with data freshness and report interactivity.

- **Power Query design**: Decisions here may fail to leverage the data source's native capabilities and therefore also fail to avoid additional work in the mashup engine.

- **Data modeling**: Decisions here may make the data model unnecessarily large, waste memory, consume more computing resources, and affect usability.

- **Inefficient DAX calculations**: Decisions here may fail to leverage the highly efficient internal VertiPaq Storage Engine and force operations in the Formula Engine.

- **Complex or inefficient row-level security**: Decisions here may create intensive calculations to resolve which rows the user can see.

- **Poorly designed reports**: Decisions here can put too much load on the user's device.

- **Data source or network latency**: Decisions here may place the data far away from the user.

Now that you have learned about the high-level areas of a solution that we need to consider to fully optimize performance, let's summarize the key learnings from this chapter.

Summary

As we have seen in this chapter, interacting with analytical reports is very similar to other web applications, so the user's level of engagement and satisfaction can be measured in similar ways. Studies of user interfaces and web browsing suggest that a report that is generated in less than 4 seconds is ideal. They also suggest that reports completing in 10-12-second durations or higher should be considered carefully as this is the point of user frustration.

You should set performance targets and be prepared for outliers by measuring against the **90th percentile (P90)**. Success may still require setting the right expectations by having different targets if you have highly complex reports.

It is important to remember that each component of Power BI and even the network itself can contribute to performance issues. Therefore, performance issues cannot be solved in isolation (for example, by only adjusting reports). This may require coordination with multiple teams and external vendors, particularly in large organizations.

In the next chapter, we will focus on the internal **VertiPaq Storage Engine** in Power BI to learn how to we can get it to optimize storage for us. We will also look at gateway optimization and general architectural advice to make sure the environment does not become a bottleneck.

2
Exploring Power BI Architecture and Configuration

In the previous chapter, we established guidelines for setting reasonable performance targets and gained an understanding of the major solution areas and Power BI components that should be considered for holistic performance management.

In this chapter, you will dig deeper into specific architectural choices, learning how and why these decisions affect your solution's performance. You will learn to consider broad requirements and make an informed decision to design a solution that meets the needs of different stakeholders. Ultimately, this chapter will help you choose the best components to host your data within Power BI. We will focus mainly on the efficient movement of data from the source system to end users by improving data throughput and minimizing latency.

We will begin by looking at data storage modes in Power BI and how the data reaches the Power BI dataset. We will cover how to best deploy Power BI gateways, which are commonly used to connect to external data sources. These aspects are important because users often demand up-to-date data, or historical data, and can number in the thousands of parallel users in very large deployments.

This chapter is broken down into the following sections:

- Understanding data connectivity and storage modes
- Reaching on-premises data through gateways
- General architectural guidance

Understanding data connectivity and storage modes

Choosing a data connectivity and storage mode is usually the first major decision that must be made when setting up a brand-new solution in Power BI. This means choosing between **Import** and **DirectQuery**, which we introduced in the previous chapter. Within Power BI Desktop, you need to make this decision as soon as you connect to a data source and before you can see a preview of the data to begin modeling.

> **Important Note**
> Not every data connector in Power BI supports DirectQuery mode. Some only offer Import mode. You should be aware of this because it means you may need to use other techniques to maintain data freshness when a dataset combines different data sources.

Figure 2.1 shows a SQL Server data source connection offering both **Import** and **DirectQuery** modes:

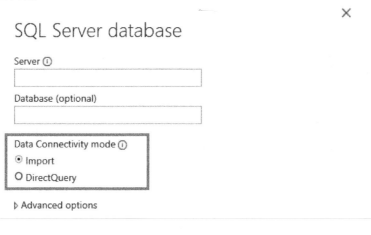

Figure 2.1 – Data connectivity options for a SQL Server source

Excel workbooks can only be configured as **Import** mode. *Figure 2.2* demonstrates this, where we can only see a **Load** button without any choices for data connectivity mode. This implies that it is **Import** mode.

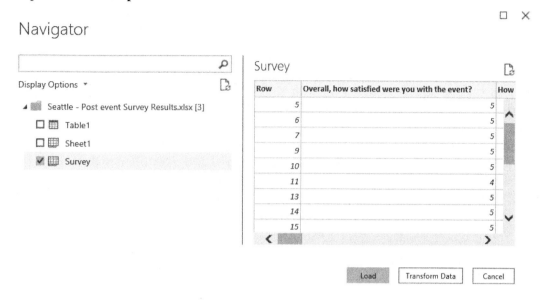

Figure 2.2 – Data connection for Excel showing no Import/DirectQuery choice

Choosing between Import and DirectQuery mode

Import data connectivity mode is the default choice in Power BI because it is the fastest, sometimes by orders of magnitude. Import mode tables store the data in a Power BI dataset, which is effectively an in-memory cache. A necessary first step for Import mode tables is to copy that source data into the Power BI Service, usually locally within the same geographical Power BI region that is processing reports. This is known as the **home region**. A DirectQuery source is not necessarily close to the Power BI home region. If it is not in the home region, the data needs to travel further to reach the Power BI report. Also, depending on how the data model is set up in DirectQuery, the Analysis Services engine may need to perform expensive processing on the data for each report interaction or analytical query.

Therefore, from a purely performance-oriented standpoint, we recommend Import mode over DirectQuery as it offers the best interactive experience. There are exceptions to this general rule, however, which we will explore in later sections.

The other reason why Import models are much faster is that they use Power BI's proprietary **xVelocity** storage also known as **VertiPaq**. xVelocity is a **column-based storage** engine, as opposed to **row-based storage** typically found in many database products. Column-based storage came about to deal with how badly row-based transactional databases handled queries from typical business reporting tools. They do many aggregations, potentially over large volumes of data while also offering detailed data exploration capability.

Row-based data storage engines physically store information in groups of rows. This works well when used by transactional systems because they frequently read and write individual or small groups of rows. They end up using most or all columns in the underlying table and were traditionally optimized to save and retrieve whole rows of data. Consider a sales management system where a new order is entered into a system – this would require writing a few complete rows in the database. Now consider the same system being used to view an invoice on screen – this would read a few rows from various tables and likely use most of the columns in the underlying tables.

Now, let's consider typical reporting and analytical queries for the same sales management system. Business staff would most often be looking at aggregate data such as sales and revenue figures by month, broken down into various categories or being filtered by them. These queries need to look at large volumes of data to work out the aggregates, and they often ignore many columns available in the underlying tables. This access pattern led to column-based storage engines, which store columns physically instead of rows. They are optimized to perform aggregates and filtering on columns of data without having to retrieve entire rows with many redundant columns that do not need to be displayed. They also recognize that there is often significant repetition within a column of data; that is, the same values can be found many times. This fact can be leveraged to apply compression to the columns by not storing the same physical values many times. The xVelocity engine in Power BI does exactly this – it applies different compression algorithms to columns depending on their data type. This concept of reducing repetition to reduce data size is not new and is the same technique you end up using when you compress or zip files on a computer to make them smaller.

The following diagram shows a simplified view of a table of data represented as rows or columns. The bold sections demonstrate how the data will be physically grouped. In column storage, repeating values such as customer ID 16 can be compressed to save space.

ROW-BASED STORAGE			
SalesOrderID	CustomerID	DateOfSale	SalesAmount
556	34	1/12/2021	5000
113	45	30/6/2021	7000
523	16	15/8/2020	5500
767	16	6/2/2021	12800

COLUMN-BASED STORAGE			
SalesOrderID	CustomerID	DateOfSale	SalesAmount
556	34	1/12/2021	5000
113	45	30/6/2021	7000
523	16	15/8/2020	5500
767	16	6/2/2021	12800

Figure 2.3 – Comparison of row and column storage

In summary, xVelocity's column-based compression technology gives you the best speed by bringing the data close to reports and squeezing that data down to significantly less than the original size. In *Chapter 10, Data Modeling and Row-Level Security*, you will learn how to optimize import models. Keeping Import models as small as possible will help you avoid hitting system limits such as the per-workspace storage limit of 10 GB in Shared capacity.

> **Important Note**
>
> A good rule of thumb is that Import mode tables using xVelocity are about 5x-10x smaller. For example, 1 GB of raw source data could fit into a 100 MB-200 MB Power BI dataset. It is often possible to get even higher compression depending on the **cardinality** of your data.

Next, we will look at legitimate reasons to avoid Import mode.

When DirectQuery is more appropriate

While Import mode offers us great benefits in terms of dataset size and query speed, there are some good reasons to choose DirectQuery instead. Sometimes, you will not have a choice and requirements will dictate the use of DirectQuery.

The main difference with DirectQuery, as the name implies, is that queries against the Power BI dataset will send queries to the source system. The advantage of this configuration is that you get the latest information all the time. Data is not copied into the Power BI dataset, which contains only metadata such as column names and relationships. This means that there is no need to configure data refresh or to wait for refreshes to complete before you can work with the latest data. Thus, it is typical to find DirectQuery datasets ranging in size from a few kilobytes to about 2 MB.

> **Important Note**
>
> Import versus DirectQuery is a trade-off. Import gives you the best query
> performance while needing data refresh management and potentially not
> having the latest data available. DirectQuery can get you the latest data and
> allow you to have data sizes beyond Power BI's dataset size limits. DirectQuery
> sacrifices some query speed and can add optimization work to the source
> system.

Here are the major reasons why you would use DirectQuery mode:

- *Extremely large data volumes*: A dataset published to a workspace on a Power BI
  Premium capacity can be up to 10 GB in size. A dataset published to a workspace on
  Shared capacity can be up to 1 GB in size. These sizes refer to the Power BI Desktop
  file (`.pbix`) that is published to the Power BI service, though in Premium datasets
  can grow far beyond the 10GB publication limit. If you have significantly more data,
  it may be impractical or simply impossible to move it into Power BI and refresh it
  regularly. DirectQuery does have a 1 million row limit per query, though this should
  not be a cause for concern as there should not be any practical use for so much
  unaggregated data in a report.

- *Real-time access to source data*: If business requirements require real-time results
  from the data source for every query, the only obvious choice is DirectQuery.

- *Existing data platform investments*: Some organizations may already have significant
  investments in a **data warehouse** or **data marts** typically stored in a central
  database. These already contain clean data, modeled in a form that is directly
  consumable by analysts and business users, and act as a single source of truth.
  These data sources are likely to be accessed by different reporting tools and
  a consistent, up-to-date view is expected across these tools. You may want to use
  DirectQuery here to fit into this central source of truth model and not have older
  copies in a Power BI dataset.

- *Regulatory or compliance requirements*: Laws or company policies that restrict
  where data can be stored and processed may require source data to remain within
  a specific geographical or political boundary. This is often referred to as data
  sovereignty. If you cannot move the data into Power BI because it would break
  compliance, you may be forced to use DirectQuery mode.

Like Import, DirectQuery mode can also benefit from specific optimization. This will be
covered in detail in *Chapter 3, DirectQuery Optimization*.

Now that we have investigated both Import and DirectQuery modes and you understand the trade-offs, we recommend bearing the following considerations in mind when choosing between them:

- How much source data do you have and at what rate will it grow?
- How compressible is your source data?
- Is Premium capacity an option that allows larger Import datasets to be hosted?
- Will a blended architecture suffice? See the following section on *Composite models.*

Composite models

Power BI does not limit you to using only Import or DirectQuery in a single dataset or .pbix file. It is possible to combine one or more Import mode tables with one or more DirectQuery tables in a **composite model**. In a composite model, the Import and DirectQuery tables would be optimized the same way you would in a strictly Import-only or strictly DirectQuery-only model. However, combined with the **Aggregations** feature, composite models allow you to strike a balance between report performance, data freshness, dataset size, and dataset refresh time. You will learn how to leverage aggregations in *Chapter 10, Data Modeling and Row-Level Security.*

LiveConnect mode

In LiveConnect mode, the report will issue queries on demand to an external Analysis Services dataset. In this way, it is like DirectQuery in that the Power BI report does not store any data in its local dataset. However, the distinction is that LiveConnect mode is only available for Analysis Services. No data modeling can be performed, and no DAX expressions can be added. The Power BI report will issue native DAX queries to the external dataset. LiveConnect mode is used in the following scenarios:

- Creating reports from a dataset available in a Power BI workspace from Power BI Desktop or Power BI Web.
- Your organization has invested in Azure Analysis Services or SQL Server Analysis Services and this is the primary central data source for Power BI reports. The top reasons for choosing this are as follows:

    a) You need a high level of control around partitions, data refresh timings, scale-out, and query/refresh workload splitting.

    b) Integration with **CI/CD** or similar automation pipelines.

    c) Granular Analysis Services auditing and diagnostics are required.

    d) The initial size of the dataset cannot fit into Premium capacity.

The following diagram highlights the scenarios that use LiveConnect:

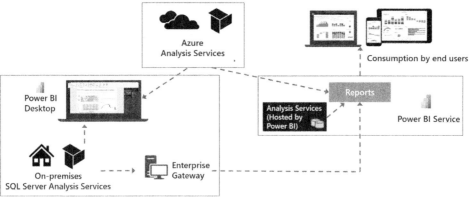

Figure 2.4 – LiveConnect scenarios

> **Important Note**
>
> Connections to Analysis Services also support Import mode, where data is copied and only updated when a data refresh is executed. The external Analysis Services dataset may itself be in Import mode, so you should consider whether LiveConnect is indeed a better option to get the latest data. Import can be a good choice if you are simply building lookup tables for a smaller data mart or temporary analysis (for example, a list of products or customers).

The way a report connects to its data source depends on where the report is being run. A connection from Power BI Desktop from a work office may take a completely different route than a connection from the Power BI Service initiated by a person using the Power BI Web portal or mobile app. When organizations need a way to secure and control communications from Power BI to their on-premises data sources (data that is not in the cloud), they deploy Power BI Gateways. In the next section, we will discuss Power BI Gateways, their role in data architecture optimization, and specific tips on getting the most out of gateways.

Reaching on-premises data through gateways

The on-premises data gateway provides a secure communications channel between on-premises data sources and various Microsoft services, including Power BI. These cloud services include Power BI, Power Apps, Power Automate, Azure Analysis Services, and Azure Logic Apps. Gateways allow organizations to keep sensitive data sources within their network boundaries on-premises and then control how Power BI and users can access them. The gateway is available in both Enterprise and Personal versions. The remainder of this section focuses on the Enterprise version.

When a gateway is heavily loaded or undersized, this usually means slower report loading and interactive experiences for users. Worse, an overloaded gateway may be unable to make more data connections, which will result in failed queries and some empty report visuals. What can make matters worse is that users' first reaction is often to refresh the failed report, which can add even more loads to a gateway or on-premises data source.

How gateways work

Gateways are sometimes thought of as just a networking component used to channel data. While they are indeed a component of the data pipeline, gateways do more than just allow data movement. The gateway hosts Power BI's **Mashup Engine** and supports Import, DirectQuery, and LiveConnect connections. The gateway service must be installed on a physical or virtual server. It is important to know that *the Gateway executes Power Query/M as needed, performing the processing locally on the gateway machine*. In addition, the gateway compresses and then encrypts the data streams it sends to the Power BI Service. This design minimizes the amount of data sent to the cloud to reduce refresh and query duration. However, since the gateway supports such broad connectivity and performs potentially expensive processing, it is important to configure and scale gateway machines so they perform well.

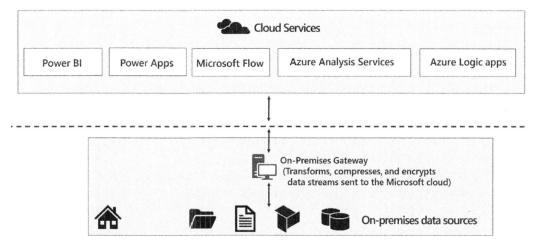

Figure 2.5 – The on-premises gateway performs mashup processing locally

Good practices for gateway performance

Some general guidelines should be applied whenever gateways are deployed. We will discuss each one in the following list and provide reasons to explain how this design benefits you:

- *Place gateways close to data sources*: You should try to have the gateway server as physically close to the data sources as possible. Physical distance adds latency because information needs to travel further and will likely need to pass through different computers and networking infrastructure components along the way. These are referred to as **hops**. Each hop adds a small amount of processing delay, which can grow when networks are congested. Hence, we want to minimize both hops and physical distance. This also means having the gateway on the same network as the data source if possible, and ensuring it is a fast network. For data sources on **virtual machines** in the cloud, try to place them in the same region as your Power BI home region.

- *Remove network throttling*: Some network firewalls or proxies may be configured to throttle connections to optimize internet connectivity. This may slow down transfers through the gateway, so it is a good idea to check this with network administrators.

- *Avoid running other applications or services on the gateway*: This ensures that loads from other applications cannot unpredictably impact queries and users. This could be relaxed for development environments.

- *Separate DirectQuery and Scheduled Refresh gateways*: Import mode connections would only be used during data refresh operations and are often used more after hours when data refreshes are scheduled. Since they often contain Power Query/M data transformations, refresh operations consume both CPU and memory and may require significant amounts for complex operations on large datasets. We will learn how to optimize Power Query/M in *Chapter 8, Loading, Transforming, and Refreshing Data*. For DirectQuery connections, in most cases, the gateway is acting as a pass-through for query results from data sources. DirectQuery connections generally consume much less CPU and memory than Import. However, since dataset authors can perform transformations and calculations over DirectQuery data, this can consume significant CPU in bursts. Deploying multiple gateways with some dedicated to DirectQuery and others to Refresh allows you to size those gateways more predictably. This reduces the chances of unexpected slowdowns for users running reports and queries.

- *Use sufficient and fast local storage*: The gateway server buffers data on the disk before it sends it to the cloud. It is saved to the location `%LOCALAPPDATA%\Microsoft\On-premises data gateway\Spooler`.

If you are refreshing large datasets in parallel, you should ensure that you have enough local storage to temporarily host those datasets. We highly recommend using high-speed, low-latency storage options such as solid-state disks to avoid storage becoming a bottleneck.

- *Understand gateway parallelism limits*: The gateway will automatically configure itself to use reasonable default values for parallel operations based on the CPU cores available. We recommend monitoring the gateway and considering the sizing questions from the next section to determine whether manual configuration would benefit you. To manually configure parallelism, modify the gateway configuration file found at `\Program Files\On-premises data gateway\ Microsoft.PowerBI.DataMovement.Pipeline.GatewayCore.dll. config`.

Set the following:

```
MashupDisableContainerAutoConfig = true
```

Now you can change the following properties in the configuration file to match your workload profile and available machine resources:

Setting	Description
MashupDefaultPoolCon tainerMaxCount	The concurrent number of **mashup containers** that run in parallel for refreshes. Most queries use a mashup container to execute. The recommended upper bound is 2x the number of gateway CPU cores. If you set this to 1, queries will execute sequentially. This may improve data sources that do not handle parallel queries well.
MashupDQPoolContaine rMaxCount	The concurrent Power BI DirectQuery limit.
MashupDQPoolContaine rMaxWorkingSetInMB	Maximum "working set" memory allowed for each Power BI DirectQuery mashup container.
MashupTestConnection PoolContainerMaxInst anceCount	Maximum mashup container count for test connections.
MashupAzureConnector sCachingPoolContaine rMaxCount	Maximum mashup container count for LogicApps, Power Apps, and Power Automate.
MashupAzureConnector sCachingPoolContaine rMaxWorkingSetInMB	Maximum "working set" memory allowed for each LogicApps, Power Apps, and Power Automate mashup container.

Figure 2.6 – A table showing available gateway configuration settings

Sizing gateways

Most organizations start with a single gateway server and then scale up and/or out based on their real-world data needs. It is very important to follow the minimum specifications suggested by Microsoft for a production gateway. At the time of writing, Microsoft recommends a machine with at least 8 CPU cores, 8 GB RAM, and multiple gigabit network adapters. Regular monitoring is recommended to understand what load patterns the gateway experiences and which resources are under pressure. We will cover monitoring later in this chapter.

Unfortunately, there is no simple formula to apply to get gateway sizing exactly right. However, with some planning and the right tools, you can get a good idea of what your resource needs will be and when you should consider scaling out.

We have already learned that the gateway supports different connection types. The type and number of connections will largely determine resource usage on the gateway server. Therefore, you should keep the following questions in mind when planning a gateway deployment:

- How many concurrent dataset refreshes will the gateway need to support?
- How much data is going to be transferred during the refresh?
- Is the refresh performing complex transformations?
- How many users would hit a DirectQuery or LiveConnect source in parallel?
- How many visuals are in the most used DirectQuery/LiveConnect reports? Each data-driven visual will generate at least one query to the data source.
- How many reports use **Automatic Page Refresh** and what is the refresh frequency?

In the next section, we will look at how to monitor a gateway and gather data to inform sizing and scaling to ensure consistent performance.

Configuring gateway performance logging

The on-premises gateway has performance logging enabled by default. There are two types of logs captured – query executions and system counters. They can be disabled by changing the corresponding value property to `True` in the gateway configuration file. The following shows the default settings:

```
<setting name="DisableQueryExecutionReport"
serializeAs="String">
  <value>False</value>
</setting>
```

```
<setting name=" DisableSystemCounterReport"
serializeAs="String">
  <value>False</value>
</setting>
```

Other settings you can adjust that affect performance logging are shown here:

- *ReportFilePath*: This is the path where the log files are stored. This path defaults to either `\Users\PBIEgwService\AppData\Local\Microsoft\On-premises data gateway\Report` or `\Windows\ServiceProfiles\PBIEgwService\AppData\Local\Microsoft\On-premises data gateway\Report`. The path depends on the OS version. If you use a different gateway service account, you must replace this part of the path with your service account name.

- *ReportFileCount*: The gateway splits log files up when they reach a predetermined size. This makes it easy to parse and analyze specific time periods. This setting determines the number of log files of each kind to retain. The default value is `10`. When the limit is reached, the oldest file is deleted.

- *ReportFileSizeInBytes*: This is the maximum size of each log file. The default value is 104,857,600 (100 MB). The time period covered in each file can differ depending on the amount of activity captured.

- *QueryExecutionAggregationTimeInMinutes*: Query Execution metrics are reported in aggregate. This setting determines the number of minutes for which the query execution information is aggregated. The default value is 5.

- *SystemCounterAggregationTimeInMinutes*: System Counters metrics are also aggregated. This setting determines the number of minutes for which the system counter is aggregated. The default value is 5.

When logging is enabled, you will start to collect information in four sets of files with the `.log` extension and numerical suffixes in the filename. The log file group names are provided in the following list.

- *QueryExecutionReport*: These logs contain detailed information on every query execution. They tell you whether the query was successful, the data source information, the type of query, how long is spent executing and data processing, how long it took to write data to disk, how much data was written, and what the average speed is of the disk operations. This information is invaluable as it can be used to work out where bottlenecks are at a query level.

- *QueryStartReport*: These are simpler query logs that provide the actual query text, data source information, and when the query started. You can see the exact query that was sent to data sources, which can be useful for performance troubleshooting, especially with DirectQuery data sources. You will learn how to optimize systems for DirectQuery in *Chapter 3, DirectQuery Optimization*.

- *QueryExecutionAggregationReport*: These logs contain aggregated query information in buckets of 5 minutes by default. They provide useful summary information such as the number of queries within the time window, the average/minimum/maximum query execution duration, and the average/minimum/maximum data processing duration.

- *SystemCounterAggregationReport*: This log contains aggregated system resource information from the gateway server. It aggregates average/minimum/maximum CPU and memory usage for the gateway machine, gateway service, and the mashup engine.

> **Important Note**
> You need to restart the gateway after adjusting any settings to apply the changes. It can take up to 10 minutes plus the `QueryAggregationTimeInMinutes` value to see log files appearing on the disk.

Parsing and modeling gateway logs

Microsoft has provided a basic Power BI **report template** to help you analyze gateway data. This template can be found at the following link: `https://download.microsoft.com/download/D/A/1/DA1FDDB8-6DA8-4F50-B4D0-18019591E182/GatewayPerformanceMonitoring.pbit`.

The template will scan your log folder and process all the files it finds that match the default naming pattern. It parses and expands complex columns, for example, JSON, and leaves you with the following data model.

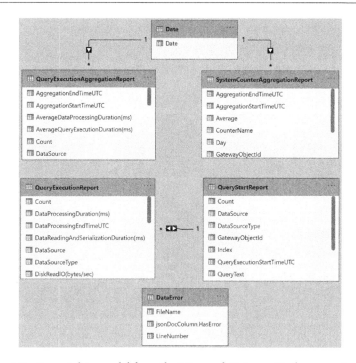

Figure 2.7 – Report data model from the Microsoft Gateway Performance template

The following figure demonstrates one of the default views in the Gateway Performance template:

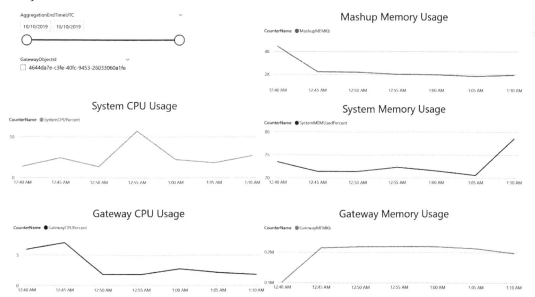

Figure 2.8 – Example of gateway performance visualization from the template

The Microsoft-provided template does a reasonable job of giving you visibility on some aggregate and detailed operations on the gateway. However, to extract further value from it, you will likely need to make some changes to the transformations, data model, and calculations. This could take some work to perfect, so it may be worth considering whether a pre-built option is feasible. If your organization uses Microsoft Premier or Unified Support, you may have access to Power BI performance assessments. These are run by experienced customer engineers who have enhanced templates to analyze gateway logs. Another option is to engage consultants who have a professional solution on the market. A web search for Microsoft partners who offer such a solution will help you identify and evaluate the costs and benefits.

If you choose to build on the Microsoft template yourself, do consider the following improvements:

- Automate the retrieval and storage of logs from the gateway server, for example, with **PowerShell** scripts.

- Build separate date and time dimensions and connect them to all the log tables so that you can build reports that can look at time-correlated activity across every log.

- Build common **dimension tables** for Query Status, Query Type, and Data Source from the log files and connect them to each log table. This will allow you to slice report pages using the same filter across different logs.

- Add a dimension table containing details of all your gateways, such as the environment, gateway ID, name, memory size, and CPU core count. Use the gateway ID to connect it to the **fact tables** log.

- Build report views that focus on trends and aggregates to highlight spikes in CPU or memory while able to distinguish between DirectQuery and Refresh queries. Further details are provided in the next section.

Next, we'll look at gateway logs.

Analyzing gateway logs

We suggest that the initial views you build on gateway logs will help you to answer high-level questions and spot problems areas quickly. Here are some important questions you should be able to answer:

- Are there any spikes in overall gateway resource usage and do the spikes recur regularly?

- When I reach high or maximum resource usage, what is the workload pattern?

- What datasets, dataflows, or reports consume the most gateway resources?

- What is the gateway throughput in terms of queries per second and bytes processed per second?

- When I see throughput drops, what operations were running in that time slice, and which contributed most from a resource perspective?

- Is the gateway performing many Refresh and DirectQuery operations in parallel? This is likely to create pressure on CPU and memory at the same time, so consider dedicated DirectQuery and Refresh gateways, spreading out Refresh operations, and scaling.

- What is the average query duration over time and what contributes to increases – gateway resource limits or growing data volume/query complexity?

- What are the slowest queries? Are they consistently slow or does the performance vary greatly? The former may suggest query or model design issues, or that optimization may be needed at the data source or even the network. The varying performance of the same queries suggests unpredictable loads on the gateway or data source are the issue.

> Tip
>
> Go back to the *Sizing gateways* section and review the high-level questions to ask when sizing the gateway. See how they connect with the detailed questions and data points we just covered. This will help you build guidance for your organization, understanding what size of gateway is needed for your workloads and data sources.

Next, we will look at when you should consider scaling and how to do so.

Scaling up gateways

It is possible to manage a gateway well but still begin to reach resource limits due to data and usage growth. Scaling up is simply adding more resources or replacing them with faster components. You know it is time to scale when your analysis shows you are hitting a memory, CPU, or disk limit and may have no more room to move in changing Refresh schedules or optimizing other layers of the solution. We will cover such optimizations in detail in subsequent chapters.

For now, let's assume that the deployed solutions are perfect, yet you are seeing performance degradation and an increase in query failures caused by excessive loads. The first choice here should be to scale up. You may choose to increase the number of CPU cores and memory independently if your analysis identified only one as the problem and you see enough headroom in the other. While CPU and memory are the common candidates for scaling up, do keep an eye on disk and network performance too. You may need to scale those up too or scale out if this is not an option.

Scaling out with multiple gateways

When you can no longer effectively scale up a single gateway machine, you should consider setting up a gateway cluster. This will allow you to load balance across more than one gateway machine. Clusters also provide high availability through redundancy in case one machine goes down for whatever reason.

To create a gateway cluster, you simply run the gateway installer on a different server. At the time of installation, you will be given the option of connecting the gateway to an existing gateway server, which acts as the primary instance. This is shown in the following screenshot:

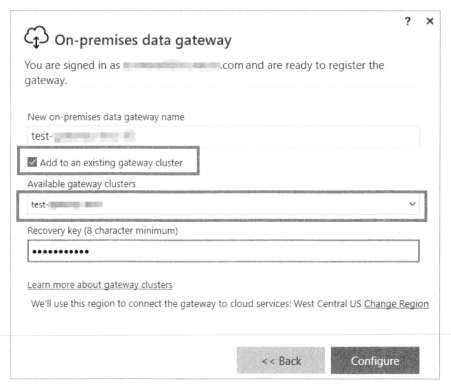

Figure 2.9 – Adding a gateway to a cluster by selecting the primary instance

All requests are routed to the primary instance of a gateway cluster. The request is routed to another gateway instance in the cluster only if the primary gateway instance is offline.

> **Tip**
>
> If a gateway member server goes down, you should remove it from the cluster using the `Remove-OnPremisesDataGateway` PowerShell command. If not, query requests may still be sent to it, which can reduce performance.

Load balancing on the gateway is random by default. You can change this to balance load based on CPU or memory thresholds. This will change the behavior so when a member is at or over the throttling limit, another member within the cluster is selected. The request will fail only if all members within the cluster are above the limits.

A gateway admin must update settings in the config file introduced earlier (the `\ Program Files\On-premises data gateway\ Microsoft.PowerBI. DataMovement.Pipeline.GatewayCore.dll.config` file).

The following settings can be adjusted to control load balancing:

- *CPUUtilizationPercentageThreshold*: A value between 0 and 100 that sets the throttling limit for CPU. 0 means the configuration is disabled.

- *MemoryUtilizationPercentageThreshold*: A value between 0 and 100 that sets the throttling limit for memory. 0 means the configuration is disabled.

- *ResourceUtilizationAggregationPeriodInMinutes*: The time window in minutes for which CPU and memory system counters of the gateway machine are aggregated. These aggregates are compared against the thresholds defined beforehand. The default value is 5.

Now that we have a good grasp of storage modes and gateway optimization, we will consider broader factors that come into play and can slow down operations in these areas.

General architectural guidance

This section presents general architectural best practices that can help with performance.

Planning data and cache refresh schedules

A sometimes-overlooked consideration is how fresh an Import dataset's sources are. There is no point refreshing a dataset multiple times a day if it relies on an external data mart that is only refreshed nightly. This adds an unnecessary load to data sources and the Power BI service.

Look at your environment to see when refresh operations are happening and how long they are taking. If many are happening in parallel, this could slow down other operations due to intense CPU and memory usage. The effect can be larger with Power BI Premium. Consider working with dataset owners to remove unnecessary refreshes or change timings so that they do not occur altogether, but are potentially staggered instead. A data refresh in progress can require as much additional memory as the dataset itself, sometimes more if the transformations are complex or inefficient. A general rule of thumb is that a refreshing dataset consumes twice the memory.

Reduce network latency

In an earlier section, we discussed how reducing the physical distance and hops between data sources helps to reduce network latency. Here are additional considerations:

- **Co-locate** your data sources, gateways, and other services as much as possible, at least for production. If you relied on Azure, for example, it would be recommended to use the same Azure region as your Power BI home tenant region.

- Consider a **cloud replica** of on-premises data sources. This incurs some cloud costs but can significantly reduce latency for Power BI if the cloud region is far from the on-premises data center.

- If your data is in the cloud, consider performing Power BI development through **remote desktop** into cloud virtual machines. Those virtual machines should ideally be in the same region as the data sources.

- Use Azure **ExpressRoute** to have a secure, dedicated, high-speed connection from your on-premises network to the Azure Cloud.

Now that you have a good understanding of the architectural choices that affect performance in Power BI, let's summarize what we've learned before we explore the next area of performance in Power BI.

Summary

In this chapter, we saw how the two storage modes in Power BI work. Import mode datasets create a local in-memory cache of the data in Power BI. DirectQuery mode datasets pass queries through to external data sources. Generally, Import mode is the fastest because it is local to Power BI, in-memory, a column-based database, and compresses data to make working with it more efficient. However, DirectQuery mode provides a way to always have the latest data returned from the source and avoid managing data refreshes. It also allows you to access very large datasets that are far beyond the capacity available in Power BI Premium. In this way, there is a trade-off between these two modes. However, Power BI also provides composite models that blend Import and DirectQuery for very good performance gains.

You have also learned the role of on-premises gateways for enterprises to allow Power BI to connect securely with on-premises data sources. Gateways host Power BI's mashup engine, where data transformations are performed locally. These can be resource hungry, especially with hundreds or thousands of users, which could translate to many connections per second. This means gateways need to be sized, monitored, and scaled. Hence, we looked at the high-level questions that should be asked, for example, relating to a simultaneous refresh or user counts. We then looked at gateway performance logging to provide data to get the answers to these questions and inform scaling. We introduced the gateway performance monitoring template provided by Microsoft and suggested improvements for better usability. Then we learned what patterns to look for when analyzing logs and questions to help drive the correlation of data. This helps us determine when to scale up a gateway or scale out to gateway clusters and load balancing.

We then explored how to plan data refresh to prevent periods of too much parallel activity. Finally, we learned how to reduce data and network latency in other ways for development and production scenarios.

In the next chapter, we will extend the topic of storage modes further by focusing specifically on optimizing DirectQuery models. This will involve guidance for the Power BI dataset and the external data source.

3
DirectQuery Optimization

Until now, we have looked at **Power BI** performance from a relatively high level. You have learned which areas of Power BI performance can be impacted by your design decisions and what to consider when making these choices. These decisions were architectural, so were about choosing the right components to ensure the most efficient movement of data to suit your data volume and freshness requirements.

However, this knowledge alone is not sufficient and will not guarantee good performance. With the gateways in the previous chapter, we saw how a single component of the solution can be configured and optimized quite heavily. This applies to most of the other areas of Power BI, so now we will begin to deep dive into how specific design decisions in each area affect user experience and what configurations should be avoided.

In *Chapter 2, Exploring Power BI Architecture and Configuration*, we looked at storage modes for Power BI datasets and learned about **Import** and **DirectQuery**. In this chapter, we will look specifically at the DirectQuery storage mode. Power BI reports issue queries in parallel by design. Each user interaction on the report can trigger multiple queries. You can have many users interacting with DirectQuery reports that use the same data source. This potentially high rate of queries to the external source must be taken into consideration when building DirectQuery models.

We will look at data modeling for DirectQuery models to reduce the chance of overwhelming the data source. You will learn how to avoid Power BI and the data source performing extra processing. We will learn about the settings available to adjust DirectQuery parallelism. We will also look at ways to optimize the external data source and leverage its strengths to handle the type of traffic that Power BI generates.

This chapter is broken into the following sections:

- Data modeling for DirectQuery
- Configuring for faster DirectQuery

Data modeling for DirectQuery

Data modeling can be thought of very simply as determining which data attributes are grouped into tables, and how those tables connect to one another. Building a DirectQuery data model in Power BI allows you to load table schema metadata and relationships from the data source. If desired, you can also define your own relationships and calculations across any compatible tables and columns.

Calculations in a DirectQuery model are translated to external queries that the data source must handle. You can check the external query that is being generated in the **Power Query Editor** by right-clicking on the query step and then choosing **View Native Query**, as shown in the following figure:

Figure 3.1 – The View Native Query option in Query Settings

You can check the native query to see how Power BI is translating your calculation to the data source's native query language to assess if it might have performance implications. The following example shows the native query for a table where a single calculation was added. The source is a **SQL** server and the calculation is a simple subtraction of two numerical columns:

```
select [_].[SalesOrderID] as [SalesOrderID],
    [_].[RevisionNumber] as [RevisionNumber],
    [_].[OrderDate] as [OrderDate],
    [_].[DueDate] as [DueDate],
    [_].[ShipDate] as [ShipDate],
    [_].[Status] as [Status],
    [_].[OnlineOrderFlag] as [OnlineOrderFlag],
    [_].[SalesOrderNumber] as [SalesOrderNumber],
    [_].[PurchaseOrderNumber] as [PurchaseOrderNumber],
    [_].[AccountNumber] as [AccountNumber],
    [_].[CustomerID] as [CustomerID],
    [_].[SalesPersonID] as [SalesPersonID],
    [_].[TerritoryID] as [TerritoryID],
    [_].[BillToAddressID] as [BillToAddressID],
    [_].[ShipToAddressID] as [ShipToAddressID],
    [_].[ShipMethodID] as [ShipMethodID],
    [_].[CreditCardID] as [CreditCardID],
    [_].[CreditCardApprovalCode] as [CreditCardApprovalCode],
    [_].[CurrencyRateID] as [CurrencyRateID],
    [_].[SubTotal] as [SubTotal],
    [_].[TaxAmt] as [TaxAmt],
    [_].[Freight] as [Freight],
    [_].[TotalDue] as [TotalDue],
    [_].[Comment] as [Comment],
    [_].[rowguid] as [rowguid],
    [_].[ModifiedDate] as [ModifiedDate],
    [_].[TotalDue] - [_].[Freight] as [TotalWithoutFreight]
from [Sales].[SalesOrderHeader] as [_]
```

Figure 3.2 – Native T-SQL query with a custom calculation

> **Tip**
>
> In DirectQuery mode, keep calculations simple to avoid generating complex queries for the underlying data source. For measures, initially limit them to sum, count, minimum, maximum, and average. Monitor the native queries generated and test responsiveness before adding more complexity, especially with CALCULATE statements.

Another point to keep in mind is that there do not need to be any physical relationships in the underlying data source to create virtual relationships in the Power BI data model. Physical relationships are created intentionally by data engineers to optimize joins between tables for common query patterns, so we want Power BI to leverage these whenever possible.

The following figure shows a simple DirectQuery model in **Power BI Desktop** with an arbitrary relationship created across two **Dimension** tables – *Person* and *Product*.

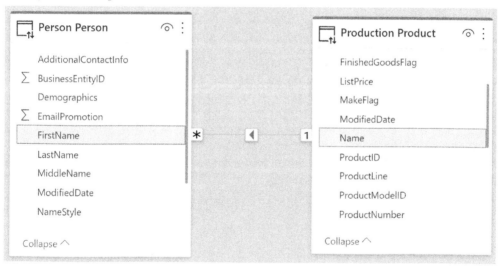

Figure 3.3 – An arbitrary relationship in DirectQuery

This trivial data model, with a single relationship, is simply for the sake of illustration. The point is that it is highly unlikely that the underlying database would have a relationship set up across these tables, and certainly not across those text columns representing the names of products and people. However, when we create such a relationship in Power BI, we are asking the data source or Power BI to perform that join on- demand. This is typically much slower as it cannot take advantage of any existing relationship optimizations at the source.

> **Tip**
>
> In DirectQuery mode, avoid creating relationships across tables and columns that do not have physical relationships and indexes already set up at the data source. If this cannot be avoided, consider limiting yourself to smaller tables, at least on one side of the relationship.

This was a good example of how the flexibility provided by Power BI can lead to unintended consequences if we do not fully understand the implication of our choices. There will be more of these as we progress through future chapters.

Optimizing DirectQuery relationships

Let's build further on physical relationships in the data source. There are likely to be existing **Primary Key** and **Foreign Key** columns with relationships, constraints, and indexes defined at the data source. *Figure 3.4* provides a simple example from a retail sales scenario, where a territory lookup table is related to a sales order table. The **TerritoryID** column in each table is used for the join:

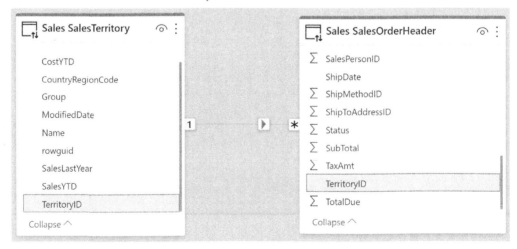

Figure 3.4 – Typical relationship to a lookup table on a numerical identifier

In cases like this, **referential integrity** may be enforced at the source. This means that the **SalesTerritory** table can be considered the master list of territories and that every entry in the **SalesOrderHeader** table must have a corresponding **TerritoryID**. This implies that there cannot be null/empty values for **TerritoryID** in either table. This is a good practice enforced in many database systems, which is important for Power BI because a DirectQuery dataset can issue more efficient queries to the remote data source if you can assume referential integrity.

In database terms, having referential integrity means Power BI can use an INNER JOIN instead of an OUTER JOIN when pulling data across more than one table. Referential integrity means a more efficient INNER JOIN can be used with a safe assumption that no rows from either table will be excluded due to a failure to match keys. You need to instruct Power BI to do this in the data model for each relevant relationship. The following figure shows where to do this in the relationship editor in Power BI Desktop for the sales example we discussed earlier:

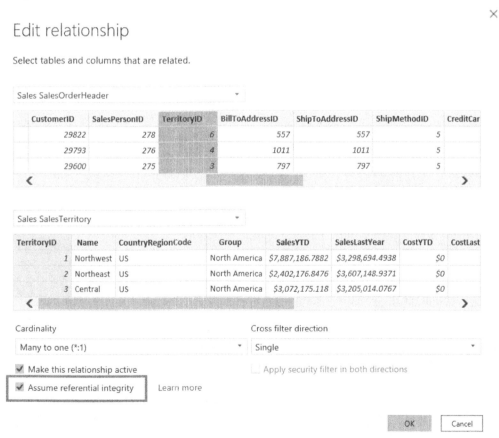

Figure 3.5 – Setting referential integrity for a DirectQuery relationship

Another convenience provided by Power BI is the ability to define calculated columns, which does work for DirectQuery tables. Power BI supports building relationships using a single column from each table. However, occasionally when data modeling it may be necessary to use a combination of columns to uniquely identify some entities. A simple modeling technique to address this is to introduce a calculated column to concatenate the relevant columns into a unique key. This key column is then used to build relationships in the Power BI model. Relationships across calculated columns are not as efficient as those across physical columns. This is especially true for DirectQuery.

> Tip
>
> In DirectQuery mode, avoid creating relationships using calculated columns. This join may not be pushed down to the data source and may require additional processing in Power BI. When possible, use COMBINEVALUES () to create concatenated columns because it is specifically optimized for DirectQuery relationships.

Other ways of pushing this column calculation to the data source are to add a computed column or materialized view.

Two more aspects of relationships to consider are **Cardinality** and **Cross filter direction** (as seen in *Figure 3.5*). A cardinality setting of *Many-to-many* will disable the referential integrity setting and might result in less efficient queries if the data does in fact support a *One-to-many* relationship instead. Similarly, having cross filter direction set to *Both* (sometimes called a **bi-directional relationship**) could result in additional queries to the data source. This is because more tables are affected by minor report actions like slicer changes, as the filter effect needs to be cascaded across relationships in more tables. Consider whether a bi-directional relationship is necessary to support your business scenario.

> Tip
>
> Bi-directional relationships are sometimes used to have slicer values in a report update as the filter state of the report changes. Consider using a measure filter on the slicer visual to achieve the same effect. Continuing with our sales scenario as an example, this technique could be used to only show values in a product slicer if the product did have some sales.

The final piece of advice on relationships in DirectQuery concerns the **Globally Unique Identifier** (**GUID**) or slightly differently defined **Universally Unique Identifier** (**UUID**). These are represented by 32 hexadecimal characters and hyphens. An example of a GUID is `123e4567-e89b-12d3-a456-426614174000`. They can be used to uniquely identify a record in a data store and are often found in **Microsoft** products and services.

> **Tip**
> Avoid creating logical relationships on GUID columns in DirectQuery. Power BI does not natively support this data type and needs to convert when joining. Consider adding a materialized text column or integer surrogate key in the data store instead and use those to define the relationship.

In the next section, we will look at configuration and data source optimization that can benefit DirectQuery.

Configuring for faster DirectQuery

There are a few settings that can be adjusted in Power BI to speed up DirectQuery datasets. We will explore these next.

Power BI Desktop settings

In the Power BI Desktop options, there is a section called **Published dataset settings** (as shown in *Figure 3.6*). The highlighted area shows the setting that controls how many connections per data source can be made in parallel. The default is 10. This means no matter how many visuals are in a report, or how many users are accessing the report in parallel, only 10 connections at a time will be made.

If the data source can handle more parallelism, it is recommended to increase this value before publishing the dataset to the **Power BI service**. However, with very busy data sources, you may find overall performance can improve by *reducing* the value instead. This is because too many parallel queries can overwhelm the source and result in a longer total execution time. A lower value means some queries will have to wait and be issued a little later, giving the data source some breathing room.

> **Important Note**
>
> Power BI Desktop will allow you to enter large numbers for the maximum connections setting. However, there are hard limits defined in the Power BI service that can differ depending on whether you are using a Premium capacity and what size your capacity is. These limits can change and are not publicly documented, so it is recommended to contact **Microsoft Support** to learn more for your scenario.

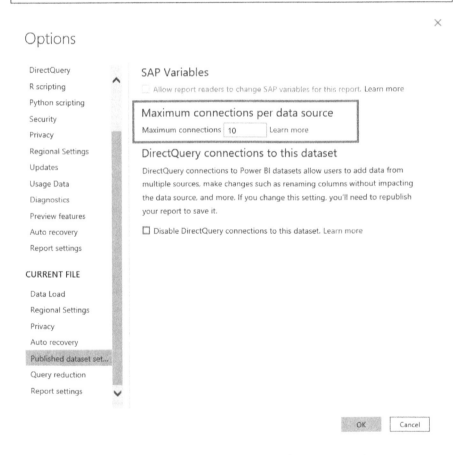

Figure 3.6 – Maximum connections per data source setting

Another useful section of Power BI Desktop options that can benefit DirectQuery is **Query reduction** (as shown in *Figure 3.7*). The figure reflects the default setting, which means that Power BI will issue queries to update visuals for every filter or slicer change a user makes in a report. This keeps the experience highly interactive but can have undesired effects with DirectQuery sources that are busy or not optimized, and with reports that have complex underlying queries. This is because the data source may not even have finished processing queries for the first filter or slicer change when the user makes further changes, which issues even more queries.

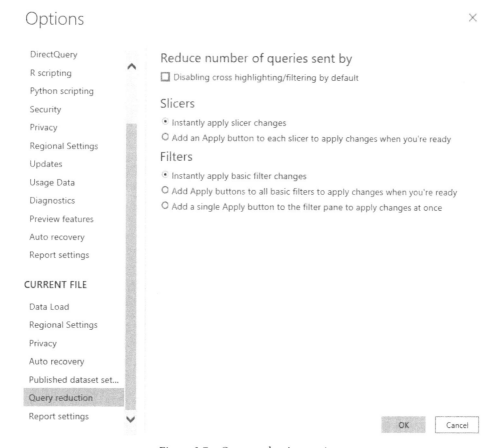

Figure 3.7 – Query reduction settings

The query reduction settings allow you to add **Apply** buttons for slicers and filters. This allows the user to make multiple selections before applying changes, so only a single set of queries will be sent. The report snippet in *Figure 3.8* shows a single slicer and the filter pane of a report after the query reduction settings have been applied:

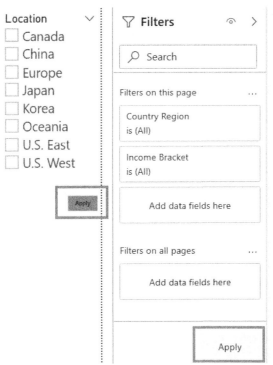

Figure 3.8 – Apply buttons added to slicers and filters

Next, let's look at how you can optimize the external data source to perform better in DirectQuery scenarios.

Optimizing external data sources

We have learned that DirectQuery datasets can perform slower than Import datasets because the external source might not be designed to handle workloads from **Business Intelligence** tools.

Regardless of what technology is powering the external data source, there are some common practices that apply to many storage systems that you should consider implementing to speed up queries for Power BI. These are as follows:

- **Indexes**: An index provides a database with an easy way to find specific records for operations such as filtering and joining. Consider implementing indexes on columns that you use for Power BI relationships or that are often used in report filters or slicers to limit data.

- **Column storage technology**: Modern data storage platforms allow you to define special indexes that use column storage instead of typical row-storage principles. This can speed up aggregate queries in Power BI reports. Try to define the index using columns that are often retrieved together for summaries in reports.

- **Materialized views**: A materialized view is essentially a query whose results are pre-computed and physically stored like a regular table of data. Whenever the base data changes, the materialized view is updated to reflect the current state. You can move transformations to a materialized view in the data source instead of defining them in Power BI. The source will have the results ready for Power BI to consume. This works well with data that does not change very frequently. Be aware that too many materialized views can have a performance impact on the source, as it must continually keep them up to date. Over-indexing can start reducing performance gains.

- **In-memory databases**: One reason Import datasets can perform very well is that they keep all data in memory instead of slower disk storage. The DirectQuery source system may have its own in-memory capabilities that could be leveraged for Power BI.

- **Read-only replicas**: Consider creating a read-only replica of your source system dedicated to Power BI reports. This can be optimized for Power BI traffic independently of the original data source. It can even be synchronized periodically if a real-time replica is not necessary, which can improve performance further.

- **Scaling up/out**: You may be able to increase the power of the source system by giving it more computing and memory resources and distributing the load across multiple servers or nodes to better handle complex parallel queries. The latter is a common pattern in **Big Data** systems.

- **Maintaining Database Statistics**: Some database systems use internal statistics to help the internal query optimizer pick the best query plan. These statistics need to be maintained regularly to ensure the optimizer is not making decisions based on incorrect cardinality and row counts.

You will need to understand what queries Power BI is sending to the external data source before you can decide what optimizations will provide the best return on investment. In *Chapter 4*, *Analyzing Logs and Metrics*, and *Chapter 5*, *Desktop Performance Analyzer*, you will learn how to capture these queries from Power BI. You can also use query logging or tracing in the external source to do this, which is more typical in production scenarios where reports are published to the Power BI service.

Let's now review the key learnings for DirectQuery datasets before we move on to discuss the sources of performance metrics available in Power BI.

Summary

In this chapter, we defined basic data modeling as a process where you choose which data attributes are grouped into entities and how those entities are related to one another. We learned that for DirectQuery, transformations in Power Query should be kept simple to avoid generating overly complex query statements for the external source system. We also learned how to use the native query viewing feature in Power Query to see the exact query Power BI will use. We saw how transformations can also be translated to native query language.

We learned that Power BI is flexible enough to allow you to define your own relationships across DirectQuery tables not necessarily matching those already in the data source. This must be used with care and some planning. It is better to leverage relationships and referential integrity that are already defined in the external data source where possible as these are likely already optimized for joining and filtering. We also explored relationship settings and their implications for DirectQuery.

Next, we explored settings in Power BI Desktop that can be used to control the level of parallelism at the data source and report level. We concluded by learning about the ways in which many widely available data platforms can be optimized and scaled to improve the performance of DirectQuery models. These external optimizations may require collaboration with other administration teams to implement options, run tests, and choose the ones that make the most sense for Power BI.

In the next chapter, we will highlight different sources of performance metrics available in Power BI, what data they make available to you and which areas of performance tuning they can help you with.

Part 2: Performance Analysis, Improvement, and Management

In this part of the book, you will learn to identify sources of performance information in Power BI and how to access them. We will also see which tools are appropriate for different layers, how to debug issues, and how to apply a structured approach to performance improvement.

This part comprises the following chapters:

- *Chapter 4, Analyzing Logs and Metrics*
- *Chapter 5, Desktop Performance Analyzer*
- *Chapter 6, Third-Party Utilities*
- *Chapter 7, Governing with a Performance Framework*

4
Analyzing Logs and Metrics

In the first part of this book, we built a solid foundation for performance management in Power BI by identifying the major architectural components that can affect your experience. We learned why your choices in these areas can slow things down, and we provided recommendations and justifications in each area.

Once these theoretical concepts have been put into practice, you will need to know how to measure performance and analyze the data. This will let you make informed decisions on where to invest time to investigate further and where to make changes for performance tuning. Hence, it is time to move into the second part of this book, where we will look at different places you can get performance-related information in Power BI and how to make sense of that data.

In this chapter, we will focus on the first part of report performance management, which is obtaining performance information. You'll learn what information is available, how to retrieve it, and what to focus on to determine the causes of bad performance.

This chapter covers the following topics:

- Power BI usage metrics
- Power BI logs and engine traces

Power BI usage metrics

In *Chapter 1, Setting Targets and Identifying Problem Areas*, we discussed how report loading performance is the most obvious factor regarding the speed of a **Business Intelligence** platform. In Power BI, a workspace administrator can get performance information using the built-in usage metrics report, though please note this is not available for **Classic** workspaces. Performance information is only available for *the New Power BI Workspace Experience* (`https://docs.microsoft.com/en-us/power-bi/collaborate-share/service-new-workspaces`) (*Workspace v2*).

You can access usage metrics using the report drop-down menu in the content list of the Power BI workspace, as shown in the following screenshot:

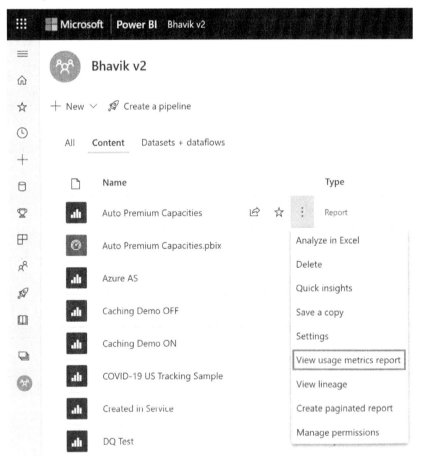

Figure 4.1 – How to view the usage metrics for a report in a workspace

You can also launch the usage metrics report from the report toolbar when viewing a report. This is shown in the following screenshot:

Figure 4.2 – How to view the usage metrics after opening a report

After you launch the usage metrics report, select the **Report performance** page. This will initially show the **Daily performance** view, visualizing how the report is performing per day for the past 30 days. This is shown in the following screenshot:

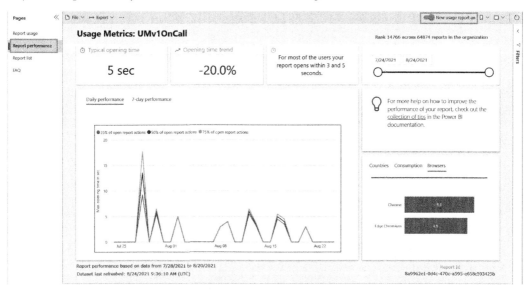

Figure 4.3 – The report performance trend in the usage metrics report

You can switch the trend visual by clicking on the **7-day performance** header. This chart smooths the trend by showing a 7-day rolling aggregate for each metric.

> **Tip**
> Power BI currently supports two versions of usage metrics. If your usage metrics report looks different from the one shown in the preceding screenshot and does not contain any performance information, check that the **New usage report on** option is enabled in the toolbar, as shown in the preceding screenshot. You can use the toggle to switch back to the classic usage metrics if needed.

The report performance page provides a few different metrics that are worth describing:

- **Typical opening time**: This is the 50th percentile (or median) of the report load duration across the selected period in the report. It represents the middle number if you sorted all the report load durations from shortest to longest. The median can provide a better approximation of the typical duration than the average because the latter can be affected by outliers and small sample sizes.

- **Opening time trend**: This shows the percentage change in typical opening time (50th percentile), comparing the value for the first half of the reporting period to the value for the second half. In the preceding screenshot, we can see that the report has become 20% faster because the opening time has been reduced.

- **For most of the users your report opens between [X] and [Y] seconds**: This statement provides you with a range of report open durations. The lower bound (X) represents the 10th percentile, while the upper bound (Y) represents the 90th percentile. Therefore, *most* here represents 80% of the total report opens. This is a good way to think about performance since it covers a broad range and will not be heavily affected by outliers. Ideally, these two numbers will not differ by too much, though there isn't a general rule to apply here. Your goal should be to have the upper bound be within your target report load duration, as discussed in *Chapter 1, Setting Targets and Identifying Problem Areas*.

- **25% of report open actions**: This is the 25th percentile of the report's load duration.

- **50% of report open actions**: This is the 50th percentile (median) of the report's load duration.

- **75% of report open actions**: This is the 75th percentile of the report's load duration.

Note the chart at the bottom right of the report performance page. It shows the typical (50th percentile) report open duration by **Country**, **Consumption Method**, and **Browser**. We recommend monitoring performance by these categories regularly to see if any scenarios stand out. There are additional data points available in the dataset that power the usage metrics report, though they are not shown in the report by default. In the next section, we'll learn how to expose and use them.

Customizing the usage metrics report

The visuals in the usage metrics report provide us with an easy way to get a quick overview of the performance of a specific report. You'll likely want to build some views of this data, so next, we'll look at ways you can adjust the report or access the raw data to build a view.

Filtering usage metrics

The usage metrics report is filtered to one report by default. You may want to look at performance for the entire workspace in aggregate or view metrics for a different report. You can achieve this by expanding the filter pane on the right, clearing any existing filters, then selecting the report name or ID that you are interested in. The following screenshot shows the expanded filter pane with the default **ReportGuid is (All)** filter cleared and the list of report names expanded. Note how the metrics report title changes to **(Multiple reports selected)** to let you know that multiple reports are in scope:

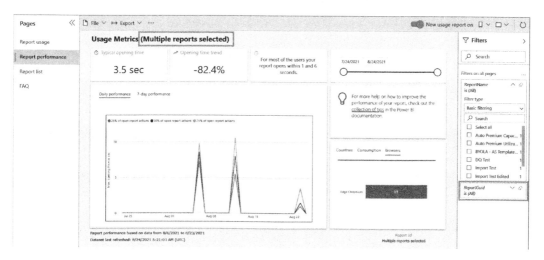

Figure 4.4 – Report load performance for the entire workspace

Now, let's learn how to open the data model behind this report and make report customizations.

Accessing raw data via an editable copy of usage metrics

The Power BI usage metrics report is managed by the system. You are not allowed to edit it and editing options will not appear in the toolbar. However, you can work around this by creating a copy of the usage metrics report. Simply use the **File** menu to **Save a copy**, as shown in the following screenshot:

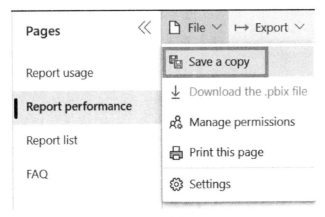

Figure 4.5 – Saving a copy of the usage metrics report

When you save a copy of the usage metrics report, it will be placed in the same workspace as the original system-managed version. You do not need to configure a refresh for this report because it is using the hidden, system-managed usage metrics dataset as a source.

To customize the copy, you can edit the report on the web in the same way you work with any regular Power BI report. Simply navigate to it and open it, then use the **Edit** button on the toolbar and make the necessary modifications. The following screenshot shows the tables that are exposed when we edit the report:

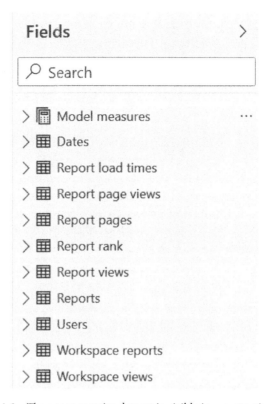

Figure 4.6 – The usage metrics dataset is visible in a customized copy

Now, we'll briefly describe the major elements of the usage metrics dataset to help you construct views that answer your common questions.

The measures include the following:

- **Model measures**: A logical container for the measures in the dataset. It contains subfolders to group the measures for better manageability.

The dimensions include the following:

- **Dates**: A common date table. We recommend using this table for filtering and visualizing by date because it is connected to all the relevant log tables and will allow you to place different metrics next to each other in the same date context.

- **Reports**: A list of all reports in the workspace by name and identifier. Use the **IsUsageMetricsReport** column to exclude any system reports from your analysis – they will be set to **True**.

- **Report pages**: A list of all the report pages by name and identifier, including a mapping to the report ID that the page belongs to.

- **Users**: A list of all **user principal names** (**UPNs**) whose activity is captured in the report. The UPN is most often an email address.

The facts include the following:

- **Report page views**: A table containing an entry for each report page view, as reported by the Power BI client. Use this table to analyze views at the report page's granularity level. It is important to note a limitation stated in the Microsoft documentation. Report page views rely on telemetry data that's sent to Power BI from the client device (for example, the web browser on a PC). *In some situations, the device or network configuration may block outgoing connections and prevent this information from reaching Power BI.*

- **Report load times**: This contains an entry for each report of the open activity, as reported by the **Power BI client** (for example, `powerbi.com` in a web browser or the Power BI mobile app on a phone). It contains *activity start* and *end timestamps*, which are used in the dataset to calculate duration. *A current limitation is that the report page is not identified, so the activity could be for any page of the report.* A workaround for this will be discussed later in this chapter.

- **Report views**: This contains an entry for each *report open activity*, as reported by the Power BI service. This will be reported by the Power BI backend each time a report is opened. This data is not affected by client/network issues and every report open activity is expected to reach Power BI.

- **Report rank**: A static ranking table listing all the reports in the workspace and the viewership rank over the entire tenant.

- **Workspace reports**: A summary of the total days with usage and usage trends for each report. Use the **IsUsageMetricsReportWS** column to exclude any system reports from your analysis – they will be set to true. This data is used to populate the **Report list** page of the Power BI usage metrics report.

- **Workspace views**: A summary of the total views for each report by user, distribution method, and consumption method. This is used to power the **Report list** page of the system-generated report.

A practical way to understand how the usage metrics dataset supports analyzing different scenarios is provided by Microsoft in the *Usage Metrics* documentation. We recommend checking out the example at the following link to see how different usage scenarios are captured and reported. This will help you interpret the usage metrics data: `https://docs.microsoft.com/power-bi/collaborate-share/service-modern-usage-metrics#worked-example-of-view-and-viewer-metrics`.

Accessing raw data with a new custom usage metrics report

You may prefer to use Power BI Desktop to author your custom performance report, or you may not want to use a copy of the system-generated usage metrics report as a base. In this case, you can create a new Power BI report in Power BI Desktop that's connected to the usage metrics dataset in the workspace you're interested in. You will find a usage metrics dataset in any workspace where the usage metrics have been accessed at least once.

To build reports over a usage metrics dataset in Power BI Desktop, choose the data source called **Power BI datasets**, then search for `usage metrics report` in the dialog box. This will list all the system-managed usage metrics datasets and allow you to connect to the one in the workspace. The following screenshot shows the result of a search where all the usage metrics datasets are listed:

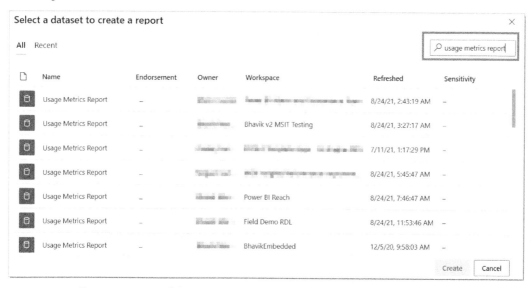

Figure 4.7 – List of usage metrics report datasets found in Power BI Desktop

Once connected to the dataset, the data model described in the previous section will be exposed and you can construct the desired views.

Raw data access via Analyze in Excel over usage metrics

Another way to access the report performance and usage data is through Excel. Here, you can use the standard **Analyze in Excel** functionality once the usage metrics report has loaded. Power BI will prompt you to download an Excel file that has the necessary connection information embedded into it:

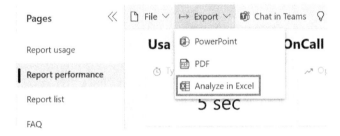

Figure 4.8 – The Analyze in Excel option for usage metrics

You can open the Excel document and construct Excel visuals over the Power BI dataset. The same dataset that we described earlier is exposed via the Excel pivotable interface. The following screenshot shows a pivot table view that was created after opening the dataset in Excel. It looks at the performance percentiles for a single report, compared by the browser:

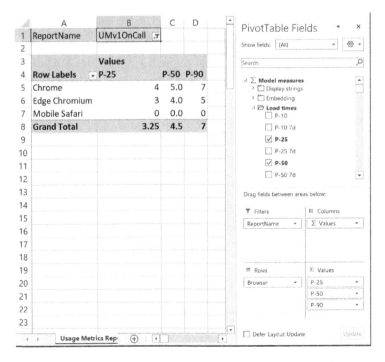

Figure 4.9 – Analyzing the usage metrics dataset in Excel

Next, we will learn about the additional details you can get from building custom views over the usage metrics dataset that Power BI provides.

Viewing granular performance data

Our coverage of the performance data available in usage metrics thus far has only dealt with aggregates, as provided in the default report. This is a good starting point, but aggregate data won't allow you to isolate issues and move closer to root cause analysis. The great news is that more granular performance (and usage) data is available in the dataset. Now that we have described the usage metrics dataset that Power BI provides, we can construct a granular performance view using the **Report load times** table.

While we will only demonstrate one option, the same result can be achieved with any of the customization methods described earlier. The following screenshot shows how a tabular and graphical view of performance can be created to analyze non-aggregated data. The goal here was to compare two reports and see how they perform over time. This can easily be extended by using the other dimensions available in the dataset:

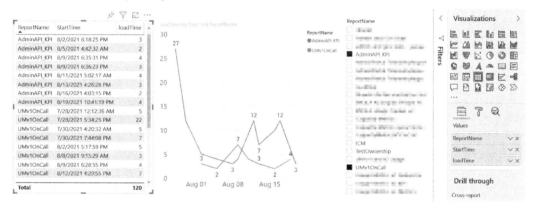

Figure 4.10 – Granular report performance view in a custom report

> **Tip**
>
> The usage metrics dataset doesn't have report page information, so you will not know which page of the report made the entry. We cannot assume that it is the default page of the report due to bookmarks and direct share links. The only workaround to identifying the page from the web service is to split the report into multiple copies with one unique page per report. This way, you can simulate the real usage of pages in isolation and be certain that the performance metrics apply to the one page. Microsoft has announced upcoming improvements to usage metrics to address this problem. At the time of writing, this update is scheduled for sometime in 2022. Please see the following link for more details: `https://docs.microsoft.com/power-platform-release-plan/2022wave1/power-bi/administrative-insights-long-term-historical-tenant-activity-retention-central-metadata-built-in-reports`.

Next, let's explore what to look for in the performance data provided by Power BI, and then consider what you might do next based on your findings.

Analyzing report performance metrics

So far, we have learned about the different ways we can access and customize views for the report performance data provided by Power BI. Now, we will provide some general guidance on how to use this data to identify issues.

If you are trying to resolve a known consistent performance issue with a specific report, you must look at visuals and queries in detail. We will employ a process and specific tools for this. These will be covered in *Chapter 5, Desktop Performance Analyzer*, and *Chapter 6, Third-Party Utilities*. For now, we are going to approach report performance from a summary level, looking for trends and anomalies and learning what the next best actions are.

You don't need to customize the report performance information to get some good insights. The built-in **Performance** page can help you answer some useful questions. The following table serves as a guide:

Question	Rationale and Next Steps
What are the slowest and fastest reports?	Identify the common characteristics of slow versus fast reports as you review them. You should focus your efforts on the slowest and most used reports. Investigate the data model, DAX, and report a visual design for problematic reports.
Is report performance consistent from day to day?	You want to determine if a report is generally slow or is being affected by user load or other system loads (more relevant for Premium). If you see that a certain period is much slower for one report, check if other reports were also affected in that period. If they were, this suggests that an external factor was the cause, not the report's design.
Is there a wide gap between lower and higher report load duration percentiles for any report?	As per the previous question, it is also useful to check if the slow runs are isolated to particular users, locations, browsers, and so on. This helps rule out report design issues.
What browsers are being used to access reports and is there a material difference in the speed?	Older browsers are officially recognized to have performance issues with Power BI. There can be a significant difference and this data can help justify decommissioning legacy browsers in large corporations that are reluctant to migrate.
Are users in certain countries or regions experiencing poor performance?	Network configuration, connection speed, and the sheer geographical distance of users from the Power BI home tenant can impact report performance. This dimension can help justify why a report can appear slow when measured in aggregate, but only because most users are far away or have poor connectivity.
Are certain platforms or distribution methods slower (for example, mobile versus the web, and embedded versus powerbi.com)?	Power BI can be deployed and consumed in various ways. Each has performance implications and may need specific optimizations. This information helps you focus your efforts on the most important scenarios for your organization.

Figure 4.11 – A guide to analyzing summary report performance data

The screenshots that follow show 1 month of real performance data of a production Power BI report that had over 60,000 views. The following screenshot shows that the report's performance appears to be quite consistent, except for 2 days where the 75th percentile seemed to increase by 5 or more seconds than the norm. This may warrant an investigation to see if any other reports were impacted and potentially by a more general issue. If other reports were fine, you should check if this report experienced high usage, which suggests its design isn't scaling well. It's also possible that only users of this report were affected. Here, you can use the country and username data to visualize and isolate these reports:

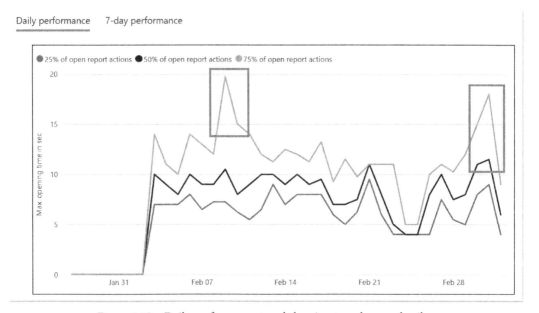

Figure 4.12 – Daily performance trend showing two abnormal spikes

The following screenshot shows the browser performance data for the same report, from the built-in usage metrics. Here, we can see that deprecated browsers are much slower than their modern counterparts for this report:

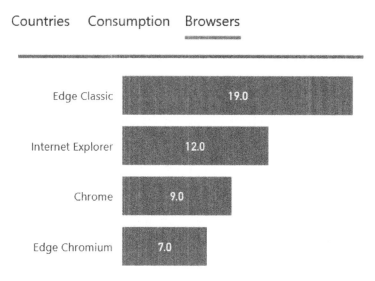

Figure 4.13 – Performance differences across browsers

Customizing the views is highly recommended. The following screenshot shows an example of a useful custom chart you can create with the metrics data. The left box shows three reports that are much slower than the rest and have reasonable usage. The right box shows a report with very high usage. While it is nowhere near the slowest report of the entire group, it has a typical opening time of 50 seconds, which is far from ideal and should be investigated:

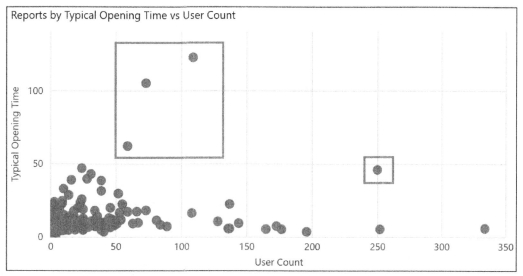

Figure 4.14 – Reports by Opening Time vs User Count – this helps prioritize investigations

Now, let's learn how to collect performance metrics from multiple workspaces.

Collecting performance metrics from multiple workspaces

At the time of writing, Power BI does not provide a single place to get report performance metrics from multiple Power BI workspaces. If you need to combine usage and performance data from multiple workspaces, you will need to perform some manual steps. Here is a suggested method:

1. Use Analyze in Excel against the built-in usage metrics to build a flat table of the performance data you need. Pick a date range that aligns with how frequently you want to run this process and get fresh data. For example, you may choose a 7-day range if you plan to update weekly, and this is assumed for the rest of the examples.

2. Repeat *Step 1* for each Power BI workspace and save the Excel file separately.

3. Use Power BI Desktop to import and combine the Excel files. Build the query in such a way that it will load all the files in a folder. This way, each week, when you get new data, you can simply add the weekly files to the folder and refresh Power BI.

4. Each week, you can reuse the previous week's Excel files and just update the date filter.

You could design a more sophisticated solution for this, such as loading the usage data into a central database and using that as a source for any data analysis. This is more suited to administrators and those with scripting ability, and we will describe this in the next section.

Power BI logs and engine traces

The report usage and performance metrics we covered in the previous section are primarily designed for workspace administrators. For **service/tenant administrators**, Power BI has raw logs that are available, though today, they do not contain report performance metrics. However, since Microsoft has stated its intention to improve logging capabilities, it is worth briefly covering these sources as they are likely to become relevant for performance tuning in the future.

Activity logs and unified audit logs

There are two sources of administrative logs from Power BI that cover activities across the entire tenant. The following table describes the major similarities and differences:

Power BI Activity Log	Unified Audit Log
Accessible via the Get Activity Events REST API and Power BI Management commandlets	Accessible via the Compliance Search interface or PowerShell commandlets
Power BI or Power Platform Service Administrator privileges required	Global Office 365 Administrator or Audit privileges required
Contains only Power BI activities	Contains activity from a range of other Microsoft products besides Power BI, such as Office 365
30 days of history	90 days of history

Figure 4.15 – Comparison of activity and audit logs

Please see the *Further reading* section for more information.

You'll need to create reports to analyze activity logs, so we suggest setting up a process like the one described earlier for workspace usage metrics. The difference with audit logs is that you will not need to use Excel documents and can save **comma-separated value (CSV)** files instead. It is also easier to automate administrative logging due to the availability of PowerShell commandlets and REST APIs.

Analysis Services server traces with the XMLA endpoint

If you are using Power BI Premium, you will have the **XMLA endpoint** available if it has been enabled in Power BI **Tenant Settings**. This is a management endpoint that can be used to perform operations on Power BI datasets by issuing commands directly to the Analysis Services Engine. This will let you initiate a server trace from **SQL Server Profiler** on the workstation and collect detailed dataset information in **near-real time**. Analysis Services data is very useful to help understand engine load, query performance, and refresh performance. We will cover engine traces in more detail in later chapters. For now, note that SQL Profiler provides a generic log capture and viewing interface, and it's not recommended. We will recommend other tools in *Chapter 6, Third-Party Utilities*. For those interested in SQL Profiler or unable to use unofficial tools, we recommend a blog post by Christopher Webb, a well-known authority on **Analysis Services** who is the author of many books on the subject. This article can be found at the following link: https://blog.crossjoin.co.uk/2020/03/02/connecting-sql-server-profiler-to-power-bi-premium/.

Integration with Azure Log Analytics

Microsoft recently released a feature that allows you to connect Power BI to Azure Log Analytics workspaces. Azure Log Analytics is a platform where you can ingest logs, retain them for up to 2 years, perform ad hoc queries on near-real-time data, set alerts, and extract data for reporting and analytics. Microsoft's public roadmap suggests that a lot of performance-related metrics are coming. This is a promising direction as it gives customers full control over their log data with detailed and granular metrics, albeit at a cost. This feature is accompanied by sophisticated downloadable report templates. Since the feature is in Public Preview at the time of writing, we will not cover any specific functionality or recommendations as these aspects may change. More information is available at the following link: `https://powerbi.microsoft.com/blog/announcing-long-term-usage-and-performance-insights-public-preview/`.

Monitoring Azure Analysis Services and Power BI embedded

Azure Analysis Services (**AAS**) and **Power BI embedded** (**PBIE**) are first-party Azure services. This means they are provisioned, managed, and billed via Azure. You can leverage these services in a standalone manner, directly integrating them with custom applications or using them as independent data tiers that can be scaled on-demand as needed. We will primarily use Azure tooling to look at data from these services.

Azure metrics for AAS

After you have provisioned an AAS instance, you can use built-in metrics to visualize your load and operations. Simply navigate to the AAS instance in the Azure portal and select the **metrics** link from the left navigation. You can then select various metrics to plot in the web interface, as described in the documentation (`https://docs.microsoft.com/en-us/azure/analysis-services/analysis-services-monitor`). Let's highlight some of the more important metrics and how they can help you:

- **Current User Sessions**: The number of concurrent active user sessions. Correlate this with known periods of poor performance to determine if user load may be a contributing factor.

- **M Engine Memory**: The memory usage that's used by mashup engine processes when you're running data refreshes. Keep an eye on this to identify spikes. See if high values coincide with reports of failures or lower than expected performance. You may need to reschedule refreshes, optimize content, or handle the higher load by scaling up or out.

- **M Engine QPU**: The processing power that's used by the mashup engine processes, measured in Query Processing Units. For example, if you have an S1 sized instance, then you have 100 QPU and should ensure that there is enough headroom for queries when you hit peak QPU usage by the M engine. The exact number depends on your scenario and can be determined by load testing when there is no refresh. We will cover load testing in *Chapter 13, Optimizing Premium and Embedded Capacities.*

- **Memory**: Memory Usage: The total memory usage by all the server processes on the instance. If this is near the maximum that's provided on the SKU, query and refresh performance will likely degrade and even result in some failures.

- **QPU**: The processing power that's used across the entire instance. A well-optimized instance should operate at peak load without reaching the maximum QPU for sustained periods, though high values are not necessarily bad.

- **Query Pool Busy Threads**: The number of processor threads being used for queries. The maximum varies by SKU. If you see this reaching a maximum number and remaining flat for extended periods, this means that there are too many reports/queries being run at the same time. Some queries will have to wait before they can start executing.

The following screenshot shows the **AAS QPU** metrics displayed in the Azure portal:

Figure 4.16 – The Azure Analysis Services QPU metrics trend in the Azure portal

There are also detailed server traces available for AAS. Some configuration is required to obtain these. We will explore this topic next.

Azure diagnostics for Analysis Services

Earlier in this chapter, we described how the XMLA endpoint can be used to connect to a Premium workspace to capture engine traces. The same concept applies to AAS, though we can use Azure diagnostic logging and Azure Log Analytics to capture and analyze this information. There are some Azure prerequisites and dependencies to satisfy before you can connect AAS to the logging service, namely provisioning a destination for the logs. This requires some administrative permissions in Azure. The setup is beyond the scope of this book, so we encourage you to read the official guidance to configure diagnostic logging, which can be found at the following link: `https://docs.microsoft.com/azure/analysis-services/analysis-services-logging`.

Azure metrics and diagnostics for PBIE

PBIE supports built-in Azure metrics that are accessed from the Azure portal in the same way we described previously for AAS. A point to note is that fewer metrics are available than with AAS. As Microsoft is transitioning its premium/embedded infrastructure from Gen1 to Gen2, the available metrics are changing. Please refer to the online documentation to get the current list. This reference also covers diagnostic logging for PBIE, which works the same way as AAS. It can be found at the following link: `https://docs.microsoft.com/power-bi/developer/embedded/monitor-power-bi-embedded-reference#metrics`.

In subsequent chapters, we will dive deeper into AS engine logs. The advice given there will apply to the AS engine within Power BI, AAS, and PBIE.

Now that we've covered the primary sources of performance information in Power BI, let's summarize what we've learned in this chapter.

Summary

Since report performance is such an important aspect of the user experience, we began by looking at Power BI's built-in workspace usage metrics, which are targeted at workspace administrators.

First, we learned how to launch the usage metrics report. We saw that it contains a report performance page where we were able to visualize report trends and break down report load duration by useful dimensions such as location, browser, or consumption method. We noted that the aggregate information it provides is a good starting point, but that more detail was required for a more complete analysis. To reach this detailed data, we learned how to copy and customize the built-in report, analyze raw data in Excel, and connect to the usage dataset from Power BI Desktop. All these methods allow you to access detail and create more useful custom views. To help with customization, we provided suggestions on how to use the tables in the metrics dataset effectively, including covering multiple Power BI workspaces. Finally, we looked at typical questions to ask of the performance data, examples of interesting metrics that you should investigate further, and what to do next based on what you find.

Then, we moved on to logs and traces, noting that there are tenant-wide logs available to those with the required administrator permissions. However, those logs do not contain performance information yet, so we focused on how to capture logs directly from the Analysis Services Engine, which is a central part of any Power BI solution. We learned that this is an important source of data for query and refresh performance. There were different ways to format this data, depending on which flavor of the AS engine you are using. When using Premium datasets, you can connect to the XMLA endpoint to start a near-real-time trace from a workstation. You also have a **PaaS**-based option to connect Power BI to Azure Log Analytics to capture the granular data in an environment you own. Log Analytics is a dedicated Azure service for high-scale log analysis with ad hoc queries, long-term storage, alerting capabilities, and support for visualization in Power BI.

For those using Azure Analysis Services or Power BI embedded, we learned that Azure metrics and diagnostic logging must be used since these are standalone Azure services. An important point is that all AS engine logs are derived from the same traces, even though they are exposed in different ways and formats.

The next part of our journey will see us diving deeper into performance analysis by using tools to analyze report and query performance data in detail, at a report page and visual level. We will begin by looking at how to use the Power BI Desktop Performance Analyzer. This is an important tool that will be referred to in later chapters as we look at the performance implications of various design choices.

Further reading

To learn more about the topics that were covered in this chapter, take a look at the following resources:

- **Get Activity Events Rest API**: `https://docs.microsoft.com/rest/api/power-bi/admin/get-activity-events`

- **Power BI Management PowerShell Commandlets**: `https://www.powershellgallery.com/packages/MicrosoftPowerBIMgmt`

- **Microsoft 365 Compliance Search**: `https://compliance.microsoft.com/`

- **Microsoft 365 PowerShell Commandlets**: `https://docs.microsoft.com/microsoft-365/compliance/search-the-audit-log-in-security-and-compliance`

5
Desktop Performance Analyzer

In the previous chapter, we looked at ways to get performance and usage information from the Power BI service through reports and logs. This is real-world data that's provided by Microsoft through various features, though there are currently some limitations as to what questions it can answer. For **Power BI reports**, we often need to know whether visuals, queries, or combinations thereof are slow. Some of this granularity isn't available from the Power BI service in production at the time of writing. However, you can get much more granular performance information in Power BI Desktop through the built-in Performance Analyzer.

As we progress through this book, you will learn how the end user report performance experience can be affected by many different factors. A good way to pinpoint these is to analyze report behavior at the level of each user interaction, and the behavior of each visual in response to that action.

Performance Analyzer is an excellent tool for this. In this chapter, we will spend some time learning about its features. We will also learn when and how to use the tool to diagnose performance problems.

This chapter will cover the following topics:

- Overview of Performance Analyzer
- Spotting and mitigating performance issues
- Exporting and analyzing performance data

Technical requirements

There are samples available for some parts of this chapter. We will mention which files to refer to in the relevant sections. Please check out the `Chapter05` folder on GitHub to get these assets: `https://github.com/PacktPublishing/Microsoft-Power-BI-Performance-Best-Practices`.

Overview of Performance Analyzer

Performance Analyzer lets you record user actions and break down report behavior by each report visual, including DAX and DQ queries. The tool provides durations for phases of a report visual's internal operations, in milliseconds. The following screenshot shows how the **Performance analyzer** pane displays statistics for a single-page refresh operation that's initiated from the tool itself.

Take note of the action that's been captured and the duration breakdowns provided. The **Copy query** functionality is especially useful when you're debugging performance related to DAX and data model design. It allows you to extract a **DAX query** or the external **Direct query** command that the visual generated. These queries can be analyzed in other tools, which we will cover in *Chapter 6, Third-Party Utilities*:

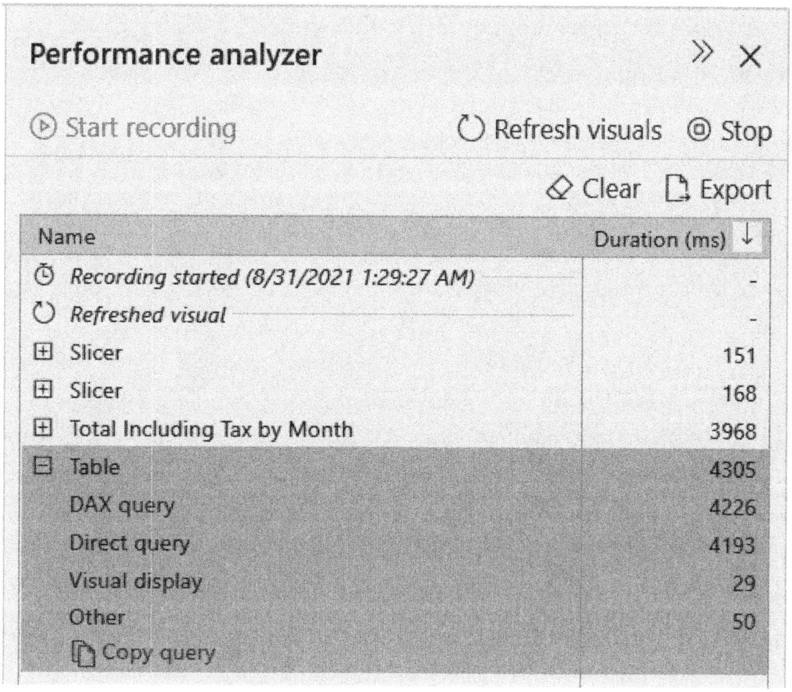

Figure 5.1 – Performance analyzer results with an expanded visual

This chapter will focus on practical examples of using the tool and nuances in Power BI's behavior that should be considered when running performance testing. If you do need an introduction to using Performance Analyzer, please review the product documentation: `https://docs.microsoft.com/power-bi/create-reports/desktop-performance-analyzer`.

Important Note

Performance Analyzer measures durations from its perspective – that is, the Power BI Desktop client. Be aware that development conditions in Power BI Desktop may be very different from those in production. Many things can differ, such as data volume, source load, user concurrency, security enforcement, location, and the inclusion of on-premises gateways. Always keep this in mind when assessing benchmarks from Performance Analyzer. The Power BI Desktop development conditions are often ideal and may not represent reality for most users.

Actions and metrics in Performance Analyzer

Performance Analyzer captures the following user actions:

- **Changed page**: This covers changing pages using the tabs provided by Power BI and custom page navigation buttons that you place in the report.

- **Cross-highlighted**: This captures typical cross-highlight activities such as selecting points or bars in visuals. Note, however, that most clicks in Power BI report visuals trigger at least a visual refresh. For example, when you click an empty space in a visual to deselect a cross-highlighted item, the visuals refresh as expected. If you click the same empty space again, you will notice a visual refresh, and this will be captured by the performance analyzer.

- **Changed a slicer**: This triggers when a slicer value is changed and is applied to the other visuals. If you are using the **Query Reduction** settings in the report to place an **Apply** button on slicers, you need to click the **Apply** button to trigger the **Changed a slicer** event. Even if you do use **Apply** buttons, interacting with slicers can trigger visual updates that the analyzer will capture.

- **Changed a filter**: This triggers when a report filter value is applied. Query reduction with **Apply** buttons on filters behaves the same way as with slicers.

Performance Analyzer contains the following breakdowns per visual:

- **DAX query**: This is only shown if a query was required. It measures the time from when the visual issued the query to when it received the results from the Analysis Services engine. This time is expected to be a bit longer than the DAX query time that's reported by the Analysis Services engine because it includes communication and other overhead. It can be affected by users' physical distance from data sources.

- **Direct query**: This is only shown for a DirectQuery data source if a query was required. It measures the time from when the Analysis Services engine issued an external query to when it received the results. This number should correspond to DirectQuery class event timings from the Analysis Services engine.

- **Visual display**: This is the time spent by the visual drawing the results on the screen. It includes time to fetch external assets such as images or perform geocoding. Poorly implemented or complex custom visuals tend to spend more time here.

- **Other**: This is a general category for any non-display-related activities that are performed by the visual, such as preparing queries or other background processing. It also includes time spent waiting for other visuals. This is because visuals all share a single user interface thread and in very simplistic terms, they all get a sequential slice of the CPU. Every time you add a new visual to a page, the higher this *other* number becomes for *every* visual. This isn't necessarily bad, but it can make visual-heavy reports more sluggish. We will explore this topic in more detail in *Chapter 9, Report and Dashboard Design*.

> **Tip**
> A visual refresh does not necessarily trigger a query in the underlying data source. The Power BI client has a local query result cache, so it can avoid re-running queries when switching back and forth between recently used filtered views. This explains why it is possible to see no DAX query for a data-driven visual. To force the query, you can use the **Refresh visuals** button in the **Performance analyzer** pane.

Determining user actions

At the time of writing, there are some interesting behaviors to note when viewing captured activity in Performance Analyzer. Some user interactions will not be logged at the action level by Performance Analyzer. If you have a **Slicer** configured as a dropdown, for example, not all your interactions with it are captured at the same granularity. This can make it difficult to work out what the user was doing after a long series of report interactions. The following screenshot shows a simple case as an example:

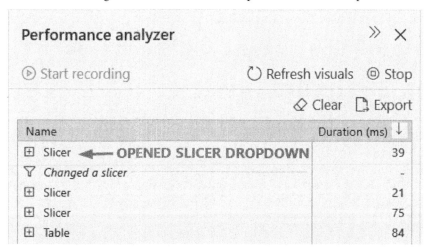

Figure 5.2 – The Slicer dropdown opened, then a selection is made

Here, first the **Slicer** dropdown is opened then the slicer value was selected, denoted as **Changed a slicer**. It is not obvious that the first item was a user action since it looks like a generic visual update. If we extend this example by opening the slicer dropdown again, it becomes even less clear. The following screenshot shows how the analyzer simply appends the drop-down action to the visuals from the previous **Changed a slicer** action:

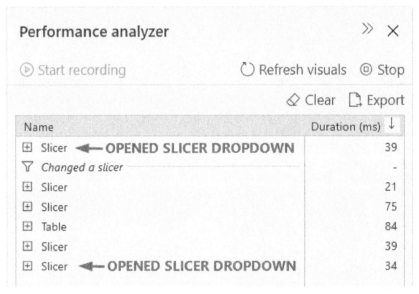

Figure 5.3 – The Slicer dropdown opened a second time

Some advanced Power BI report development techniques are not captured as formal user actions by Performance Analyzer. For example, if you use image visuals and bind the action to a report bookmark (such as a pop-up slicer panel), this will just register as a series of visual updates. The following screenshot shows an example of such a report, where a pop-up slicer has appeared and the report content in the background has been dimmed:

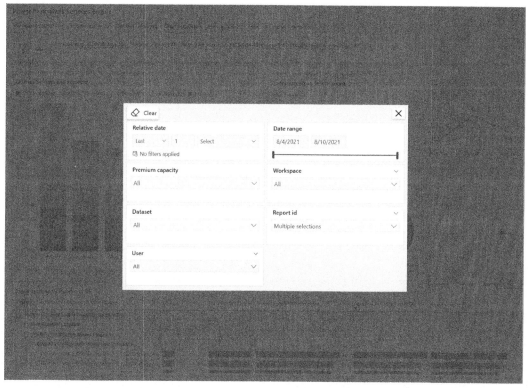

Figure 5.4 – Example of a pop-up slicer panel triggered by an action on an image

The following screenshot shows what **Performance analyzer** would capture for this pop-up slicer. The highlighted area shows the activities associated with showing the **Slicer** panel. They are directly below the activities from the previous user action (a visual refresh initiated from the analyzer):

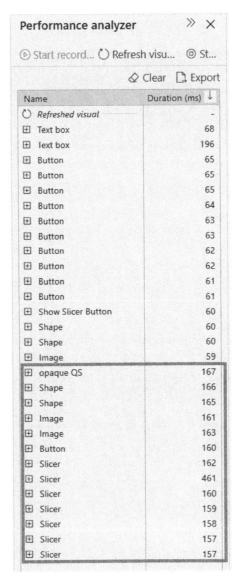

Figure 5.5 – Highlighted area showing how to activate the Slicer panel

Next, we'll look at some tips for using Performance Analyzer, examples of performance issues you might uncover using the tool, and what the data suggests.

Spotting and mitigating performance issues

First, we will cover some recommended practices in working with Performance Analyzer to ensure you are comparing the same thing each time you test. This is important, so you should try to eliminate as many variables as possible and simulate the same conditions, whatever you can reasonably control.

Achieving consistency in tests

When you have a `.pbix` file open in Power BI Desktop, the dataset has already been loaded into memory. For import models, the file could be quite large, easily a few **gigabytes** (**GB**). You are likely to have noticed that Power BI Desktop takes longer to start up when opening a very large file. Much of this time is taken by the dataset being loaded from disk into memory. This concept applies in the **Power BI service** too, after you deploy datasets there.

The Power BI service does not keep all datasets in memory all the time. The service applies some heuristics to decide when to free up memory. If you haven't used a dataset for some time, you can incur a model load delay when you first run the report. Even though Microsoft uses efficient storage and transfer technologies behind the scenes, this delay is not negligible for datasets that are multiple GB in size. This can push the first-time load too far beyond the 8–10-second recommendation for the maximum report load duration, which was given in *Chapter 1, Setting Targets and Identifying Problem Areas*. Bear this model's load time in mind when comparing Desktop and service performance and consider removing this outlier from your performance metrics when appropriate. User expectations may also need to be set for this first run scenario for large models, especially if the reports serve critical needs or audiences.

Any discussion about performance tends to touch on the topic of caching. Caching is a proven mechanism that's been used in computing for decades as a simple way to boost the performance of frequently used scenarios by storing some results locally for fast reuse. Power BI benefits from caching in many areas too. However, this can affect your tests because the very first run of a report and its queries are typically slower than subsequent reloads, which benefit from caches.

When you open an existing file in Power BI Desktop, you start with the last report page that was open when the file was saved. This page would likely be populated with some visuals, which will load, fire queries, and render before you can interact with Power BI Desktop. Even if you start Performance Analyzer immediately and start investigating behavior, you are already benefiting somewhat from caches in the client and Analysis Services to some extent. A good way to observe and account for this caching in Power BI Desktop is through blank report pages.

> **Tip**
> Add a blank page to your report when doing performance testing in Power BI Desktop. Save the file with that blank page open and then exit Power BI Desktop. Open the file in Power BI again, observing that it opens on the blank page again. Now, you are in a state where no queries have run against the dataset, so it has not had a chance to populate caches.

The following screenshot shows the effect of opening a file on a blank page and then switching to the report to check performance, compared to using the visual refresh button on the **Analyzer** panel. The first *cold* load spends over 1 second in **Other**, whereas this category is negligible in the subsequent visual refresh. DAX queries had very little impact. This is due to some visual initialization that only occurs the very first time the visual is displayed. You can influence this category by reducing the number of visuals in the report. There is no recommended limit, but noticeable delays start to occur when the report uses 30-50 visuals or more, especially those that run queries. We will look at visual reduction techniques in *Chapter 9, Report and Dashboard Design*:

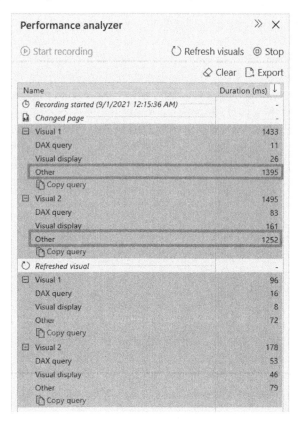

Figure 5.6 – More time was spent in "Other" on the first load

The Power BI Desktop client will cache queries in local memory. If you're accessing reports through the Power BI web portal, this is done using your web browser. If you switch away from a report page and back to it again, Power BI will not issue new queries and will render visuals from the local query cache. This is demonstrated in the following screenshot, where a report page was viewed, we switched to a blank page, and then we switched back to the original report page again. We expanded the activities for the same two visuals, noting that no DAX queries were fired the second time:

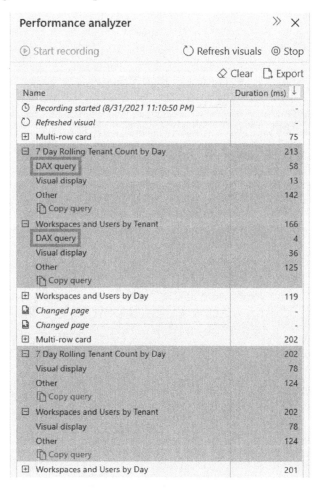

Figure 5.7 – DAX queries were only fired the first time the page loaded

One final matter worth considering is what else you are running on the machine at the same time as Power BI Desktop and Performance Analyzer. Combinations of large datasets and complex queries can require significant CPU and memory resources for short bursts. If you are running many other applications on the machine while performance testing, it may affect your measurements.

You can see the effects of slower CPU speed on visuals by adjusting the power settings on your computer. In Microsoft Windows, you can slow down your processor through the **Advanced settings** section of **Power Options**, as shown in the following screenshot. Depending on how your processor handles this setting, you could see noticeable increases in duration by lowering the **Maximum processor state** setting. This is a somewhat crude but useful tool to simulate how the reports will perform on older, slower devices:

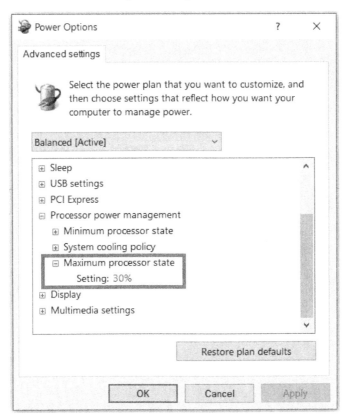

Figure 5.8 – Adjusting Power Options in Windows to reduce CPU power

> **Tip**
> Web browsers have built-in developer tools that can also simulate slow and low power devices. We recommend doing a web search for the browser you are using to learn how.

Now, let's learn about the areas that can affect report performance that Performance Analyzer cannot fully address.

Understanding Performance Analyzer's strengths and limitations

Performance Analyzer can help you optimize your report's design, data model's design, and DAX formulas to achieve the best balance of functionality and performance. Excluding external factors such as DirectQuery load, Premium capacity load, or network conditions, you might assume that once you get the best speed in Desktop, the same experience will be achieved in the service. This is often true, so performance optimization in Desktop is an excellent first step in any performance journey.

There are still scale-related issues that can affect performance in production. When dealing with large data volumes, it is a good practice to limit data volumes when you're still in development, to speed up the process. You would point to the large production data sources when publishing reports to the broader organization. Queries will generally run faster on smaller data volumes, so if the difference is significant, the results from Desktop could be unrealistic. Some DAX expressions or visuals may only slow down when you're dealing with large volumes of data, so performance degradation may not be consistent across visuals or pages, even in the same report. Again, this must be considered when you're doing performance testing and comparisons.

> **Tip**
> When conducting performance tests in Performance Analyzer, if you cannot connect to the production datasets directly, replicate the data source as closely as possible. Try to have the same data or similar volumes in your testing environment.

Another factor to be aware of when using Performance Analyzer is your geographical location. If all your users are accessing Power BI from a single physical office, you can safely run all performance tests from that office. However, if you have multiple locations, **virtual private networks** (**VPNs**), or remote users over the public internet, you should consider running tests from those locations to account for network conditions. What you choose to optimize will depend on your users' roles and the impact of poor performance.

> **Tip**
> If you have users in multiple geographical locations and it is not feasible to physically run performance tests in all of them, you might be able to create similar network conditions by using a **virtual machine** (**VM**) in the same region as those users. You can provision these VMs on demand from any established cloud provider and pay a very small amount for a few hours of testing.

A limitation of the Performance Analyzer user interface in Desktop is the absence of timestamps or an overall duration for the operation. This makes it difficult to work out the total duration of your action, from start to finish. We will partly address this limitation later in this chapter when we look at logs.

Next, let's look at examples of problems you can identify with Performance Analyzer.

Interpreting and acting on Performance Analyzer data

Performance Analyzer excels at identifying slow queries and slow visuals. We will look at some results where these appear slow and consider what to do next.

Dealing with slow queries

There are a variety of reasons why a query could be slow. When testing in Desktop, you will be looking primarily at model and DAX efficiency, especially if you are using a local dataset contained within a .pbix file. Excluding external factors typically found in production use, here are some reasons a query might be slow:

- It requests a wide and deep set of results

- It contains complex or inefficient measures

- It is operating on a large dataset, possibly with high cardinality joins

- The data model is not following recommended practices

- Combinations of all these factors

The following figure shows two table visuals from a report showing sales and product counts grouped by account number. There is a simple sum measure (**LineTotal**), along with a distinct count of red products. The slow and fast measures give the same results, though the underlying DAX is a little different:

AccountNumber	LineTotal	UniqueRedProducts_Slow		AccountNumber	LineTotal	UniqueRedProducts_Fast
AW00011000	8,248.99			AW00011000	8,248.99	
AW00011001	6,383.88	3		AW00011001	6,383.88	3
AW00011002	8,114.04	1		AW00011002	8,114.04	1
AW00011003	8,139.29	1		AW00011003	8,139.29	1
AW00011004	8,196.01	1		AW00011004	8,196.01	1
AW00011005	8,121.33	1		AW00011005	8,121.33	1
AW00011006	8,119.03			AW00011006	8,119.03	
AW00011007	8,211.00	1		AW00011007	8,211.00	1
AW00011008	8,106.31	2		AW00011008	8,106.31	2
AW00011009	8,091.33	3		AW00011009	8,091.33	3
AW00011010	8,088.04	1		AW00011010	8,088.04	1
Total	**109,846,381.40**	**79**		**Total**	**109,846,381.40**	**79**

Figure 5.9 – Tables with the same results but from using different measures

The following screenshot shows the results of Performance Analyzer for the tables previously. Observe how one query took over 26 seconds, whereas the other took under 1.5 seconds:

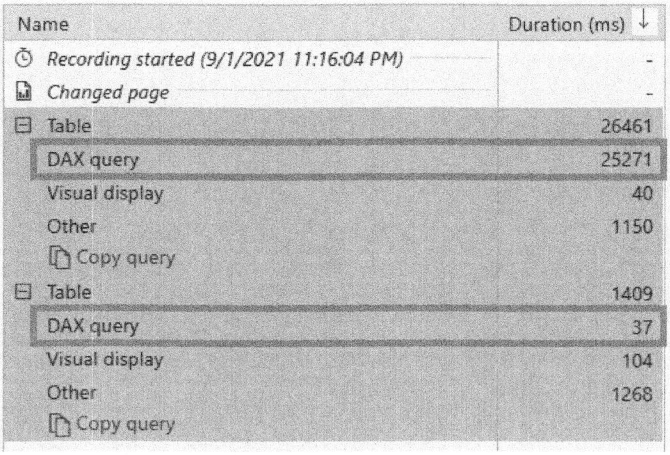

Name	Duration (ms) ↓
⏱ *Recording started (9/1/2021 11:16:04 PM)*	-
🖺 *Changed page*	-
⊟ Table	26461
DAX query	25271
Visual display	40
Other	1150
🗐 Copy query	
⊟ Table	1409
DAX query	37
Visual display	104
Other	1268
🗐 Copy query	

Figure 5.10 – Vastly different query durations for the same visual result

Now, let's view the DAX code behind these measures:

```
UniqueRedProducts_Slow =
CALCULATE (
DISTINCTCOUNT ('SalesOrderDetail' [ProductID]),
FILTER (
'SalesOrderDetail',
RELATED ('Product' [Color]) = "Red"))
UniqueRedProducts_Fast =
CALCULATE (
DISTINCTCOUNT ('SalesOrderDetail' [ProductID]), 'Product' [Color]
= "Red")
```

These definitions look very similar, and we can assume a relationship between `SalesOrderDetail` and `Product`. Hence, it might not be obvious why one is so much slower. The reason is that the slow version is forcing a *row context* through the `RELATED` function. We will return to this example in the next chapter, where we will capture the query traces. If you were starting with just the slow version and saw this 26-second query, a recommended action would be to look at **Analysis Services** engine traces to discover why. In the case of slow queries here, you should also review the data model and DAX for best practices. These will be covered in dedicated chapters later in this book. You can explore this in the sample `Slow vs Fast Measures.pbix` file.

Dealing with slow visuals

There are often occasions where the DAX query's duration is only a small portion of the total visual duration. Visuals could be slow for the following reasons:

- They fetch external visual content such as images.
- They retrieve data from APIs, such as a map visual's geocoding coordinates.
- They are performing complex calculations on many data points.
- They are not optimized, which can be the case with some uncertified custom visuals.

The following screenshot shows a map visual of some **inspection sites** around the USA. The dataset contains over 27,000 latitude and longitude coordinates. The visual applies a point reduction algorithm and geocodes the data:

Inspection Sites

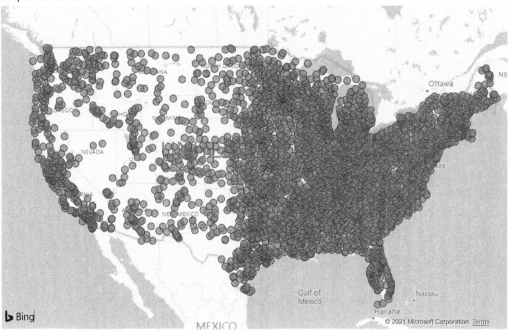

Figure 5.11 – A map with many points

The following screenshot shows the analyzer trace for the same map visual. It was the only visual on the report page, and we switched there from a blank page. Notice how the **Visual display** and **Other** durations add up to over 4 seconds, which is most of the visual's overall duration:

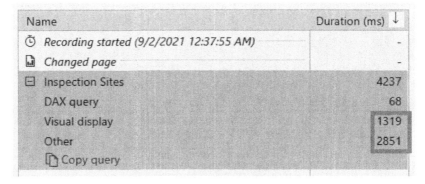

Figure 5.12 – Significant amount of time spent on non-query activities

In this specific case, even though 4 seconds is reasonable, you might change the visual configuration or apply filters to speed the visual up. This advice generally applies to other slow visuals too and is worth exploring. You can explore this map in the sample files, in `Map with Many Points.pbix`.

If the problematic visual can't be improved, you could replace it with a similar one that performs better, albeit with some compromises. Alternatively, you could think about telling the story a different way, through a different set of visualizations.

The effect of adding more visuals

Earlier in this chapter, we mentioned how the **Other** category increases as you add more visuals. This can be seen in Performance Analyzer. To show how things can get to the more extreme end, we created a report with six simple unique visuals. Then, we duplicated these 19 times for a total of 120 visuals. After, we changed the different filter combinations for the visuals so that each would generate a unique query. These six visuals are shown in the following screenshot:

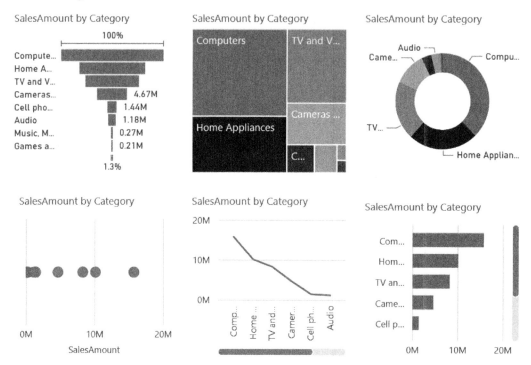

Figure 5.13 – Visuals that were duplicated for the test

The following screenshot shows a few of the visual performance results when the page containing 120 visuals was tested. Note how the DAX queries are extremely fast, while a lot of time is spent in **Other**:

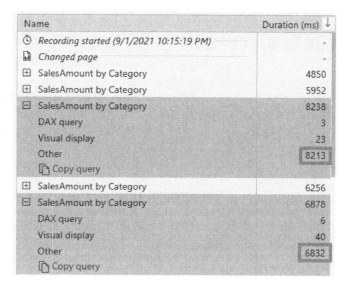

Name	Duration (ms) ↓
⏱ *Recording started (9/1/2021 10:15:19 PM)*	-
📄 *Changed page*	-
⊞ SalesAmount by Category	4850
⊞ SalesAmount by Category	5952
⊟ SalesAmount by Category	8238
DAX query	3
Visual display	23
Other	8213
📋 Copy query	
⊞ SalesAmount by Category	6256
⊟ SalesAmount by Category	6878
DAX query	6
Visual display	40
Other	6832
📋 Copy query	

Figure 5.14 – Significant time spent in "Other" with 120 visuals (not all shown)

If your reports have this issue with many visuals, the best advice is to reduce the number. You won't necessarily compromise on the experience, and in many cases, this can improve it. We will cover specific guidance for report optimization in *Chapter 9, Report and Dashboard Design*.

Now, let's conclude this chapter by exploring the log export capability of Performance Analyzer.

Exporting and analyzing performance data

Earlier in this chapter, we came across a few limitations regarding the information that Performance Analyzer provides. A great way to dive deeper into these logs is to import and parse them in Power BI itself so that you can analyze the data. In this section, you will get some guidance on how to import and transform the logs and use the additional information they provide.

The Power BI Performance Analyzer log is a JSON file with the following properties:

- All user actions and events generated by visuals are at the top level of the JSON document, contained in an events element.

- Some events contain a metrics element, which can have multiple properties such as query duration, query text, and visual metadata, such as ID and type.

- Events have an id and a parentid, both of which can be used to define a parent-child hierarchy of events, allowing you to visualize the tree.

The following screenshot shows the first few entries in a Performance Analyzer log file:

```
{
    "version": "1.1.0",
    "events": [
        {
        {
            "name": "User Action",
            "component": "Report Canvas",
            "start": "2021-09-03T03:53:28.246Z",
            "id": "cc7f4683c7eae2856ba2",
            "metrics": {
                "sourceLabel": "UserAction_ChangePage"
            }
        },
        {
            "name": "Visual Container Lifecycle",
            "component": "Report Canvas",
            "start": "2021-09-03T03:53:28.420Z",
            "end": "2021-09-03T03:53:30.665Z",
            "id": "0aeda8bb1e877969ee3f-9ab27e40bdc010c9196c",
            "metrics": {
                "status": 1,
                "visualTitle": "Slicer",
                "visualId": "0aeda8bb1e877969ee3f",
                "visualType": "slicer",
                "initialLoad": true
            }
        },
        {
            "name": "Query",
            "component": "Report Canvas",
            "start": "2021-09-03T03:53:28.422Z",
            "end": "2021-09-03T03:53:30.636Z",
            "id": "393e8e690c654094ca0c",
            "parentId": "0aeda8bb1e877969ee3f-9ab27e40bdc010c9196c"
        },
```

Figure 5.15 – The first few elements of the Performance Analyzer log file

Some transformation work is required before you can get value out of the data. We mentioned earlier that the user actions and visual events are at the same level in the file. Events themselves are not associated with the user action because user actions have no children. First, we must assume that after a user action, the next few events in the time sequence are the visual changes caused by that action. To visualize the events like a tree, we must derive some new columns to group each user action's events together and parent them to that action. We can also calculate a duration by subtracting the start and end timestamps.

The following screenshot shows a simple DirectQuery report that we will use to analyze the log files:

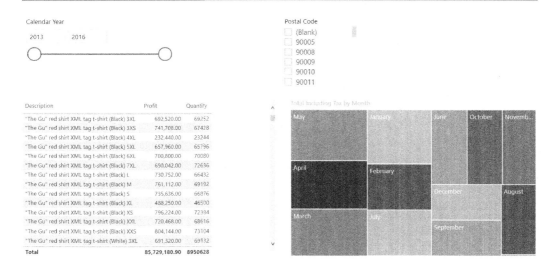

Figure 5.16 – DirectQuery report with four visuals

The performance log is generated by switching to this page from a blank page, then performing a visual refresh in the analyzer. There is a total of two user actions. The log from the user interface is shown in the following screenshot:

Name	Duration (ms) ↓
⏱ *Recording started (9/2/2021 8:53:22 PM)*	-
🔖 *Changed page*	-
⊞ Slicer	2245
⊞ Slicer	1350
⊞ Total Including Tax by Month	4087
⊞ Table	5014
◌ *Refreshed visual*	-
⊞ Slicer	107
⊞ Slicer	132
⊞ Table	4118
⊞ Total Including Tax by Month	3297

Figure 5.17 – A Performance Analyzer trace for the two user actions

We exported this data and then worked on it in the sample `Analyzing Desktop Performance Logs.pbix` file. When the data has been shaped to our needs, we can build a simple chronological view, allowing us to filter out various event types and visuals. You can use this to investigate the sequence and duration of the events:

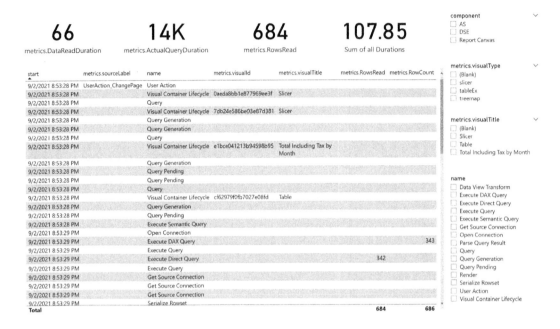

Figure 5.18 – Sequence of events and performance metrics

The following screenshot shows how to build a tree view for each user action. In this example, we used the slicer to select one user action. Now, we can see its statistics and event tree:

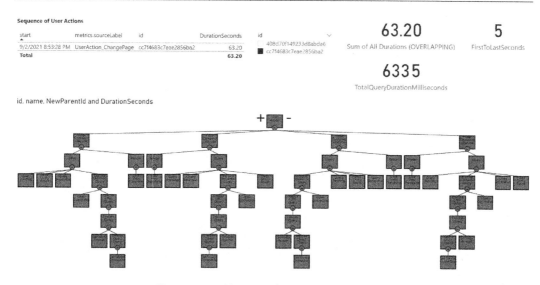

Figure 5.19 – Tree visualization of a user action

This view contains a **FirstToLastSeconds** calculation, which is from the earliest start time to the latest end time of events in scope. It tries to give you an idea of the duration of the user action itself until the last activity is completed. This addresses one gap in the Desktop UI.

> **Important Note**
>
> Calculating the duration of the user action using this custom method is not officially documented and should be considered approximate only. You should use it to compare the relative changes in performance from one design to another.

The transformation methods that were used in the sample file are quite basic and rely on you manually hardcoding line numbers in the file to partition user actions. This is intentional, to illustrate the structure of the JSON in a small file. You can point this sample to your log file and make changes as necessary to make it more automatic over much larger performance log files.

Now that we have finished looking at Performance Analyzer, it is time to summarize what we've learned in this chapter.

Summary

In this chapter, we introduced Performance Analyzer as a built-in tool to help you assess performance for every report user action, on a per-visual basis. It breaks visual processing into query, visual, and other components to help you focus on your performance tuning efforts. It also provides durations and other metrics to help you assess behavior. It lets you copy DAX and DQ queries for analysis in other tools. You can also export the whole performance log file for analysis.

We learned about the types of user actions that the analyzer captures and what metrics it provides in the user interface. We also pointed out some scenarios that can make it difficult to distinguish actions.

Next, we covered some good practices for performance testing in Power BI Desktop, such as using blank report pages, ensuring consistency in tests, and trying to replicate production scenarios as closely as possible. We learned that even if we optimized performance a lot in Desktop, it may not reveal issues that arise with high user or data scale. It cannot help much with external factors that affect the speed of published reports in the Power BI service.

Then, we learned that the analyzer is good at identifying slow visuals or queries and provided practical examples of both. We learned why these could be slow and what next steps you could take to resolve such issues. We also learned that a very high number of visuals can slow down a report due to processor contention, regardless of query speed or individual visual speed.

We concluded this chapter by looking at the extra information we can get from the exported performance log files. It was possible to work out sums of durations and the length of user actions, though there are caveats as this is not officially documented. It was also possible to transform the data to visualize the event hierarchy as a tree. These techniques increase the value of the analysis you do in Performance Analyzer.

In the next chapter, we will look at freely available third-party utilities that complement Performance Analyzer and help you optimize your report, data model, and DAX queries.

6
Third-Party Utilities

In the previous two chapters, we used tools and data provided by Microsoft to get insights into report performance. In this chapter, we will cover some popular freely available third-party utilities that complement the built-in offerings and improve your productivity when investigating report performance issues.

These tools have a range of features, such as documenting our solutions, analyzing them to give recommendations, the ability to modify Power BI artifacts, capturing performance traces, and running queries. It is beyond the scope of this book to cover the full functionality of these tools, so we will limit our coverage to features and techniques that help us assess and improve performance.

The utilities introduced in this chapter are largely maintained by community contributors and are often **open source**. All the utilities described in this chapter are widely used to the point where they are formally acknowledged by Microsoft. Power BI Desktop will recognize them if they are installed on your computer and allow you to launch them from its **External Tools** menu, sometimes even connected to the .pbix file you are working on. At the time of writing, these utilities are actively maintained, and the releases are generally of high quality.

However, while the development of these open source tools is often stewarded by experts who run their own Power BI consulting and training businesses, they are not always officially supported, so you should bear this in mind. Your organization may have policies against the use of such tools. If you do use them, be aware that you may not be able to get prompt dedicated assistance as you normally would with a support case for a paid commercial offering.

All the utilities in this chapter can connect to Analysis Services datasets running within Power BI Desktop, Azure Analysis Services, or the Power BI service. Therefore, we will simply refer to these tools connecting to Analysis Services datasets for most of the chapter.

This chapter is broken into the following sections:

- Power BI Helper
- Tabular Editor
- DAX Studio and VertiPaq Analyzer

Technical requirements

There are samples available for some parts of this chapter. We will call out which files to refer to. Please check out the `Chapter06` folder on GitHub to get these assets: `https://github.com/PacktPublishing/Microsoft-Power-BI-Performance-Best-Practices`.

Power BI Helper

Power BI Helper has a range of features that help you explore, document, and compare local Power BI Desktop files. It also lets you explore and export metadata from the Power BI service, such as lists of workspaces and datasets and their properties. Power BI Helper can be downloaded from the following link: `https://powerbihelper.org`.

In previous chapters, we discussed how important it is to keep Power BI datasets smaller by removing unused tables and columns. Power BI Helper includes features to help you do this, so it could be a useful tool to incorporate into standard optimization processes before production releases.

Identifying large columns in the dataset

In general, having a smaller model speeds up report loads and data refresh, which is why it is good to be able to identify the largest items easily. For now, we simply want to introduce this capability so you are aware of this technique. We will learn about dataset size reduction in detail in *Chapter 10, Data Modeling and Row-Level Security*. Complete the following steps to investigate dataset size:

1. Open your .pbix file in Power BI Desktop, then connect Power BI Helper to the dataset.

2. Navigate to the **Modeling Advise** tab.

3. Observe how Power BI Helper lists all columns sorted by their dictionary size from largest to smallest.

    The dictionary size is how much space in MB is taken by the compressed data for that column. The following figure shows the result of this tab:

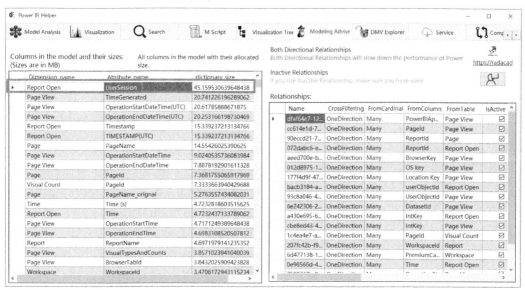

Figure 6.1 – Modeling Advise tab of showing largest column

In this example, the **UserSession** column (referred to as an attribute) takes up about 45 MB. The .pbix file was 172 MB. From these sizes, we can calculate that this one column contributes to approximately 25% of the file size, which is significant. You should try to remove large columns like this from the dataset. If you need it for reporting, relationship, or calculation purposes, try optimizing it using techniques from *Chapter 10, Data Modeling and Row-Level Security*.

> **Tip**
>
> A Power BI Desktop file in Import mode contains a complete copy of the source data. The data is contained within the `.pbix` file as an Analysis Services backup file (`.abf`). Even though the `.pbix` file size is not the same as the size of the dataset when it is loaded into memory, it can be used for a quick approximation to judge the impact of column and table sizes on the overall dataset size.

Identifying unused columns

Power BI Helper can identify all the unused columns in your model. You simply navigate to the **Visualization** tab and observe them in a list. You can remove them from the dataset by right-clicking the items and selecting **Delete**. This is shown in the following figure:

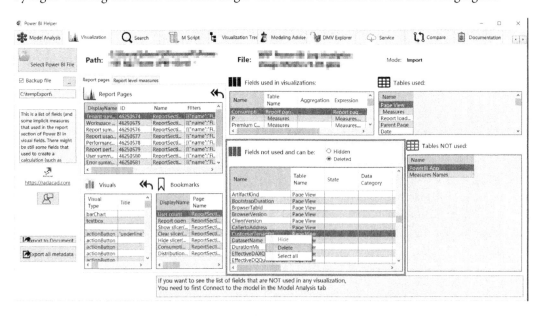

Figure 6.2 – Unused columns showing the ability to delete from Power BI Helper

Note that any changes applied in Power BI Helper will be applied to the `.pbix` file you have open immediately. By default, Power BI Helper will back up your original file to the location specified at the top left, as shown in the previous figure. It is recommended to use this backup feature to recover from accidental deletions.

Identifying bi-directional and inactive relationships

The **Modeling Advise** tab we referred to in *Figure 6.1* has a relationships section on the right-hand side. You can use this to conveniently identify all bi-directional relationships in your dataset. These can slow down queries and might have unintentional filter consequences, so it's a good idea to review each one to ensure it is really needed.

Identifying measure dependencies

Power BI Helper visualizes measure dependencies via the **Model Analysis** tab. Measures can be reused within other measures, and this is the best practice for maintainability. In a chain of measure dependencies, the start of the chain is often referred to as the **base measure**. Base measures may be used in many other measures and Power BI Helper lets you easily identify all those reverse dependencies. You can use this information to get a better return on investment when performance tuning because optimizing base measures that are used in many other measures could have a large overall impact. Conversely, you may have a complex measure that uses many other measures. In this case, Power BI Helper helps you identify all the measures it uses so you know which to consider when optimizing.

We have seen how Power BI Helper can help us identify a few common dataset design issues. Next, we will look at **Tabular Editor**, another freely available tool that can go in more depth into dataset design guidance.

Tabular Editor

Tabular Editor is available as both a commercial offering and an open source version. The paid version offers some advanced development functionality and even dedicated support, which professional Power BI developers may find useful. The good news is that the free version contains all the useful core features at the time of writing, and it can be downloaded at the following GitHub link: `https://github.com/TabularEditor/TabularEditor`.

Tabular Editor is a productivity tool aimed at improving many aspects of the development experience offered by Power BI Desktop or Microsoft Visual Studio. These core features are out of scope for this book. Due to the sheer popularity of the tool with experienced BI developers, you are encouraged to learn more about Tabular Editor if you expect to build and maintain complex enterprise models over many months or even years. Please follow the product documentation to become familiar with the interface and functionality of Tabular Editor. We are going to focus on a specific feature of Tabular Editor called the Best Practice Analyzer.

Using Tabular Editor's Best Practice Analyzer

Tabular Editor has a powerful extension called the **Best Practice Analyzer** (**BPA**). This extension lets you define a set of modeling rules that can be saved as collections. An example of a rule is to avoid using floating-point data types for numerical columns. Once you have a set of rules defined, you can use the BPA to scan an Analysis Services dataset. It will check all objects against applicable modeling rules and generate a report in the process.

After you have installed Tabular Editor, open the **Tools** menu. Here you will find the options to launch the BPA and manage its rules, as shown in the following figure:

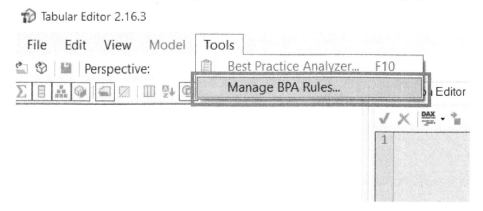

Figure 6.3 – How to manage BPA rules in Tabular Editor

If this is the first time you are using Tabular Editor, you will find that there are no rules included with the installer. The best way to start is to use a default set of best practices that Microsoft helped define, and you need to perform some brief manual steps to load in some default rules. For reference, you can find the rules included within the Tabular Editor project on GitHub, at the following location: `https://github.com/TabularEditor/BestPracticeRules`.

To install the rules, you simply copy the `BPARules.json` file found at the previous link into the `%localappdata%\TabularEditor` folder on your computer. You can paste this exact location into Windows File Explorer to get to the appropriate place.

Alternatively, you can use the Advanced Scripting functionality of Tabular Editor to download and copy the rules to the location for you. Simply paste the following script into the tool, run it, then restart Tabular Editor to have the rules available:

```
System.Net.WebClient w = new System.Net.WebClient();
string path = System.Environment.GetFolderPath(System.
Environment.SpecialFolder.LocalApplicationData);
string url = "https://raw.githubusercontent.com/microsoft/
Analysis-Services/master/BestPracticeRules/BPARules.json";
```

```
string downloadLoc = path+@"\TabularEditor\BPARules.json";
w.DownloadFile(url, downloadLoc);
```

> **Note**
>
> You need to connect to an Analysis Services dataset in Tabular Editor before you can run any scripts; otherwise, the option will be disabled in the toolbar.

The following figure shows the result of running the BPA download script in Tabular Editor, highlighting the script execution button and the successful result shown in the status bar:

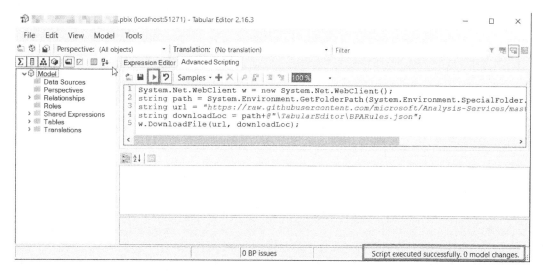

Figure 6.4 – BPA rules successfully loaded via the Advanced Scripting feature

Once you have the rules loaded, you can view, modify, and add rules as you please. The following screenshots show what the interface looks like after rules are imported:

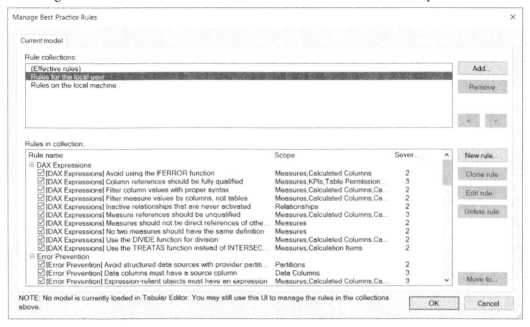

Figure 6.5 – BPA rules loaded into Tabular Editor

The next screenshot shows the rule editor, after opening an existing rule:

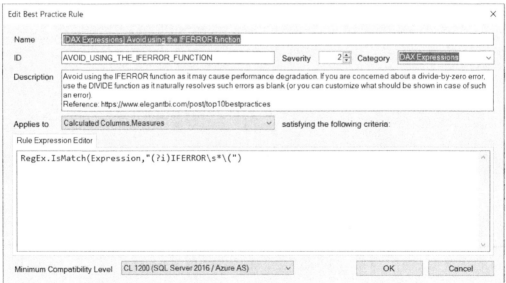

Figure 6.6 – Editing a best practice rule

When you want to run the BPA rules against your dataset, connect to it using one of the supported methods in Tabular Editor. Once connected, run the BPA by pressing *F10* or by selecting it from the **Tools** menu, which was introduced in *Figure 6.3*.

A sample of results that can be obtained from running the BPA on a dataset is shown in the following figure. It highlights three useful toolbar buttons that are available for some rules:

- Go to object: This will open the model script at the definition of the offending object.

- Generate fix script: This will generate a script you can use to apply the change and copy it to the clipboard.

- Apply fix: This will apply the fix script to your model immediately. Be careful with this option and make sure you have a backup in place beforehand.

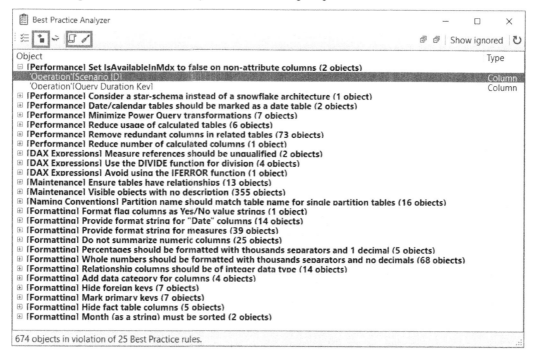

Figure 6.7 – BPA results, highlighting context-sensitive toolbar actions

Once you have the BPA results, you need to decide which changes to apply. It might seem like a great idea to simply apply all changes automatically. However, we advise a careful review of the results and applying some thought to which recommendations to apply and in what order.

The default BPA rules are grouped into six categories:

- **DAX Expressions**
- **Error Prevention**
- **Formatting, Maintenance**
- **Naming Conventions**
- **Performance**

For performance optimization, we advise focusing on the **Performance** and **DAX Expressions** categories. These optimizations have a direct impact on the query and refresh performance. The other categories benefit usability and maintenance.

Tip

The best way to be certain that performance optimizations have had the expected impact is to test the effect of each change in typical usage scenarios. For example, if you plan to optimize three independent DAX measures, change one at a time and check the improvement you get with each change. Then check again with all changes applied. This will help you identify the most impactful change and not assume that every change will result in a measurable difference when stacked with others. This will also help you learn the relative impact of design patterns, so you know what to look for first next time around to get the best return on investment when optimizing designs.

Thus far, we have been introduced to some utilities that help us identify dataset design issues. Next, we will look at DAX Studio and VertiPaq Analyzer. These are complementary tools that give us more dataset information and help us debug and resolve dataset and DAX performance issues, with the ability to customize DAX queries and measure their speed.

DAX Studio and VertiPaq Analyzer

DAX Studio, as the name implies, is a tool centered around DAX queries. It provides a simple yet intuitive interface with powerful features to browse and query Analysis Services datasets. We will cover querying later in this section. For now, let's look deeper into datasets.

The Analysis Services engine has supported **Dynamic Management Views (DMVs)** for many years. These views refer to SQL-like queries that can be executed on Analysis Services to return information about dataset objects and operations.

VertiPaq Analyzer is a utility that uses publicly documented DMVs to display essential information about which structures exist inside the dataset and how much space they occupy. It started life as a standalone utility, published as a Power Pivot for an Excel workbook, and still exists in that form today. In this chapter, we will refer to its more recent incarnation as a built-in feature of DAX Studio.

It is interesting to note that VertiPaq is the original name given to the compressed column storage engine within Analysis Services (*Verti* referring to columns and *Paq* referring to compression).

Analyzing model size with VertiPaq Analyzer

VertiPaq Analyzer is now built into DAX Studio as the **View Metrics** feature, found in the **Advanced** tab of the toolbar. You simply click the icon to have DAX Studio run the DMVs for you and display the statistics in a tabular form. This is shown in the following figure:

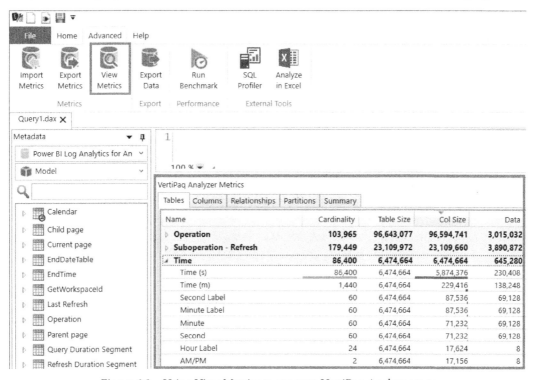

Figure 6.8 – Using View Metrics to generate VertiPaq Analyzer stats

You can switch to the **Summary** tab of the **Vertipaq Analyzer Metrics** pane to get an idea of the overall total size of the model along with other summary statistics, as shown in the following figure:

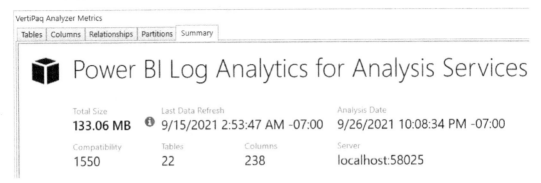

Figure 6.9 – Summary tab of VertiPaq Analyzer Metrics

The **Total Size** metric provided in the previous figure will often be larger than the size of the dataset on disk (as a `.pbix` file or Analysis Services `.abf` backup). This is because there are additional structures required when the dataset is loaded into memory, which is particularly true of Import mode datasets.

In *Chapter 2, Exploring Power BI Architecture and Configuration*, we learned about Power BI's compressed column storage engine. The DMV statistics provided by VertiPaq Analyzer let us see just how compressible columns are and how much space they are taking up. It also allows us to observe other objects, such as relationships.

The **Columns** tab is a great way to see whether you have any columns that are very large relative to others or the entire dataset. The following figure shows the columns view for the same dataset we saw in *Figure 6.9*. You can see how from 238 columns, a single column called **Operation-EventText** takes up a staggering 39% of the whole dataset size! It's interesting to see its **Cardinality** (or uniqueness) value is about four times lower than the next largest column's:

Table-Column	Rows	Cardinality	Col Size	Data	Dictionary	Hier Size	% Table	% DB	Encoding	Data Type
Operation-EventText	103,965	24,729	54,493,308	97,480	54,197,956	197,872	56.41%	39.06%	HASH	String
Time-Time (s)	86,400	86,400	5,874,376	230,408	4,952,720	691,248	90.73%	4.21%	HASH	DateTime
StartTime-Time	86,400	86,400	5,874,376	230,408	4,952,720	691,248	90.89%	4.21%	HASH	DateTime
EndTime-Time	86,400	86,400	5,874,376	230,408	4,952,720	691,248	90.89%	4.21%	HASH	DateTime

Figure 6.10 – One column monopolizing the dataset

In the previous figure, we can also see that **Data Type** is **String**, which is alphanumeric text. These statistics would lead you to deduce that this column contains long, unique text values that do not compress well. Indeed, in this case, the column contained DAX and DQ query text from Analysis Services engine traces that were loaded into Power BI. A finding such as this may lead you to re-evaluate the need for this level of detail in the dataset. You'd need to ask yourself whether the extra storage space and time taken to build the compressed columns and potentially other structures is worth it for your business case. In cases of highly detailed data such as this where you do need long text values, consider limiting the analysis to shorter time periods, such as days or weeks.

Now let's learn about how DAX Studio can help us with performance analysis and improvement.

Performance tuning the data model and DAX

The first-party option for capturing Analysis Services traces is SQL Server Profiler. When starting a trace, you must identify exactly which events to capture, which requires some knowledge of the trace events and what they contain. Even with this knowledge, working with the trace data in Profiler can be tough since the tool was designed primarily to work with SQL Server database traces. The good news is that DAX Studio can start an Analysis Services server trace then parse and format all the data to show you relevant results well presented within its user interface. It allows us to both run and measure queries in a single place and provides bespoke features for Analysis Services that make it a good alternative SQL Profiler for tuning Analysis Services datasets.

Capturing and replaying queries

The **All Queries** command in the **Traces** section of the DAX Studio toolbar will start a trace against the dataset you have connected to. The following figure shows the result when a trace is successfully started:

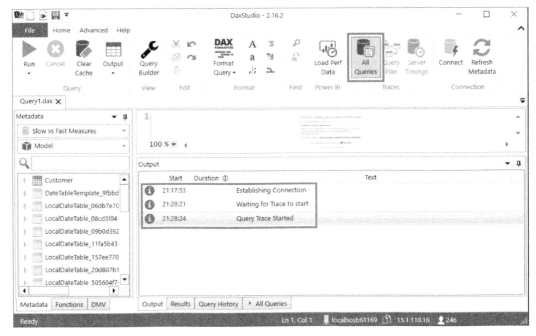

Figure 6.11 – Query trace successfully started

Once your trace has started, you can interact with the dataset outside DAX Studio and it will capture queries for you. How you interact with the dataset depends on where it is. For a dataset running on your computer in Power BI Desktop, you would simply interact with the report. This would generate queries that DAX Studio will see. The **All Queries** tab at the bottom of the tool is where the captured queries are listed in time order with durations in milliseconds. The following figure shows two queries captured when opening the **Unique by Account No** page from the Slow vs Fast Measures.pbix sample file:

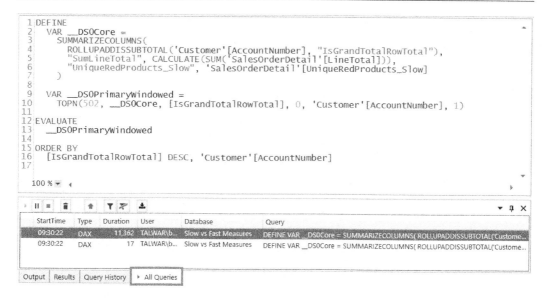

Figure 6.12 – Queries captured by DAX Studio

In *Chapter 5, Desktop Performance Analyzer*, we presented *Figure 5.9* in the section entitled *Interpreting and acting on performance analyzer data*. It showed two visuals that generated the same output onscreen. The previous screenshot shows us that the fast version took only 17 ms whereas the slow version tool took more than 11.3 seconds. In the screenshot, the query selected in blue was double-clicked to bring its DAX text into the editor above. You can now modify this query in DAX Studio to test performance changes. We learned in the previous chapter that the DAX expression for the UniqueRedProducts_Slow measure was not efficient. We'll learn a technique to optimize queries soon, but first, we need to learn about capturing query performance traces.

Obtaining query timings

To get detailed query performance information, you can use the **Server Timings** command shown in *Figure 6.12*. After starting the trace, you can run queries and then use the **Server Timings** tab to see how the engine executed the query, as shown in the following figure:

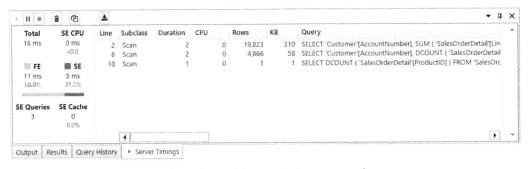

Figure 6.13 – Server Timings showing detailed query performance statistics

The previous figure gives very useful information. **FE** and **SE** refer to the **formula engine** and **storage engine**. The storage engine is fast and multi-threaded, and its job is fetching data. It can apply basic logic such as filtering data to retrieve only what is needed. The storage engine is single-threaded and it generates a query plan, which is the physical steps required to compute the result. It also performs calculations on the data such as joins, complex filters, aggregations, and lookups. We want to avoid queries that are spending most of the time in the formula engine, or that execute many queries in the storage engine. The bottom-left section of *Figure 6.14* shows that we executed almost 5,000 SE queries. The list of queries to the right shows many queries returning only one result, which is suspicious.

For comparison, we look at timings for the fast version of the query and we see the following:

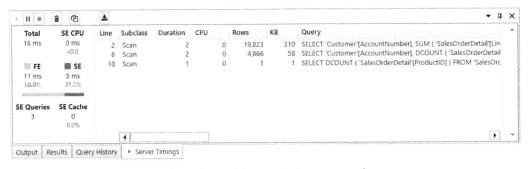

Figure 6.14 – Server Timings for fast version of query

In the previous screenshot, we can see that only three server engine queries were run this time, and the result was obtained much faster.

> **Tip**
> The Analysis Services engine does use data caches to speed up queries. These caches contain uncompressed query results that can be reused later to save time fetching and decompressing data. You should use the **Clear Cache** button in DAX Studio to force these caches to be cleared and get a proper worst-case performance measure. This is visible in the menu bar in *Figure 6.12*.

We will build on these concepts when we look at DAX and model optimizations in later chapters. Now let's look at how we can experiment with DAX and query changes in DAX Studio.

Modifying and tuning queries

Earlier in the section, we saw how we could capture a query generated by a Power BI visual then display its text. A nice trick we can use here is to use **query-scoped measures** to override the measure definition and see how performance differs.

The following screenshot shows how we can search for a measure, right-click, then pull its definition into the query editor:

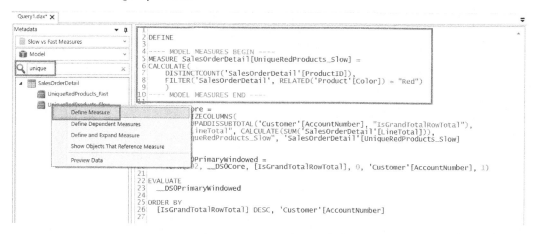

Figure 6.15 – Define Measure option and result in Query pane

We can now modify the measure in the query editor, and the engine will use the local definition instead of the one defined in the model! This technique gives you a fast way to prototype DAX enhancements without having to edit them in Power BI and refresh visuals over many iterations.

Do remember that this technique does not apply any changes to the dataset you are connected to. You can optimize expressions in DAX Studio, then transfer the definition to Power BI Desktop/Visual Studio when ready. The following screenshot shows how we changed the definition of `UniqueRedProduct_Slow` in a query-scoped measure to get a huge performance boost:

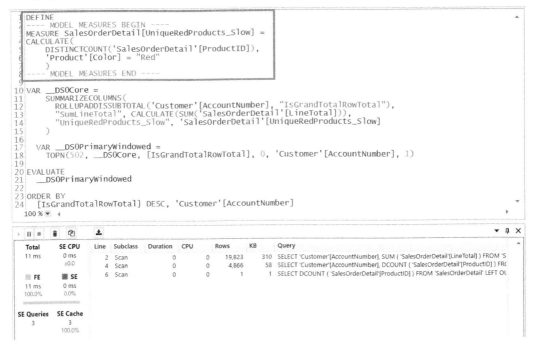

Figure 6.16 – Modified measure giving better results

The techniques described here can be adapted to model changes too. For example, if you wanted to determine the impact of changing a relationship type, you could run the same queries in DAX Studio before and after the change to draw a comparison.

Here are some additional tips for working with DAX Studio:

- **Isolate measures**: When performance tuning a query generated by a report visual, comment out complex measures and then establish a baseline performance score. Then add each measure back to the query individually and check the speed. This will help identify the slowest measures in that query and visual context.

- **Work with Desktop Performance Analyzer traces**: DAX Studio has a facility to import the trace files generated by Desktop Performance Analyzer. You can import the trace files using the **Load Perf Data** button located next to **All Queries** highlighted in *Figure 6.11*. This trace can be captured by one person then shared with a DAX/modeling expert who can use DAX Studio to analyze and replay their behavior. The following figure shows how DAX Studio formats the data to make it easy to see which visual and component is taking the most time. It was generated by viewing each of the three report pages in the `Slow vs Fast Measures.pbix` sample file:

#	Visual	QueryStart	QueryEnd	Rows	Query Ms	Render Ms	Total Ms	Query
1	Table	10:35:12	10:35:12	4	44	80	124	DEFINE VAR __DS0Core = SUMMARIZECOLUMNS
2	Table	10:35:12	10:35:12	4	39	130	169	DEFINE VAR __DS0Core = SUMMARIZECOLUMNS
3	Table	10:35:18	10:35:54	502	35,527	73	35,600	DEFINE VAR __DS0Core = SUMMARIZECOLUMNS
4	Table	10:35:18	10:35:18	502	38	160	198	DEFINE VAR __DS0Core = SUMMARIZECOLUMNS
5	Filter: Sales by Date	10:35:58	10:35:58	1,124	9	2,045	2.054	DEFINE VAR __DS0Core = SUMMARIZECOLUMNS
6	Customers by Group	10:35:59	10:35:59	3	9	93	102	DEFINE VAR __DS0Core = SUMMARIZECOLUMNS
7	Card	10:35:59	10:35:59	1	13	16	29	EVALUATE ROW("SalesAmount", 'SalesOrderDeta
8	Card	10:35:59	10:35:59	1	10	30	40	EVALUATE ROW("CountSalesOrderID", CALCULA
9	Card	10:35:59	10:35:59	1	9	41	50	EVALUATE ROW("Customer_Coverage", 'Custome
10	Slicer	10:36:00	10:36:00	1	9	81	90	EVALUATE ROW("MinTotalDue", CALCULATE(MIN
11	Slicer	10:36:00	10:36:00	10	0	46	46	DEFINE VAR __DS0Core = VALUES('Product'[Colo
12	Slicer	10:36:00	10:36:00	6	0	34	34	DEFINE VAR __DS0Core = VALUES('SalesTerritory'
13	Slicer	10:36:00	10:36:00	101	15	26	41	DEFINE VAR __DS0Core = VALUES('ProductMode
14	Bonus by FirstName	10:36:01	10:36:01	17	7	116	123	DEFINE VAR __DS0Core = SUMMARIZECOLUMNS
15	SalesAmount by Product Category	10:36:01	10:36:01	21	32	50	82	DEFINE VAR __ScopedCore0 = SUMMARIZECOLU

Figure 6.17 – Performance Analyzer trace shows slowest visual caused by slow query

- **Export/import model metrics**: DAX Studio has a facility to export or import the VertiPaq model metadata using `.vpax` files. These files do not contain any of your data. They contain table names, column names, and measure definitions. If you are not concerned with sharing these definitions, you can provide `.vpax` files to others if you need assistance with model optimization.

We have now seen how we can use useful free tools to learn more about our Power BI solutions and identify areas to improve. Let's summarize and review our learnings from the chapter.

Summary

In this chapter, we introduced some popular utilities that use different methods to analyze Power BI solutions and help us identify areas to improve. They are complementary to those provided by Microsoft and can enhance our optimization experience.

We learned that these tools are mature and have a broad range of functionality beyond performance improvement, so you are encouraged to explore all their features and consider incorporating them into your development cycle. One caveat is that free versions of these tools are often community projects and are not officially supported.

We learned about Power BI Helper and its ability to identify large columns, unused columns, bi-directional relationships, and measure dependencies. These are all candidates for performance improvement.

Next, we learned about Tabular Editor and its built-in BPA. This gave us an easy way to load in default rules provided by experts, then scan a dataset for a range of performance and other best practices. BPA could even apply some fixes immediately if desired.

Then we were introduced to DAX Studio and VertiPaq Analyzer. DAX Studio is a complete query development and tuning utility that can capture real-time query activity from Power BI datasets, including server timings. We learned how to generate dataset metrics that give us detailed information about the objects in the dataset and how much space they occupy. We then moved on to query timings, so we learned about the roles of the formula engine and the storage engine and how to see how much time is spent in each. We could also see the internal VertiPaq queries that were executed. The ability to use query-scoped measures in DAX Studio gives us a fast and powerful way to prototype DAX and model changes and see their impact on the engine timings.

At this point in the book, we learned about optimizing Power BI largely from a high-level design perspective. We also learned about tools and utilities to help us measure performance. In the next chapter, we will propose a framework where you will combine processes and practices that use these tools to establish, monitor, and maintain good performance in Power BI.

7
Governing with a Performance Framework

We began this book by introducing performance management and how to set reasonable targets, borrowing from user interface research. We identified that areas of Power BI can affect report and dataset refresh performance, then we walked through architectural concepts and optimization choices. *Chapters 4*, *5*, and *6* focused on sources of information and tools that can help us monitor report and query performance.

The metrics and tools in earlier chapters are essential building blocks for performance management. However, success is more likely with a structured and repeatable approach to build performance-related thinking into the entire Power BI solution life cycle. This chapter provides guidelines to set up data-driven processes to avoid sudden scaling issues with new content and prevent the degradation of existing content.

You could consider performance management as having two distinct phases. The first involves monitoring and identifying areas that are slowing you down. The second involves root cause analysis and remediation. The technical topics covered prior to this chapter are sufficient to give you a great head start with Power BI performance management, mainly from a reporting perspective. Since report usage is the most common use case of a business intelligence system, we'll intentionally cover the governance framework now before going deeper into detailed best practices for each product area.

We intend to give you sufficient knowledge to tackle the first phase of performance management after completing this and the previous six chapters. Once you know you have a problem and where it is, you can move on to the second phase. Subsequent chapters focus on the second phase and will provide specific advice on how to optimize a specific layer such as the report design, dataset design, and M query design.

This chapter consists of the following sections:

- Establishing a repeatable, pro-active performance improvement process
- Knowledge sharing and awareness

Establishing a repeatable, pro-active performance improvement process

In *Chapter 1, Setting Targets and Identifying Problem Areas*, we learned about the potential negative impacts of poor business intelligence system performance. It is great to have knowledge, metrics, and tools to resolve performance issues. However, a behavior that I have seen all too often is that these are usually leveraged reactively after an issue has had enough of an impact on the business that it is formally raised and brought to the attention of developers and administrators. This is not a good situation to be in for reasons described in the following points:

- Changing production systems is non-trivial, it requires careful change management, and can involve more than just deploying new technical artifacts. One example is that users may need training and documentation may need to be updated if there are significant report or dataset level changes.
- There may be short deadlines for the business to resolve performance issues, especially from leadership. Root cause analysis, evaluating enhancements, and deploying changes can be time-consuming by nature so this time pressure can affect the quality of work and introduce other unrelated issues through human error.

- There may be limited expertise to resolve complex issues, due to a lack of expert skills within the organization or limited availability of those staff members. This could delay a resolution indefinitely, increasing user frustration.

Now, let's cover the performance management cycle.

The performance management cycle

We recommend minimizing performance enhancement efforts by being pro-active about performance management. We can achieve this by thinking of performance management as a continuous cycle as shown in the following figure:

Figure 7.1 – Performance management cycle

Let's look at each of these phases in more detail to understand what they involve.

Establish/update baselines and targets

You cannot improve performance without being able to compare results from different scenarios or different system conditions. We first need to know what a reasonable expectation is for a specific scenario, ideally under known and controlled conditions. This is what we refer to as a **baseline** and it serves as the standard against which you would compare real-world measurements.

Let's put this into practical terms. Suppose we have occasional complaints about a slow report from two users. We find that the first user has report performance of around 15 seconds while the other is about 45 seconds. If we had no other information available to us, we might spend a lot of time with both users trying to work out why the issue occurs. While 15 seconds is not a good report load time, we don't know if that is within the expected range for that user's scenario. The same applies to the 45-second duration. Therefore, we recommend using baselines to help you both set expectations and understand the relative change when something slows down. Here are some guidelines to help you establish good baselines:

- A baseline metric should be an average of multiple data points for the same scenario. A minimum of three is recommended, though more is better.

- Create a baseline per dataset and report page combination. Page granularity is important because visual designs can vary, and one page of a report can be more complex and slower than others.

- For reports, establish baselines for reports both in Power BI Desktop and after publishing to the service. Comparing both metrics before and after any changes can help identify architectural or configuration issues.

- For reports, have a separate baseline metric for a full cold start where Power BI is not open, and the dataset is not in memory. This will perform differently to a warm load where the user is already in Power BI and the dataset has been recently used so is already in memory.

- For reports or queries, consider security conditions in your baseline by simulating real users' roles. Row-level security can impact performance and it may be necessary to have separate baselines for some groups with known complexity.

- Consider separate baselines for different times of the day or geographies to cater to variable network and system load conditions.

- Use the same hardware for baselines wherever possible. This eliminates the test machine as a factor.

- Maintain a record of when changes are deployed and what they were. This will set a clear point in your trend analysis where different results are expected. It also helps if changes need to be re-assessed and compared to the original baseline.

Some of the previous guidelines apply specifically to Power BI reports. However, you can and should apply the concepts to other areas of Power BI. For example, you can establish baselines for dataset refresh, both in Power BI Desktop and the Power BI service.

The baseline establishment step is both the start and the end of the cycle because any performance-related work could change the overall behavior of the system for all users, not just the ones who had problems. Hence, your baseline needs to be adjusted accordingly.

Monitor and retain history

At the time of writing this book, there are 30 days of historical performance information available for Power BI reports. For datasets on Premium workspaces, you can get the 60 most recent refreshes per dataset from the admin portal. This may not be sufficient to build a good trending view and spot gradual performance degradation, so it is recommended to extract the metrics and retain the historical data to build a long-term view as described in the *Customizing the usage report* section of *Chapter 4, Analyzing Logs and Metrics*. This can also help identify seasonal issues, for example, extra load caused by end of month processing. You should review performance against baselines and targets regularly. We recommend reviewing performance against baselines at least weekly, and you can consider plotting rolling averages to smooth out small fluctuations.

Identify problems and prioritize

This part is straightforward. Here you will compare your actual results to baselines and targets. Those that do not meet the standard should be flagged and prioritized in terms of user impact and business impact. Try to address the items that will help the most people and the most critical business process. Sometimes this can be out of your hands and driven by executive priorities.

Diagnose and fix

The artifact with the problem must be investigated and profiled as we described in the previous two chapters. The initial goal here is to work out which part of the process is problematic. Using a report as an example, you should work out if certain visuals are slow, if a measure is performing badly, or if a security filter expression is the issue. Detailed examples of what to look for in each area will be given in later chapters.

> **Tip**
> When resolving a report performance issue, it is a good idea to start with the visual layer. Even if DAX or model optimizations can help, these changes could take longer to implement safely since there could be many dependencies on the dataset. However, the report layer can often be optimized independently and even in parallel.

Set preventative measures

An important part of being pro-active about performance management is to learn from your experiences and try not to repeat mistakes. This step is about updating standards, checklists, training, and other related materials used by the development team to raise awareness.

> **Tip**
> We recommend building performance-tuning routines into your regular development cycle, at an appropriate level for the user. Enforce best practices at the initial development stage and use Power BI Desktop and third-party utilities to profile and optimize your content before deploying it to users. Also consider scale testing before going live. We cover this in the final chapter of the book.

Next, we will explore ways to socialize performance practices within your organization.

Knowledge sharing and awareness

In the previous section, we talked about the importance of being pro-active about performance management. Since there are many areas to cover, some being quite technical, we need to have the right level of complexity and relevance for the audience. We will introduce these groups in general then summarize with role-specific advice.

Helping self-service users

One of Power BI's greatest strengths is its approachability and ease of use for non-technical users or analysts who are not professional BI developers. The drawback of this is that lack of knowledge can lead to poorly optimized solutions. We recommend using the guidance in later chapters to create the following:

- **Report Design Guide** – This will incorporate style, theme, and design choices to avoid. These can even be supplied as a Power BI template file (`.pbit`).

- **Data Modeling/Loading Guide** – This will have common guidance such as the basics of **dimensional modeling**, relationship pitfalls, removing unnecessary data, and Power Query tips.

- **Custom Links to Guides** – Power BI allows you to customize help links so users can reach your documentation directly.

Let's move on to leveraging professional developers.

Leveraging professional developers

You can establish rules about why self-service content or data subject areas need a formal performance review before going live. This can be done by embedded champions and subject matter experts or central experts that would typically work in an enterprise BI team or Centre of Excellence.

This is simply a detailed and formal performance review that covers every relevant layer of the solution – including things such as DAX tuning, which may not be left to self-service users. The point is to enforce the performance review as part of the development cycle before going live. This is especially relevant to complex IT managed solutions that serve many users.

Approaching performance improvement collaboratively

By now you can see that there are many different skillsets required to build and optimize a large Power BI solution. Therefore, oftentimes, various roles must collaborate to manage performance effectively. Unfortunately, it is easy to get into a situation where one area takes all the blame. Report developers may feel pressure to fix reports without realizing measures are slow. Data engineers may feel pressure to fix slow dataset refreshes without knowing the source system is under heavy load. These are just two of many similar examples.

We recommend you set up a process to assist with performance tuning. Nominate champions or specialists who have specific strengths to be involved in reviews. These could be technical (for example, modeling, DAX, or report design) and business domain SMEs (for example, finance, inventory management, or drilling).

Lastly, try to stay on top of product changes through documentation updates and blogs. A good example is DAX performance. Improvements made by Microsoft are sometimes via the release of new functions with different names since the old ones are left unchanged for backward compatibility.

Now that we have understood the phases of the performance management cycle and different skill levels, we will describe different usage scenarios and the responsibilities various roles should have.

Applying the performance management cycle to different usage scenarios

Business intelligence tools are used by everyone from individuals to large global corporations. Naturally, you would expect the ways in which analytics are developed and maintained to change as an organization grows. The larger the organization is, the more the need for governance and central control grows. In our opinion, even in large organizations, a healthy business intelligence environment is one that balances the needs of individuals and small teams with centralized corporate data management practices. Individuals and small groups need to frequently perform new analyses or data mashups and prefer to have minimal technical friction and standards imposed because it slows them down. This can clash with organizational goals of standardization, usability guides, and best practices around modeling and design, which can affect performance.

These conflicting needs are often referred to as the balance between self-service BI and corporate or IT-led BI. It is beyond the scope of this book to recommend how best to balance these needs, noting similar-sized organizations could adopt quite different approaches with their own trade-offs. However, we will describe the common scenarios in an organization, identify typical roles that work within them, and recommend their responsibilities to help apply the performance framework.

Self-service BI

This refers to a model where business users access and analyze data even if they do not have formal training in statistics or data analysis. Self-service BI is intentionally and often the fastest and least governed way to gain insights. Users can load, manipulate, mash up and visualize data to suit their tactical needs. They may use a mixture of formal and informal sources of data, including information from external service providers (for example, population stats or weather data). This can be thought of as primarily a "pull model," where users find what they want and create their own reporting.

An example here is someone working for a cloud software provider who wants to test the hypothesis that demand for one of their services is higher following a public holiday. They need to quickly combine internal usage data with holiday dates from a public website. Depending on the governance model, the analysis may be shared with other individuals, teams, or even the entire organization, which has performance implications

Team or domain-based BI

This refers to a model where a group with a shared function or goal is looking to perform analytics on a set of known themes or initiatives. Some examples here are a company division such as procurement wanting to analyze supplier efficiency or a virtual team for a special project such as a marketing campaign that wants to understand the ROI for each channel used in the campaign. There will be business subject matter experts in the team and potentially data subject matter experts who can play a role in applying best practices that help performance. Like self-service, team-based BI may employ a mix of data sources, and indeed self-service BI frequently occurs within these teams. Groups like this usually build analytics for their own use and for management reporting.

Corporate/IT-led BI

This is a model where a central team builds common artifacts for use by many different parts of the organization – datasets, semantic models, reports, dashboards, and so on. This can be thought of as a "push model" because a central team manages distribution largely to pure consumers. There is a higher level of governance and standardization here for everything from naming conventions and data modeling standards to report design guides and corporate themes. A central BI team also often defines the infrastructure, architecture, processes, and controls that support team and self-service BI.

> **Note**
>
> The previous descriptions of BI usage scenarios suggest that a common pathway for analytics in terms of solution maturity starts with self-service BI, which can evolve into corporate BI. This is true because businesses usually identify new analytical needs but as the reach and scale of the solution grows, there is a need to apply some governance that needs guidance from IT. Therefore, we stress again the importance of applying relevant performance management for all these scenarios to reduce the overall performance remediation effort.

We'll now list typical roles involved in business intelligence projects that have a stake in solution performance. We suggest what they can do to help each other build solutions with performance in mind regardless of the scenario or user skill level. Since performance management is largely about implementation in Power BI, we omit roles such as data stewards. Do note the table does not suggest that only certain roles are involved in each scenario. Every role can have a part to play in all scenarios, but we simply focus on the primary roles and what they can do in that scenario. This is because self-service BI influences corporate BI, and vice versa.

Self-Service	Business User	• Use Performance Analyzer to help eliminate issues • Check for acceptable performance after publishing with prod data
Team/ Domain Role	Business User	• As per self-service, plus: • Decision makers establish performance criteria • Leverage guidance from subject matter experts and technical teams and review together before publishing
	Business and Data Subject Matter Experts	• Maintain a central definition of common business logic such as calculations • Establish recommended practices for data sourcing and transformation
		Responsibilities
	Data Analyst/ Report Developer	• Document common pitfalls and workarounds for loading, modeling, and visualizing • Leverage logs and third-party utilities to optimize artifacts

	Role	Responsibilities
Corporate/IT-led	Business User	• As per team-based
	Business and Data Subject Matter Experts	• As per team-based, but in collaboration with developers
	Data Analyst/Report Developer	• As per team-based, but likely more focused on visualization • Review content for performance issues before broad publication
	Data modeler	• Establish and document modeling standards, including domain-specific special cases that do not follow theory exactly • Review content for performance issues before broad publication • Leverage logs and third-party utilities to optimize artifacts
	ETL developer	• Establish and document data loading and transformation standards • Review content for performance issues before broad publication • Leverage logs and third-party utilities to optimize artifacts
	Solution Architect	• Establish and document architectural options • Leverage logs and third-party utilities to inform architectural changes and future designs • Be aware of new product developments that can improve performance (the same applies to other specialist roles)
	BI Manager/Analytics Lead	• Establish processes, roles, and responsibilities for performance management. • Collaborate with all parties to establish realistic performance targets • Track solution performance over time and refine process and performance guidance assets with team

Figure 7.2 – Roles and responsibilities of solution architect and BI manager/analytics lead

Let's now summarize the learnings from the chapter.

Summary

In this chapter, we introduced a repeatable process to help you manage performance pro-actively in your organization. This is important for consistency and the overall satisfaction of users. If we can catch and repair issues before they become widespread, we can save a lot of time and money.

We looked at how to establish baselines as a starting point and how it's important to have the correct granularity of model, report page, timeframe, user permissions, and other factors for the baselines. We talked about maintaining performance history so that you can establish meaningful trends and spot seasonal issues. When problematic content is identified, we recommended that the remediation work is prioritized based on business value and user impact to maximize return on investment. That investment involved metrics and tools we described in previous chapters that help profile the system and highlight slow areas. We then learned that taking learnings from any fixes back into standards and common practices helps to reduce future issues.

We completed the chapter by looking at ways to share knowledge and awareness of performance issues with the developer community, and how to leverage guidance documentation and expert help to improve the solutions created by self-service users. We learned about typical scenarios and roles for BI consumption in modes ranging from self-service to governed corporate deployments. Since self-service artifacts can mature into organization-wide solutions, we stressed the importance of building relevant performance guidance into the workflows for each role. We also suggested typical responsibilities for these roles to relate them to the stages of the performance cycle.

In the next chapter, we begin to dive deep into each area of a Power BI solution. Any BI solution starts with data, so we will look at how to optimize data loading and M queries in Power BI.

Part 3: Fetching, Transforming, and Visualizing Data

In this part, you will understand how the M Query engine behaves and how resources are consumed when loading, transforming, and refreshing data. You will learn to what extent the different aspects of report design slow down performance, what to avoid, and whether there are alternatives.

This part comprises the following chapters:

- *Chapter 8, Loading, Transforming, and Refreshing Data*
- *Chapter 9, Report and Dashboard Design*

8
Loading, Transforming, and Refreshing Data

So far, we have focused a lot on performance monitoring and investigation. We have now reached the next phase of our journey into Power BI performance management. Here, we will begin looking at what actions we can take to remedy the performance issues we discovered while using the tools that were introduced in previous chapters. From here on, each chapter will look deep at a specific area of a Power BI solution and will provide performance guidance. The first of these is loading data into Power BI.

Loading new data periodically is a critical part of any analytical system, and in Power BI, this applies to *Import mode* datasets. Data refresh and its associated transformations can be some of the most CPU and memory-intensive operations. This can affect user activities and cause refresh failures. Large datasets that occupy a significant portion of a host's memory, and that have complex data transformations, are more prone to resource contention. Poorly designed transformations contribute to high resource usage and can result in refresh failures. They can even affect development productivity by slowing down or, in extreme cases, crashing Power BI Desktop.

In this chapter, we will learn how Power BI's **Power Query** transformation engine works and how to design queries with performance in mind. Additionally, we'll learn how to use the strengths of data sources and avoid pitfalls in query design with the aim of reducing CPU and memory use. This provides benefits when the datasets are still in development and when they are deployed to production.

In this chapter, we will cover the following main topics:

- General data transformation guidance
- Folding, joining, and aggregating
- Using query diagnostics
- Optimizing dataflows

Technical requirements

There are examples available for some parts of this chapter. We will call out which files to refer to. Please check out the `Chapter08` folder on GitHub to get these assets: `https://github.com/PacktPublishing/Microsoft-Power-BI-Performance-Best-Practices`.

General data transformation guidance

Power Query allows users to build relatively complex data transformation pipelines through a *point* and *click* interface. Each step of the query is defined by a line of **M** script that has been autogenerated by the UI. It's quite easy to load data from multiple sources and perform a wide range of transformations in a somewhat arbitrary order. Suboptimal step ordering and configuration can use unnecessary resources and slow down the data refresh. Sometimes, the problem might not be apparent in Power BI Desktop. This is more likely when using smaller subsets of data for development, which is a common practice. Hence, it's important to apply good Power Query design practices to avoid surprises. Let's begin by looking at how Power Query uses resources.

Data refresh, parallelism, and resource usage

When you perform a data refresh for an Import mode dataset in the Power BI service, the dataset stays online. It can still be queried by published reports or even from Power BI Desktop and other client tools such as Excel. This is because a second copy of the dataset is refreshed in the background, while the original one is still online and can serve users. However, this functionality comes at a price because both copies take up memory. Furthermore, transformations that are being performed on the incoming data also use memory.

> **Tip**
> For a full refresh, you should assume that a dataset will need at least two times its size in memory to be able to refresh successfully. Those with complex or inefficient transformations might use significantly more memory. In practical terms, this means a 2 GB dataset would need at least 4 GB of memory available to refresh.

The actual work of loading and transforming data in Power BI is performed by the Power Query **mashup engine**. The *host*, as mentioned at the beginning of the chapter, refers to the machine where this mashup engine is running. This host could be Power BI Desktop, the Power BI service, a Premium capacity, or a gateway. Each table being refreshed runs in an **evaluation container**. In Power BI Desktop, each container is allocated 432 MB of physical memory by default. If a container requires more physical memory than this, it will use virtual memory and be paged to disk, which dramatically slows it down.

Additionally, the number of containers executing in parallel depends on the host. In Power BI Desktop, the number of containers running in parallel defaults to the number of logical cores available on the machine. This can be adjusted in the **Data Load** section of the Power Query settings pane. Also, you can adjust the amount of memory used by each container. These settings can be seen in the following screenshot:

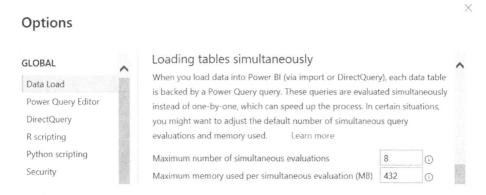

Figure 8.1 – The Power Query parallel loading settings

Some data transformations require a lot of memory for temporary data storage. If the container memory is completely used up, the operation pages to disk, which is much slower.

> **Tip**
>
> You can use **Resource Monitor**, which is built into Windows to observe the memory usage of Power Query . In the *memory* section, look for a process name such as `Microsoft.Mashup.Container`. If you see a **Commit** value that is much higher than the **Working Set**, that means paging is occurring. To avoid paging in Power BI Desktop, one option is to increase the amount of container memory. Be aware that setting this too high could use up all available memory and affect your system's responsiveness. Before increasing memory, you should optimize your query, as we will describe later.

There probably isn't much benefit in increasing the number of containers in Power BI Desktop significantly beyond the default. The default setting will assign one container per available logical core, and they will all run in parallel. Depending on the complexity of the transformations and what else is running on the development computer, this might have a reasonable load. Having too many containers could end up slowing down the overall refresh operation by trying to run too many things in parallel and creating CPU contention. Each CPU core ends up juggling multiple queries. Finally, the data source also needs to handle that many simultaneous connections. It might have its own connection limits or policies in place.

For Power BI Premium, Power BI Embedded, and Azure Analysis Services, you cannot modify the number of containers or memory settings through any UI. The limits depend on the SKU and are managed by Microsoft. However, using the **XMLA endpoint**, you can manually override the setting for how many tables or partitions can be processed in parallel. This is done by using the `sequence` command in a **TMSL** script. You can use a tool such as **SQL Server Management Studio** to connect to your dataset and execute it. The following example uses a `sequence` command to enable 10 parallel evaluation containers. Note that only one table is listed as an example. You can simply modify this script and specify more tables/partitions in the area indicated:

```
{
    "sequence":{
      "maxParallelism":10,
      "operations":[
        {
          "refresh":{
            "type":"full",
```

```
    "objects":[
        {
            "database":"ExampleDataset",
            "table":"ExampleLogs",
            "partition":"ExampleLogs202112"
        }

        // specify further tables and partitions here
    ]
        }
    }
]
}
}
```

Now, let's see how to make working with queries faster in Power BI Desktop.

Improving the development experience

When working with significant data volumes, complex transformations, or slow data sources, the Power BI Desktop development environment can occasionally slow down or become non-responsive. One reason for this is that a local data cache is maintained to show you data previews for each transformation step, and Power BI tries to refresh this in the background. It can also be caused if there are many dynamic queries being driven by a parameter. When properly used, query parameters are a good Power Query design practice. However, a single parameter change can cause many previews to be updated at once, and this can slow things down and put excess load on the data source.

If you experience such issues, you can turn off **Background Data** in the Power Query settings, as shown in *Figure 8.2*. This will cause a preview to only be generated when you select a query step. The appropriate setting is shown in the following screenshot. The screenshot also shows a setting to prevent **Parallel loading of tables**. This is very useful in scenarios where you are running many complex queries and know for certain that the source would handle sequential queries better. Often, this is the case when using handwritten native queries for a data source with many joins, transformations, and summarizations:

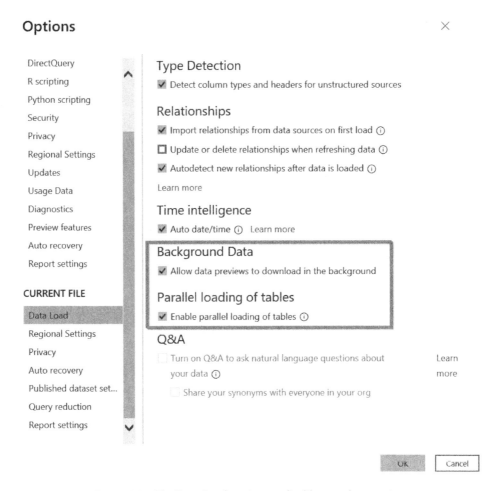

Figure 8.2 – The Data Load settings to disable complex queries

Another method for reducing the load on the source while still in development is to use a simple toggle parameter to limit the amount of data returned. The following screenshot shows how a **Binary** parameter, called **DevelopmentFlag**, appears when given possible values of **0** and **1**:

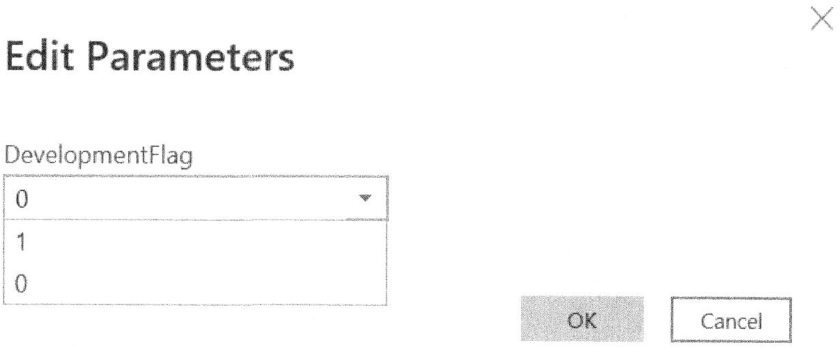

Edit Parameters

DevelopmentFlag

0	▼
1	
0	

OK   Cancel

Figure 8.3 – A toggle parameter showing possible values

Once the parameter is ready, you can use it in queries. In the following screenshot, we show how a conditional statement can be used in **Advanced Editor** to leverage this toggle. When the toggle is set to 1, Power Query only gets data prior to June 1, 2013, from the #**"Filtered Rows"** step. If the toggle is set to 0, it will pick up the result from the previous **Fact_Transaction** step instead. This is a practical example of a useful ability in Power Query to reference previous states of queries:

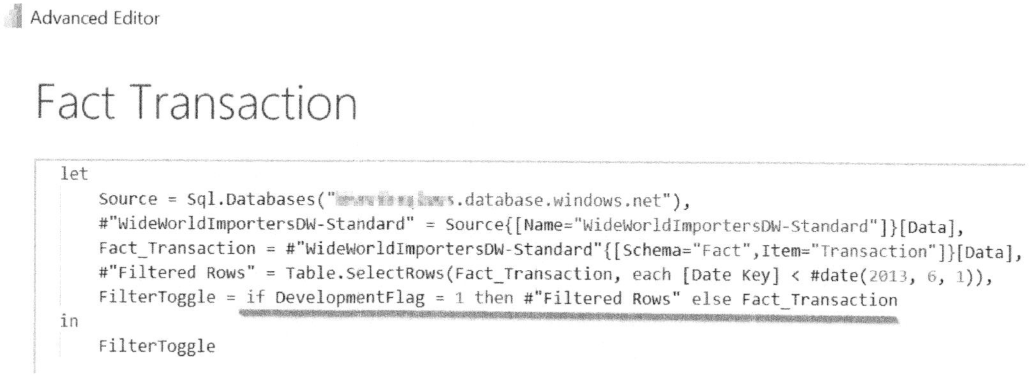

Advanced Editor

Fact Transaction

```
let
    Source = Sql.Databases("                .database.windows.net"),
    #"WideWorldImportersDW-Standard" = Source{[Name="WideWorldImportersDW-Standard"]}[Data],
    Fact_Transaction = #"WideWorldImportersDW-Standard"{[Schema="Fact",Item="Transaction"]}[Data],
    #"Filtered Rows" = Table.SelectRows(Fact_Transaction, each [Date Key] < #date(2013, 6, 1)),
    FilterToggle = if DevelopmentFlag = 1 then #"Filtered Rows" else Fact_Transaction
in
    FilterToggle
```

Figure 8.4 – Using the toggle parameter to reduce data

If you are using multiple data sources and are using values from one source to control the queries of another, you can experience lower performance with the default privacy settings. This is because Power Query prevents any leakage of data from one source to another for security reasons. For example, if you use values from one database to filter data from another, the values you pass could be logged and viewed by unintended people. Power Query prevents this leakage by pulling all the data locally and then applying the filter. This takes longer because Power Query must wait to read all the data. Also, it can't take advantage of any optimizations at the source through indexing and other techniques.

If you are comfortable with the risks associated with data leakage, you can disable the **Privacy Levels** setting, as shown in the following screenshot. This shows a global setting. However, note that you can also set this individually for each `.pbix` file much lower down in the settings (not shown):

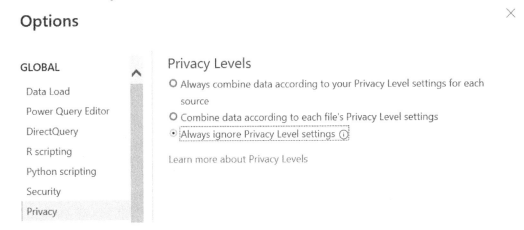

Figure 8.5 – Ignoring the privacy level settings can improve performance

Another helpful Power Query technique is using the reference feature to use one query to start a new query. This is useful when you need to split a data stream into multiple formats or filter and transform subsets differently. A common mistake is to leave this referenced table available in the data model even though it is never directly used in reports. Even if you hide it from users, it will still be loaded and occupy memory. In such cases, it's better to turn off the **Enable Load** option, which can be found by right-clicking on the query. Disabling the load will only temporarily keep the table during refresh and reduce the dataset's memory footprint. In the following screenshot example, the **CSVs** source contains two different groups of records, **Student** and **Course**. Once these groups are separated out into their own tables, the starting table does not need to be loaded:

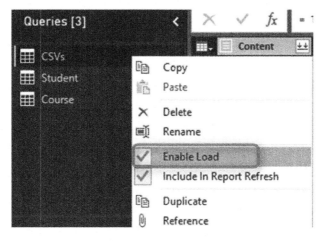

Figure 8.6 – How to turn off loading intermediate tables

A technique that can help you with complex transformations that happen in Power Query is the use of **buffer functions**. Power Query has two flavors that are relevant to us, Table.Buffer() and List.Buffer(). You can wrap these around a **Table** object or a **List** object in Power Query to force it to be loaded into memory and kept there for later use instead of streaming it in small batches. This can be useful when dealing with certain transformations, such as extracting entire tables from single columns (for example, JSON documents) or pivoting/unpivoting dynamically over large numbers of unique values, especially with multiple levels of nested functions. A good time to consider buffer functions is when you get refresh failures indicating that the resources were exhausted.

A final tip is to consider whether you really need the automatic date/time feature in Power BI. When enabled, it will create a hidden internal date table associated with every date or date/time field found in the dataset. This can take up significant space if you have a wide range of dates and many date fields. A better practice is to use your own date dimension tables that are connected to only the meaningful dates that need aggregations to month and year:

Options

GLOBAL		
Data Load	Maximum number of simultaneous evaluations	8
Power Query Editor	Maximum memory used per simultaneous evaluation (MB)	432
DirectQuery		
R scripting	**Time intelligence**	
	☑ Auto date/time for new files ⓘ Learn more	

Figure 8.7 – Time intelligence in the Power Query settings

Next, we'll look at ways to leverage the strengths of large data stores to offload work from Power Query and reduce refresh times.

Folding, joining, and aggregating

While Power Query has its own capable data shaping engine, it can push down certain transformations to data sources in their native query language. This is known as **Query Folding**, and formally, it means that the mashup engine can translate your transformation steps into a single SELECT statement that is sent to the data source.

> **Tip**
> Query Folding is an important concept as it can provide huge performance benefits. Folding minimizes the amount of data being returned to Power BI, and it can make a huge difference for refresh times or DirectQuery performance with large data volumes of many millions of rows.

There is a bit of knowledge and trial and error required to get the best folding setup. You know a query step is folded when you can right-click on it and see the **View Native Query** option enabled, as shown in the following screenshot:

Figure 8.8 – View Native Query indicates that folding has occurred

Ideally, you will want to see the last step of your query that allows you to view the native query because this means the entire query has been folded. This seems straightforward enough, but it's important to understand which operations can be folded and which can break a chain of otherwise foldable operations. This depends on the individual data source, and the documentation is not comprehensive. Not every source supports viewing a native query; one example is **Odata**, which is a standard for building and consuming **REST APIs**. You can use Query Diagnostics in such cases to learn more about what each step is doing. We will cover Query Diagnostics in the next section.

The following list of operations are typically foldable:

- Filtering rows, with static values or Power Query parameters

- Grouping and summarizing

- Pivoting and unpivoting

- Simple calculations such as arithmetic or string concatenation that translate directly to the data source

- Removing columns

- Renaming or aliasing columns

- Joining tables on a common attribute

- The non-fuzzy merging of queries based on the same source

- Appending queries based on the same source

The following list of operations are typically not foldable:

- Changing a column data type

- Adding index columns

- Merging queries based on different sources

- Appending queries based on different sources

- Adding custom columns with complex logic that have no direct equivalent in the data source

> **Tip**
> Perform all foldable transformations at the beginning of your query to ensure they all get pushed down to the data source. Once you insert a step that cannot be folded, all subsequent steps will occur locally in Power Query, regardless of whether they can be folded. Use the technique described in *Figure 8.7* to walk through your steps in sequence, and reorder them if necessary.

Specifically, you should look out for any group, sort, or merge operations in Power Query that have not been folded. These operations require whole tables to be loaded into Power Query, and this could take a long time with large datasets and can lead to memory pressure. If a group operation cannot be pushed down, but you know the source is already sorted on the grouping column, you can improve performance by using an additional parameter to the `Table.Group()` function, called `GroupKind.Local`. This will make Power Query more efficient, as it will know a group is complete when the value changes in the next row that is processed. It can do this because it assumes the values are contiguous.

> **Tip**
>
> If you are fluent in the native language of the data source and are comfortable writing your own query, you can use a custom query instead of letting Power Query generate one for you. This can be a last resort to ensure that everything possible has been pushed down. It is particularly useful when you know the source data characteristics such as frequency and distribution and can use source-specific capabilities such as query hints to improve speed. Complex joins and aggregations might not be completely pushed down to the source and might benefit from being implemented within a custom query.

Leveraging incremental refresh

For data sources that support being pushed down, Power Query supports **Incremental Refresh**. This is a useful design pattern to consider for optimizing data refresh operations. By default, Power BI requires a full load of all tables when a dataset is using Import mode. This means all of the existing data in the table is discarded before the refresh operation. This ensures that the latest data is loaded into Power BI. However, often, this results in unchanged historical data being loaded into the dataset each time it is refreshed. If you know that you have source data that is only ever appended and historical records are never modified, you can configure individual tables in a Power BI dataset to use incremental refresh to load only the most recent data. The following steps should be followed in sequence to enable incremental refresh:

1. Before you can use the incremental refresh feature, you must add two date/time parameters, called **RangeStart** and **RangeEnd**, to control the start and end of the refresh period. The setup of the parameters is shown in the following screenshot.

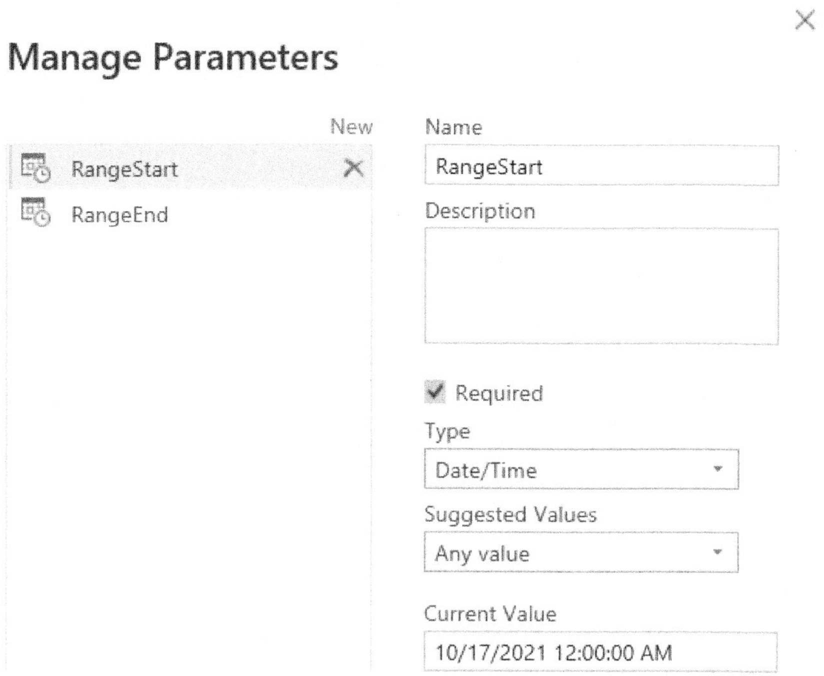

Figure 8.9 – The date/time parameters required for incremental refresh

2. Next, you must use these parameters as dynamic filters to control the amount of data returned by your query. An example of this configuration is shown in the following screenshot, where the **Invoice Date key** column is used for filtering:

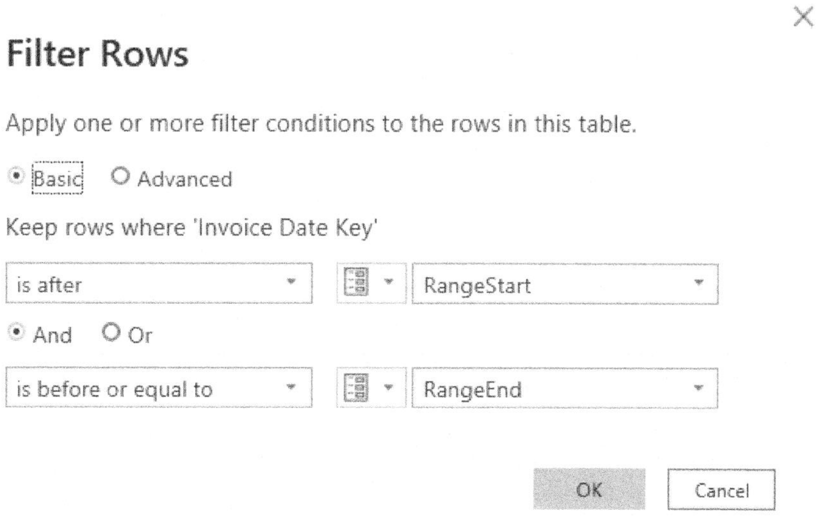

Figure 8.10 – Filter configuration to support parameterized date ranges in a query

3. Once you have a query configured to use the date range parameters, you can enable incremental refresh. You simply right-click on the table name in **Power BI Desktop** and select the **Incremental refresh** option. The following screenshot shows how the UI allowed us to select 6 months of historical data to retain, along with 1 day of new data upon each refresh, for a table called **Fact Sale**:

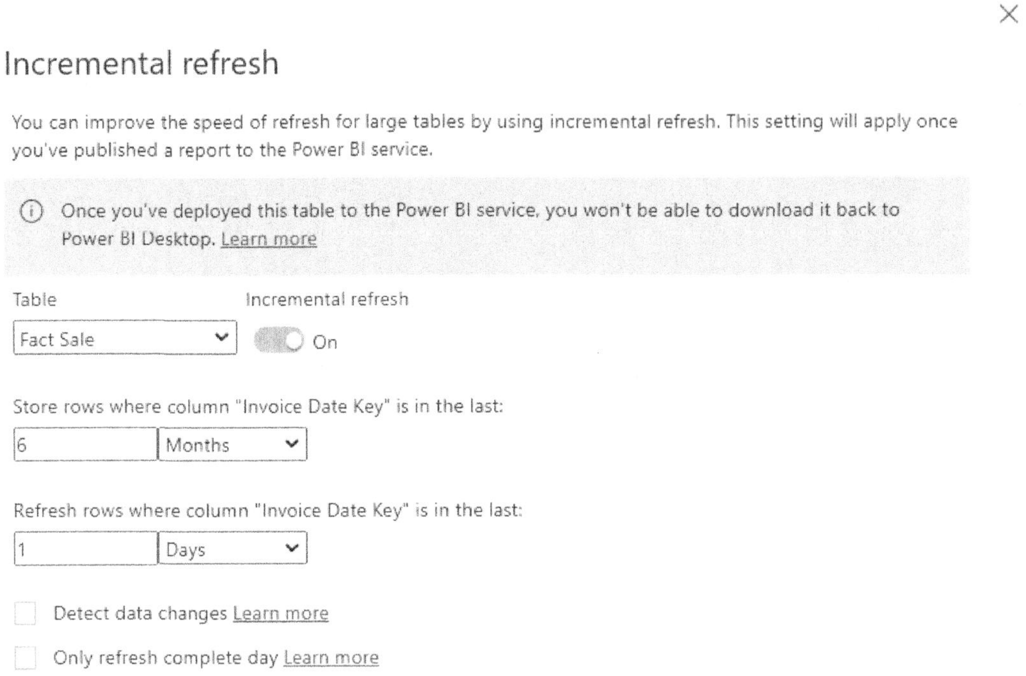

Incremental refresh

You can improve the speed of refresh for large tables by using incremental refresh. This setting will apply once you've published a report to the Power BI service.

ⓘ Once you've deployed this table to the Power BI service, you won't be able to download it back to Power BI Desktop. Learn more

Table   Incremental refresh

Fact Sale   ∨   ◯ On

Store rows where column "Invoice Date Key" is in the last:

6   Months   ∨

Refresh rows where column "Invoice Date Key" is in the last:

1   Days   ∨

☐ Detect data changes Learn more

☐ Only refresh complete day Learn more

Figure 8.11 – Incremental refresh configured within a table

There are two options available in the incremental refresh setup dialog that enable you to have more control:

- **Detect data changes**: This will allow you to choose a timestamp column in the source database that represents the last modified date of the record. If this is available in the source, it can further improve performance by allowing Power BI to only select changed rows within the refresh period.

- **Only refresh complete day**: This will ensure that only the most recent complete day of data will be refreshed. This is required to ensure the accuracy of some business metrics. For example, calculating daily average users for a web application would not be accurate if considering incomplete days. In practical terms, let's suppose you schedule a data refresh at 2 a.m. daily because it will have the lowest impact on the source system. Enabling this setting will instruct Power Query to only collect data from before midnight.

Next, we will see how the built-in query diagnostics can help us to spot and resolve performance issues.

Using query diagnostics

In Power BI Desktop, you can enable query diagnostics to get a detailed understanding of what each step of your query is doing. Even with seemingly simple queries that have few transformations, if performance is bad, you will need to know which part is slowing you down so that you can concentrate your optimization efforts. **Diagnostics** needs to be enabled in the Power Query settings, as shown in the following screenshot. You might not need all the traces that are shown in the following screenshot. At a minimum, enable the **Aggregated** diagnostics level and **Performance counters**:

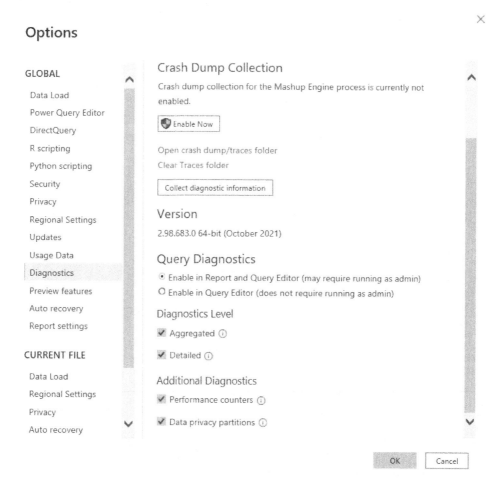

Figure 8.12 – Query Diagnostics enabled in the Power Query settings

There are up to four types of logs that are available:

- **Aggregated**: This is a summary view that aggregates multiple related operations into a single log entry. The exclusive durations are summed per entry.

- **Detailed**: This is a verbose view with no aggregation. It is recommended for complex issues or where the summary log doesn't provide enough to determine a root cause.

- **Performance counters**: Every half second, Power Query takes a snapshot of the current memory use, CPU utilization, and throughout. This might be negligible for queries that are fast or push all the work to the data source.

- **Data privacy partitions**: This helps you to identify the logical partitions that are used internally for data privacy.

Next, we will learn how to collect the traces and explore the information contained within them.

Collecting Power Query diagnostics

Diagnostic traces are not automatically collected after the settings, as shown in *Figure 8.13*, have been enabled. To save trace data to disk, you need to start diagnostics from the **Tools** menu of the **Power Query Editor** screen, as shown in the following screenshot:

Figure 8.13 – The Power Query diagnostic controls

Select the **Start Diagnostics** button to enable data collection. From this point on, any query or refresh operations will be logged to disk. You can perform as many operations as you want, but nothing will be visible until you use the **Stop Diagnostics** button. After stopping the diagnostics, the logs are automatically added to the query editor, as shown in the following screenshot:

Figure 8.14 – The query logs are automatically loaded

You can only collect traces from the Query Editor UI. It will capture any activity, even loading previews and working on a single query step. Additionally, you can capture activity from the **Report** view, which is great for tracing a full table or dataset refresh. The choice you make will depend on the scenario you are trying to debug. You can select a single query step and use the **Diagnose Step** button to run a single step, which will create a dedicated trace file that is named after the step.

> **Tip**
>
> Query logs can become quite large and might become difficult to work with. The **Power Query Editor** UI performs background operations and caching to improve the user experience, so all steps might not be properly represented. We recommend that you only capture diagnostics for the operations or tables you are trying to debug to simplify the analysis. Start diagnostics, perform the action you want to investigate, then stop diagnostics immediately after and analyze the files.

Analyzing the Power Query logs

The Power Query log files have different schemas that might change over time. We recommend that you check out the online documentation to understand what each field means. It can be found at `https://docs.microsoft.com/power-query/querydiagnostics`.

We are mostly interested in the **Exclusive Duration** field found in the aggregate and detailed logs. This tells you how long an operation took in seconds, and it helps us to find the slowest items. The Microsoft documentation describes how you can slice the log data by the step name or ID. This is an easy way to find the slowest element, but it doesn't help you to understand which operation dependencies exist. The logs contain a hierarchical parent-child structure with arbitrary depth depending on your operation complexity. To make it easier to analyze this, we provide a Power Query function that can be used to flatten the logs into an explicit hierarchy that is easier to analyze using the decomposition tree visual. Please see the `ParsePQLog.txt` example file. This function is adapted from a blog post that was originally published by Chris Webb: `https://blog.crossjoin.co.uk/2020/02/03/visualising-power-query-diagnostics-data-in-a-power-bi-decomposition-tree/`.

We have provided examples of how the parsed data can be visualized. The following screenshot is a snippet of the `Query Diagnostics.pbix` example file and shows how a decomposition tree is used to explore the most expensive operation group and its children. From the tooltip, we can see that the **Level 2** step took about 29 seconds and loaded over 220,000 rows. Additionally, we can see the exact SQL statement sent to the data source to confirm that folding occurred:

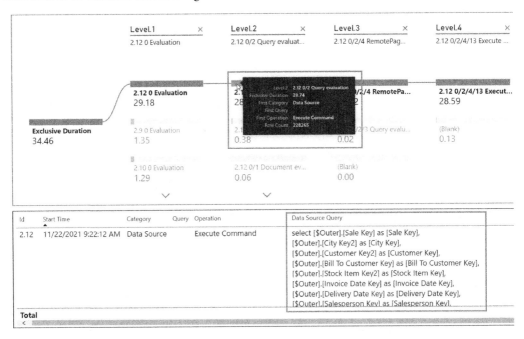

Figure 8.15 – A hierarchical view of a query log after flattening

Next, we will look at an example where the same query logic is performed in two different ways, that is, by only changing a data source. We'll see how this affects folding and how to investigate the impact on performance.

In this scenario, we have a data warehouse and want to create a wide **de-normalized** table as a quick stopgap for an analyst. We need to take a sales fact table and enrich it with qualitative data from four dimensions, such as customer and stock. The data is all in SQL Server. For the sake of this example, these tables are loaded individually into Power BI Desktop, as shown in the following screenshot. We dumped the database-hosted fact table inside a .CSV file and named it **Fact Sale_disk** to provide an alternative data source to perform the comparison:

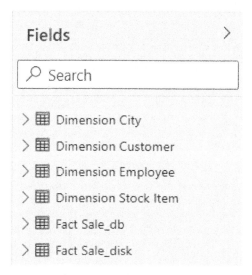

Figure 8.16 – The starting tables loaded into the dataset

We perform a merge from the fact to the dimensions, expanding the columns we need after each merge. We expect this version to be folded. Additionally, we create a second version that uses the file as a source for the fact table. We expect the disk version to not be folded because the joins and filters are applied directly to the CSV on disk. The difference between these is shown in the comparison of query steps that follow. Note how `FlattenedForAnalyst_NotFolded` has the **View Native Query** option disabled, which confirms this difference:

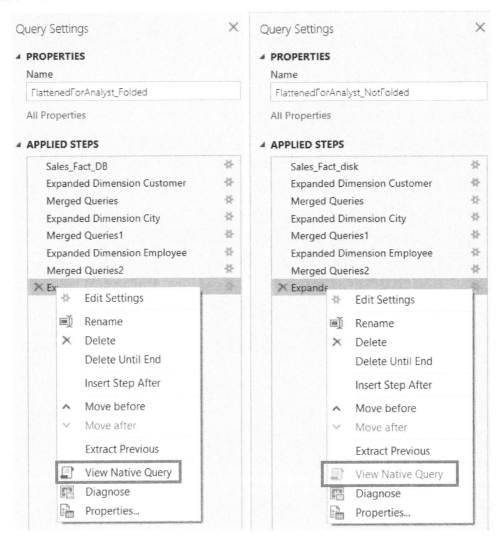

Figure 8.17 – A comparison of the same query logic using different sources

In the following screenshot, we compare the high-level activities and durations of these two refresh operations. We can clearly see that the pure database method was significantly faster – about 10 seconds compared to about 34 seconds for the mixed database and file method. This should not be a surprise when we think about how the mashup engine works. For the pure database method, all logic was folded and sent to the data source as a single query. However, when using the fact table from the file and dimensions from the database, Power Query needs to execute queries to fetch the dimension data so that it can perform the join locally. This explains why we see significantly more activities:

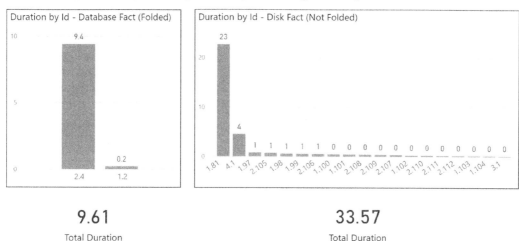

Figure 8.18 – A shorter duration and fewer operations with the folded query

Now we have gained useful fundamental knowledge and analytical methods to help identify slow operations in Power Query. Next, we will explore performance tuning for dataflows.

Optimizing dataflows

A Power BI **Dataflow** is a type of artifact contained within a Power BI workspace. A dataflow contains Power Query data transformation logic, which is also defined in the M query language that we introduced earlier. The dataflow contains the definition of one or more tables produced by those data transformations. Once it has been successfully refreshed, the dataflow also contains a copy of the transformed data stored in **Azure Data Lake**.

A dataflow might seem very similar to the query objects you define in Power BI Desktop, and this is true. However, there are some important differences, as noted in the following points:

- A dataflow can only be created online through the Power BI web application via **Power Query Online**.

- A dataflow is a standalone artifact that can exist independently. It is not bundled or published with a dataset, but dataset items can use the dataflow as a standard data source.

- There are some UI and functionality differences between Power Query in Power BI Desktop compared to Power Query Online.

- A dataflow can be used by datasets or even other dataflows to centralize transformation logic.

The last point in the preceding bullet list is important since it describes a key reason that dataflows exist in the first place. They are designed to promote data reuse while avoiding duplicated data transformation operations and redundant processing. Let's explore this using a practical example. Let's suppose an organization encourages self-service report development so that business users can get insights quickly. They realize that many different people are trying to access a list of customers with properties from two different source systems: a **Finance system** and a **Customer Relationship Management** system. Rather than let every person try to figure out how to transform and consolidate customer data across two systems, they could build one standard customer dataflow and have every user leverage this dataflow.

> **Tip**
>
> Dataflows are a great way to centralize common data transformation logic and expose the final tables to users in a consistent way. This means that the processing does not need to be duplicated for every dataset. It reduces the total amount of data refreshes and speeds up report development by giving developers pre-transformed data. Additionally, you can update the dataflow to ensure that all downstream objects benefit from the changes without needing changes themselves (assuming that the output table structure is unchanged).

The dataflow query design benefits from all the performance optimization recommendations we provided for Power Query. You are encouraged to apply the same learnings when building dataflows. However, dataflows have some backend architectural differences that provide additional opportunities for optimization. These are detailed in the following list:

- *Separate dataflows for ingestion and transformation*: This allows you to load untransformed data into a dedicated dataflow, typically referred to as **staging**. This can speed up downstream transformations by having source data available locally, potentially reused for many independent downstream transforms for added benefits.

- *Separate dataflows for complex logic or different data sources*: For long-running or complex operations, consider putting each of them in a single dedicated dataflow. This allows the entity transformations to be maintained and optimized separately. This can make some entities available sooner, as they do not have to wait for the entire dataflow to be completed.

- *Separate dataflows with different refresh cadences*: You cannot select individual entities to refresh in a dataflow, so all entities will refresh when scheduled. Therefore, you should separate entities that have different refresh cadences to avoid redundant loading and processing.

- *Consider Premium workspaces*: Dataflows running on Premium capacity have additional features that increase performance and reusability. These are covered in the next list.

The following performance-enhancing features for dataflows are highly recommended. Please note that the following items are only available for dataflows running on Premium capacity:

- *Incremental refresh*: This works for dataflows in the same way as described earlier for Power Query. Configuring this can greatly reduce dataflow refresh time after the first load.

- *Linked entities*: You can use one dataflow as a data source for a different dataflow. This allows you to break your logic into groups of transformations, into multiple phases, and reuse the data from any stage. This reduces development effort and minimizes duplicate transforms and refreshes. The following screenshot shows how the UI uses a link icon indicator when another dataflow has been used as a source. In this example, the **Audit Log Files** entity contains JSON log records from the Power BI activity log, as described in *Chapter 4, Analyzing Logs and Metrics*. The user wants to parse this log into subsets with different columns depending on the activity type. A linked entity is a good way to reuse the log data without importing it into Power BI for each subset:

Figure 8.19 – A linked entity indicated visually

- *Enhanced Compute and Computed Entities*: Premium dataflows can take advantage of the Enhanced Compute Engine, which is turned on by default for Premium. This can dramatically reduce refresh time for long-running transformations such as performing joins, using distinct filters and grouping. Power BI does this by using a SQL-like cache that can handle query folding. The following screenshot shows the dataflow settings page and where to enable enhanced compute:

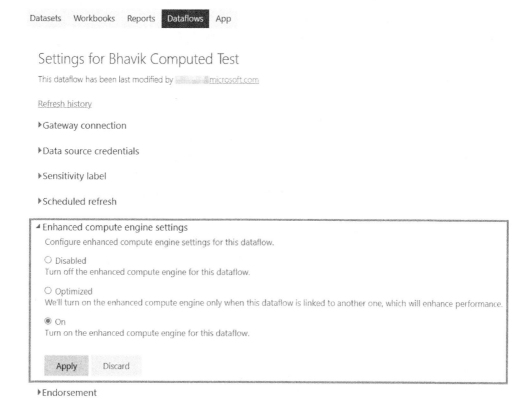

Figure 8.20 – Enhanced compute in the dataflow settings

> **Note**
>
> The enhanced compute engine setting only works when using other dataflows as a source. You can tell that you have a computed entity when you see the lightning symbol on top of its icon, as shown in the following screenshot. It also shows how Power BI provides a tooltip when hovering over the **Source** step, which indicates it will be evaluated externally.

The following screenshot highlights how computed entities are displayed in the UI:

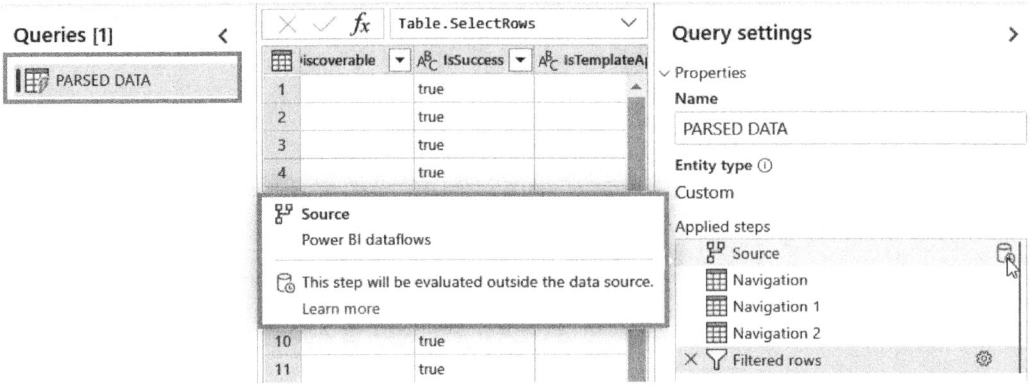

Figure 8.21 – A computed entity indicated visually

- *DirectQuery for dataflows*: When using computed entities as a source for Power BI datasets, it is possible to use them in DirectQuery mode. This is useful when you have many refreshing datasets that rely on a dataflow. Even though the dataflow is only loaded from the external data source into Power BI once, switching to DirectQuery could reduce the load on both Power BI and the source. In **Kimball** dimensional modeling terms, this is useful when you have large dimensions but often query a relatively small number of them and don't need most of their attributes. We will discuss dimensional modeling in further detail, in *Chapter 10, Data Modeling and Row-Level Security*.

DirectQuery mode is configured when accessing a dataflow as a data source in Power BI Desktop. You do this with the **Power BI Dataflows connector**, and you will be provided with the option to select Import mode or DirectQuery mode, the same as with other data sources that support both storage modes. Currently, there are some limitations to DirectQuery dataflows, such as the inability to use them with Import/DirectQuery composite models. Please refer to Microsoft's online documentation to check whether your scenario is supported.

We now have a great understanding of how data gets transformed in Power BI and how we can minimize refresh operations and make them faster. Let's wrap up the chapter with a summary of our learnings.

Summary

In this chapter, we began to dive deeper into specific areas of an actual Power BI solution, starting from transforming and loading data. We saw how Power Query and the mashup engine take center stage in this part of the pipeline, powered by the M query language. We learned how memory and CPU are important for data refresh operations. This meant that poor Power Query design can lead to failed or long-running data refreshes due to resource exhaustion.

Additionally, we learned about parallelism and how you can change the settings in Power BI Desktop to improve performance. There are also settings that can be adjusted in Power BI Desktop to speed up the developer experience and optimize data loading in general. We also learned how to customize refresh parallelism in Power BI Premium, Embedded, and Azure Analysis Services.

Then, we moved on to transformations, focusing on typical operations that can slow down with large volumes of data such as filtering, joining, and aggregating. We introduced the mashup engine's ability to perform query folding and why we should leverage this as much as possible because it pushes typically resource-intensive operations down to the data source. Such operations can often be performed far more efficiently at the data source. We learned how to see where folding is occurring in Power BI Desktop and examined how to configure incremental refresh to reduce the amount of data loaded.

The Power Query diagnostic logs contain information about each query step and its resource usage. We saw how these were not easy to parse and structure, but they do offer a lot of detail that can provide valuable insights into slow query steps or data sources.

We concluded the chapter by learning how dataflows can be used to reduce data loading and transformation by centralizing common logic and data. Also, we learned how dataflows benefit from the same performance guidance as Power Query tables. However, dataflows do have their own optimization tips with specific performance features such as enhanced compute.

Now that we have learned how to get data into Power BI efficiently, in the next chapter, we will look at report and dashboard design tips to provide a better user experience while reducing data consumption.

9
Report and Dashboard Design

In the previous chapter, we looked at how to load data into Power BI efficiently to reduce system resource use and reduce the amount of time taken to load data. Slow data refreshes generally do not impact a user's report performance experience directly because they usually occur in the background and are scheduled at off-peak times.

Now, we will shift our focus to the visual layer of Power BI. Here, inappropriate choices can directly affect the end user experience, from both a performance and usability perspective. While we will continue to focus on design patterns that improve performance, we will point out when performance guidance can also improve usability.

In this chapter, we will learn how the Power BI visual framework works within reports and how these relate to queries and engine load. This will give us fundamental knowledge on report behavior, which will help identify what to optimize. We will then go through a range of common design pitfalls and will recommend alternative solutions that can provide better performance, covering the three options for creating visual content in Power BI.

This chapter consists of the following sections:

- Optimizing interactive reports
- Optimizing dashboards
- Optimizing paginated reports

Technical requirements

There are samples available for some parts of this chapter. We will call out which files to refer to. Please check out the Chapter09 folder on GitHub to get these assets: https://github.com/PacktPublishing/Microsoft-Power-BI-Performance-Best-Practices.

Optimizing interactive reports

When we use the term **interactive report**, we refer to the primary report implementation experience available in Power BI where authoring is performed in Power BI Desktop. These reports have dynamic visuals designed primarily for viewing on screens. The report elements can resize and react to screen dimension and resolution changes, and the authoring experience is **What You See is What You Get** (**WYSIWYG**).

The term *interactive report* is unofficial and used in this book for convenience and clarity. Microsoft specifically differentiates interactive reports from **paginated reports** by name – only the latter is a documented term. Paginated reports are based on **SQL Server Reporting Services** (**SSRS**) and use a different paradigm, which we will describe further in the final section of the chapter.

> **Note**
> From here on, we will only specifically call out paginated reports. If this distinction is not made, please assume we are referring to interactive reports.

Interactive reports are built by placing individual visuals on one or more predetermined report pages. Most visuals are data-driven, which means they need to be supplied with data to render meaningful content. The Power BI visual frontend is a modern JavaScript application that executes in the client browser. Therefore, in general, a faster client device will execute the JavaScript code faster and result in a better-performing report. Do bear this in mind when considering reporting performance issues on much older hardware. However, be aware that a faster computer will usually give you less of a performance boost than spending time properly optimizing the report and its underlying dataset.

Next, we will explore the relationship between visuals and queries to learn how this affects performance.

Controlling the visuals and associated queries

An important point to note is that visuals in Power BI are designed to execute in parallel. This has interesting implications for performance. When you open an interactive Power BI report, all visuals execute at once. Data-driven visuals will each issue at least one query to the underlying dataset, and these queries are sent in batches to be executed in parallel where possible. Even visuals that do not issue queries (such as a textbox) need some CPU time. An unfortunate side-effect of Power BI being a JavaScript application is caused by how browsers execute JavaScript code. Even though visuals execute in parallel, they are executed on a single CPU thread, which means time is divided up between the visuals. Therefore, technically, only one visual is doing work on the CPU at any instant. This limitation applies to any JavaScript application. For Power BI, it means that the more visuals you have on a page, the more time they can spend waiting for the CPU, due to contention with all the other visuals.

> **Note**
>
> There is a direct relationship between the number of visuals and the load generated by a report. Higher load often results in poorer performance. This load will be spread over two areas – both the client device executing visuals and the dataset that is responding to queries. This includes queries sent to external data sources in DirectQuery mode. Therefore, you should strive to reduce the total number of visuals on a page wherever possible, especially knowing that the more you have, the more work you are asking of a single CPU thread. You should also configure visuals in a way that avoids complex queries and try to return the least amount of data – only what is needed for the scenario.

There is no specific number of visuals beyond which a Power BI report will slow down. Some guidance online suggests around 20 visuals being a concern, but we do not wish to go down this path. The reason for this is that the visual type, configuration, and underlying dataset and DAX designs will have the largest effect on performance, and two reports with the same number of visuals may have vastly different performance characteristics. Instead, we recommend driving report and dataset optimization based on pre-established targets and thresholds that take user requirements and report complexity into account. This guidance was covered in *Chapter 7, Governing with a Performance Framework*, in the first, *Performance governance framework* section, where we talked about establishing baselines and targets.

Let's now cover in detail the recommended visual-related design patterns to improve report performance:

- *Have default slicer/filter selections for the initial landing experience* – If you have a very large dataset, it can take a while to return results even after optimization. By default, Power BI will not select any values for filters and slicers. To make the initial experience faster, you can consider preselecting values for slicers or filters to limit the query space and reduce the amount of data scanned. Preselect the most frequently used set of attributes to cater for the broadest set of users. Even if some users need to change the slicer selections to get the desired context, this can save them a lot of time because they can avoid waiting for a very slow initial report load. To set default filter and slicer selections, simply save the report with the filters already applied.

- *Avoid detailed tables with many columns in the initial experience* – Users often need to see detailed source data. However, this isn't usually the starting point of data analysis. It's better to summarize important information and allow drilling to details within a narrow specific context. This concept is sometimes referred to as **master-detail report design**. You can build a dedicated drill target page that forces context and avoids issuing queries that return many rows of data. Let's look at a practical example. Suppose you wanted to build a report to investigate user behavior from an event log. Instead of building a single report page with a table showing the event level detail, a master-detail design is likely to work better here, both for performance and usability. An alternate design is to split this report into a master summary page that focuses on a smaller number of interesting users and a detail page at the event level that is designed to look at one user only. The following figure demonstrates a summary page that aggregates data by users in two different visuals:

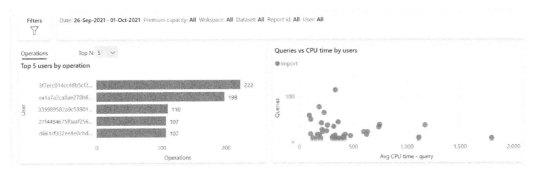

Figure 9.1 – Summary visuals showing the aggregates and the top five users

The next figure shows a detailed drill-through page that can be the target of either summary visual in the previous *Figure 9.1*:

User details

Start date/time	User	Scenario	Detail	Report id	CPU time (ms)	Duration (ms)	Status	Event text
27-Sep-2021 02:39:13 AM	3f7ecc014cc48b5cf26b13ef6e9abb75	Discover completed	DiscoverProperties		0	0	Succeeded	<pii><RestrictionList xmlns="u
27-Sep-2021 02:39:13 AM	3f7ecc014cc48b5cf26b13ef6e9abb75	Discover completed	DiscoverProperties		0	0	Succeeded	<pii><RestrictionList xmlns="u
27-Sep-2021 02:39:13 AM	3f7ecc014cc48b5cf26b13ef6e9abb75	Discover completed	DiscoverProperties		0	0	Succeeded	<pii><RestrictionList xmlns="u
27-Sep-2021 02:39:13 AM	3f7ecc014cc48b5cf26b13ef6e9abb75	Discover completed	DiscoverProperties		0	0	Succeeded	<pii><RestrictionList xmlns="u
27-Sep-2021 02:39:13 AM	3f7ecc014cc48b5cf26b13ef6e9abb75	Query completed	DAXQuery	602e4211-...	94	189	Succeeded	DEFINE MEASURE 'DataSetRe
27-Sep-2021 02:39:13 AM	3f7ecc014cc48b5cf26b13ef6e9abb75	Query completed	DAXQuery	602e4211-...	78	94	Succeeded	DEFINE MEASURE 'DataSetRe
27-Sep-2021 02:39:14 AM	3f7ecc014cc48b5cf26b13ef6e9abb75	Query completed	DAXQuery	602e4211-...	547	770	Succeeded	DEFINE VAR __DS0FilterTable
27-Sep-2021 02:39:14 AM	3f7ecc014cc48b5cf26b13ef6e9abb75	Query completed	DAXQuery	602e4211-...	500	1,020	Succeeded	DEFINE VAR __DS0FilterTable
27-Sep-2021 02:39:14 AM	3f7ecc014cc48b5cf26b13ef6e9abb75	Query completed	DAXQuery	602e4211-...	531	1,193	Succeeded	DEFINE VAR __DS0FilterTable
27-Sep-2021 02:39:14 AM	3f7ecc014cc48b5cf26b13ef6e9abb75	Query completed	DAXQuery	602e4211-...	1,094	1,646	Succeeded	DEFINE VAR __DS0FilterTable
27-Sep-2021 02:39:15 AM	3f7ecc014cc48b5cf26b13ef6e9abb75	Query completed	DAXQuery	602e4211-...	969	1,551	Succeeded	DEFINE VAR __DS0FilterTable
30-Sep-2021 08:46:45 AM	3f7ecc014cc48b5cf26b13ef6e9abb75	Discover completed	DiscoverProperties		0	0	Succeeded	<pii><RestrictionList xmlns="u
Total					41,374	50,599		

Figure 9.2 – A detailed drill-through visual, showing an event detail for only one user

- *Combine individual cards into multi-row cards or tables* – A common report practice is to use many individual card visuals to display some summary metrics in a row. We now know that each of these visuals will issue a query. When measures are at the same scope, data storage engines (including Power BI's Analysis Services) can often retrieve data and calculate multiple measures in a single batch. However, when issued by separate visuals, these measures are requested in separate independent queries and may not benefit from optimizations at the data source. To avoid this problem, you can use a single multi-row card or table visual to group all the measures. This means you will only need to initialize one visual and issue one query.

You can see how one visual only needs one query using Power BI Desktop's Performance Analyzer in the following figures, taken from the Many cards.pbix sample file. *Figure 9.3* that follows shows how each of the five card visuals issues a DAX query, and each takes approximately 2 seconds to execute:

Figure 9.3 – Five separate card visuals issuing five independent queries

Figure 9.4 shows how the same measures can be placed in a multi-row card to issue only one query:

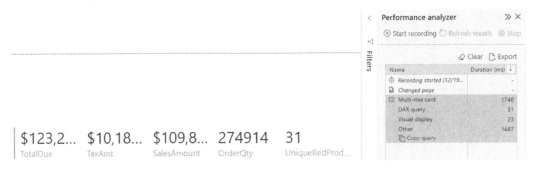

Figure 9.4 – Measures combined into a multi-row card only issue one query

Figure 9.5 shows how the same measures can be placed in a table visual, again issuing only one query:

Figure 9.5 – Measures combined into a table only issue one query

The example dataset used in the previous three figures is small, so the difference to an end user is negligible. However, with larger datasets and measures of higher complexity, significant performance gains can be realized with this technique.

- *Use Top N filters to limit data in the report* – When looking at summary information, it is a good practice to highlight items with the highest or lowest values instead of listing every single one. For example, a customer satisfaction-related visual can be limited to just the 10 customers who had the lowest satisfaction score. This reduces the amount of data returned and can speed up the report. There are two ways you can implement **Top N** filtering. The simplest method is to use the out-of-the-box **Top N** filtering available for Power BI visuals in the **Filters** pane. This can be seen in the following *Figure 9.6* where the left-side visual is in the default state, whereas the right-side visual has been configured to show the top five **Manufacturer** names ranked by **SalesAmount**:

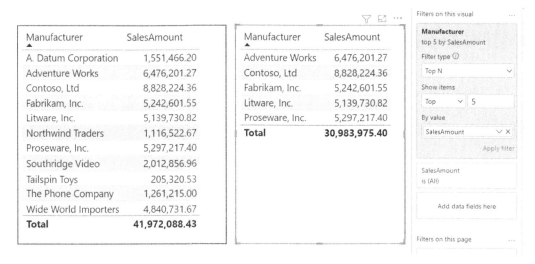

Figure 9.6 – The left visual in the default state and the right visual configured to show the top five items

Another way to implement top N is to write measures that explicitly use ranking functions. While this approach requires more effort, it allows you to perform dynamic ranking through slicer or filter values. This allows a user to choose from a list of pre-determined group sizes such as 5, 10, and 20. Whichever approach you use, we still recommend testing with and without top N enabled. There can be cases where the ranking calculation itself is expensive, and this can cause the visual to be slower when limited by top N.

- *Move infrequently used slicers to the filter pane* – It is tempting to include many different slicers on a report to provide a user with a range of options to set their context when analyzing data. A slicer is a regular Power BI visual that needs to query a dataset to populate its values. When a slicer selection is made, the default behavior in Power BI is to update all other slicers to reflect the selection made to give you a better idea of how data is distributed. The other slicers execute queries to make this update. While this functionality is useful, it can slow down reports if you have a lot of slicers with large datasets. In such cases, consider moving the least frequently used slicers to the **Filters** pane. This reduces the number of queries executed during report interaction because a filter only queries the data source to fetch values after user interaction and is not affected by slicer selections.

- *Remove unnecessary visual interactions* – When you select a data point on a Power BI visual, the default behavior is to cross-filter all other visuals. Sometimes, this might not add any value to the analysis. Therefore, we recommend reviewing report interactions for every visual and removing those that are unnecessary. This will reduce the number of queries issued because a selection in one visual no longer affects every other one. This technique also applies to slicers interacting with each other. The following figure shows how this can be configured by selecting a visual and then using the **Edit interactions** option in the **Format** menu. The slicer is selected and has its interactions edited so that it no longer affects the right-hand side visual. When editing interactions, visuals indicate their behavior with small icons at the top right, as highlighted:

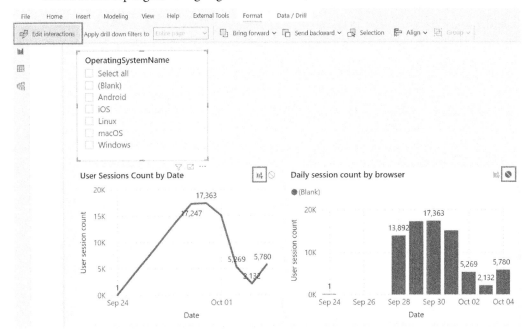

Figure 9.7 – A slicer will only affect the right-side visual, as shown by the icons

- *Use tooltips to reduce query result volume and query complexity* – Some analyses might need many different measures. In such cases, report developers tend to use tables or matrices with all the measures displayed. If measures are complex and data volumes are large, this can make the query quite slow. A good workaround is to only display the critical measures and move the rest to **Tooltips**. Most Power BI visuals support tooltips, which are a popup overlay shown when a user hovers over a data point and will only load data on demand. Tooltips are set via the properties of a visual and can be either a list of attributes or a report page. We recommend making users aware of the tooltip functionality as part of their onboarding and report familiarization training.

The following *Figure 9.8* shows a visual where a report page Tooltips type has been displayed when hovering over the second row in the table. It also shows the tooltip configuration properties, indicating that the report page called **TT-Visual count** is used as the tooltip:

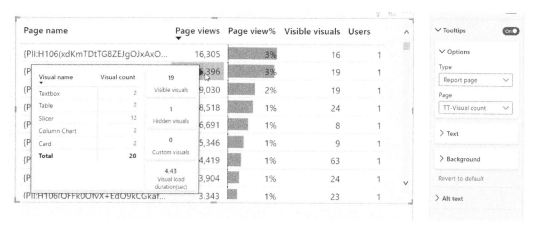

Figure 9.8 – Tooltips used to provide information that is not needed immediately

- *Performance-test custom visuals and prioritize certified custom visuals* – One of Power BI's strengths is the wide range of custom visuals available to extend your analytical capability. Some are not well-optimized or may not be updated to take advantage of improvements in the visual framework. Such visuals can perform slowly even if you have a fast dataset. We recommend testing custom visuals in isolation with the Power BI Desktop Performance Analyzer to determine their performance characteristics. Use realistic data volumes when testing and compare them with out-of-the-box visuals for typical report interactions, such as cross-highlighting and filtering. We also recommend using **Power BI certified visuals**, which are reviewed and validated by Microsoft. If a custom visual is too slow, we recommend exploring other ways of presenting the same information, possibly using multiple interacting visuals to be analyzed together. However, we acknowledge that some custom visuals are unique and cannot be easily replaced.

- *Leverage query reduction for complex reports* – Another way to reduce the number of queries and improve report performance is to change the default behavior of interactions, slicers, and filters. You can set configure query reduction in Power BI Desktop from the options screen. This will allow you to disable visual interactions by default and lets you add an **Apply** button to slicers and filters. This will let users change many slicers and filters without issuing new queries for each change. Only one final set of queries will be sent when the **Apply** button is used. The options are shown in *Figure 9.9* that follows:

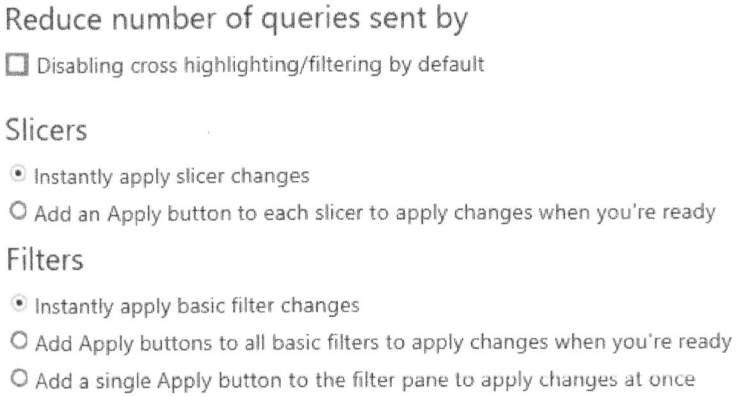

Reduce number of queries sent by

☐ Disabling cross highlighting/filtering by default

Slicers

⦿ Instantly apply slicer changes

◯ Add an Apply button to each slicer to apply changes when you're ready

Filters

⦿ Instantly apply basic filter changes

◯ Add Apply buttons to all basic filters to apply changes when you're ready

◯ Add a single Apply button to the filter pane to apply changes at once

Figure 9.9 – The query reduction options in Power BI Desktop

Report visuals can be pinned to create Power BI dashboards, so next, we will look at how we can optimize dashboards.

Optimizing dashboards

A Power BI dashboard lets users curate a collection of reports and visuals to show on a single page through an action called **pinning**. It is an easy way to create a customized view of the most important elements from different and potentially unrelated reports into a single dashboard. Dashboards in Power BI were designed to be fast and behave differently to reports because, where possible, they cache the query result and visual beforehand. This greatly reduces dashboard load time because it avoids most on-demand processing. Power BI does this by executing queries and preparing dashboard tiles when the underlying data has been updated.

> **Note**
> Visuals are cached when pinned to a dashboard, but reports (called live report tiles) are not. Therefore, we recommend only pinning individual visuals to dashboards instead of report pages to take advantage of caching.

There is also the potential to add significant background load on a system when using dashboards. This is because dashboard tiles must respect security context. If you are using row-level security, there will be different roles/contexts, so Power BI will need to generate a unique tile cache for each security context. This happens automatically after a dataset refresh for Import mode. For DirectQuery datasets, tiles are refreshed hourly.

With large datasets and many contexts, there is the potential to generate hundreds or thousands of background queries in a short time span. If you are not using Premium capacities, the most likely effect is *increased data refresh duration* because the tile refresh is performed at the end. However, if you are using Premium capacity, you have a fixed set of resources, and these background operations have a higher likelihood of impacting interactive users.

Since tile refresh is automatic and there are no settings available to configure it, we recommend testing without row-level security to determine whether tile refresh is the cause of a suspected performance issue.

In the final section, we will cover paginated reports.

Optimizing paginated reports

Paginated reports in Power BI use the mature SSRS technology. A paginated report implements the XML-based **Report Definition Language** (**RDL**) to define reports. They are known as *pixel-perfect*, referring to the fact that they are designed with printing in mind. They are designed with a pre-determined page size (often a standard letter or A4), and the designer will lay out elements exactly where they need to appear on a page by specifying element sizes. They are very good at handling operational-style reports with many rows and pages, such as a group of sales invoices, by providing features such as page headers, footers, and margins. The designer often does not know how many pages the report will generate, as more content simply overflows to a new page. Paginated reports have a dedicated authoring tool called Power BI Report Builder.

Paginated reports can use relational or analytical data sources, which can be hosted in the cloud or on-premises. The latter refers to multidimensional sources such as Power BI datasets, and we will explore their optimization in detail in the next chapter. For the remainder of this chapter, we will focus on relational sources – typically, transactional database systems such as SQL Server and Oracle Database.

The following points provide guidance on optimizing paginated reports:

- *Use cloud data sources* – On-premises sources are likely to be geographically distant and need to be accessed through a gateway. This can be much slower than a cloud source, especially if it is in the same region as Power BI.

- *Use the DAX query designer for analytical sources* – Power BI Report Builder offers an Analysis Services DAX query designer and an Analysis Services MDX query designer. **Data Analysis Expressions (DAX)** and **Multi-dimensional Expressions (MDX)** are different query languages supported by Analysis Services. These designers can be used for Power BI dataset data sources or any Analysis Services model. We recommend using the DAX designer for better performance, especially over tabular models.

- *Leverage stored procedures in the relational source* – Stored procedures are encapsulated pieces of business logic. They can be reused across multiple reports and parameterized to deal with various input. They can contain complex logic, such as loops and temporary tables. They generally perform well due to optimizations applied at the data source, such as cached execution plans.

- *Only retrieve required data* – A paginated report allows you to aggregate and filter data within a visual report control, such as a table or chart. However, this can result in slower queries and higher data volumes loaded into the report. It can also require more report processing overhead to render the results. Therefore, we recommend performing aggregation and filtering at the source in the stored procedure or by customizing the relational query. These are likely to perform better than relying on the paginated report engine.

- *Dataset filtering versus parameterization* – Paginated reports can apply filters over already retrieved data (filtering) or pass a filter directly to the data source (parameterization). Let's illustrate via an example. Suppose we have a sales report that can be filtered to different countries. With dataset filtering, the report will retrieve all country data upfront. When a user selects a specific country, it will perform the filtering without needing to issue new queries to the data source. With dataset parameterization, changing the country will issue a new query and retrieve only the results for the selected country.

  We recommend dataset filtering when you expect a different subset of the dataset rows will be reused many times – in our example, the user may switch between countries often. Here, you recognize that the cost of retrieving a larger dataset can be traded off against the number of times it will be reused. However, caching large datasets on a per-user basis may negatively impact performance and capacity throughput.

- *Avoid calculated fields* – A paginated report allows you to define your own custom fields within a query result. For example, you might concatenate values or perform some arithmetic. We recommend doing this at the data source instead so that the calculation will be done beforehand and be readily available for the report. This can have a significant impact if the query returns many rows.

- *Optimize images* – Keep image file sizes as small as possible by using the lowest resolution that still gives you good quality. Compressed formats such as JPG will help reduce size, and some graphics programs will let you adjust compression settings to balance size with quality.

  Try to avoid embedded images, as they can bloat the report size and slow down rendering. A better alternative is to use images stored on web servers or a database, which improves maintainability through central storage. However, be aware that when using web servers, the images may load slowly if they are from an external network.

Let's now summarize what we have learned from this chapter.

Summary

In this chapter, we looked focused on the visual layer of Power BI where we design the report content. We learned that there are two types of reports in Power BI. Interactive reports consist of a collection of visuals such as charts and slicers and are more commonly used. Paginated reports are based on mature SSRS technology and provide pixel-perfect reports designed for print media.

Interactive reports are comprised of visuals that execute queries to fetch data to render. Power BI is a modern JavaScript application where each visual can be thought of as a code block that executes in parallel. This means that the more visuals you have on a page, the more work the data source needs to do. Browsers do not actually execute JavaScript in parallel, since the work is all assigned to a single CPU thread. This means that the more visuals a report has, the more each visual needs to wait to get a slice of the CPU. Hence, we described how visual reduction is a good design goal because it reduces CPU contention.

We also learned that user actions in interactive reports often result in multiple queries being executed. This can provide a bad experience with large datasets, many visuals, and complex measures because every click results in multiple complex queries that overwhelm the source. To combat this, we learned about different ways to design the report to reduce visual and query counts, using principles such as master-detail and query reduction features in the product.

We then learned how Power BI dashboards provide a way to aggregate content from different reports and how they use caches for visuals but not live report tiles. Here, we learned that tile refresh after scheduled refresh can impact the overall refresh times or the user report interaction experience, more so on Premium capacities.

We completed the chapter by exploring paginated reports and learned how to take advantage of the relational data source.

In the next chapter, we will get into data modeling, which is one of the most important sections of the book. A poorly performing data model can affect the reporting layer significantly and negate the guidance we covered in this chapter.

Part 4: Data Models, Calculations, and Large Datasets

In this part, you will build data models that are efficient and intuitive, avoiding slowing down queries with sub-optimal relationships or DAX calculations. You will also learn how to use aggregations and composite models for very large datasets.

This part comprises the following chapters:

10
Data Modeling and Row-Level Security

In the previous chapter, we looked at the visual layer in Power BI, where a key point was to reduce the load on data sources by minimizing the complexity and number of queries. We learned that this area is usually the easiest and quickest place to apply performance-related fixes. However, experience working with a wide range of Power BI solutions has shown that issues with the underlying dataset are very common and typically have a greater negative performance impact. Importantly, this impact can be amplified because a dataset can be used by more than one report. Dataset reuse is a recommended practice to reduce data duplication and development effort.

Therefore, in this chapter, we will move one layer deeper, into modeling Power BI datasets with a focus on Import mode. Dataset design is arguably the most critical piece, being at the core of a Power BI solution and heavily influencing usability and performance. Power BI's feature richness and modeling flexibility provide alternatives when you're modeling data and some choices can make development easier at the expense of query performance and/or dataset size. Conversely, certain inefficient configurations can completely slow down a report, even with data volumes of far less than 1 GB.

We will discuss model design, dataset size reduction, building well-thought-out relationships, and avoiding pitfalls with **row-level security** (**RLS**). We will also touch on the tools and techniques we learned about in the previous chapters to look at the impact of design decisions.

In this chapter, we will cover the following topics:

- Building efficient data models
- Avoiding pitfalls with row-level security

Technical requirements

Some samples are provided in this chapter. We will specify which files to refer to. Please check out the `Chapter10` folder in this book's GitHub repository to get these assets: `https://github.com/PacktPublishing/Microsoft-Power-BI-Performance-Best-Practices`.

Building efficient data models

We will begin with some theoretical concepts on how to model data for fast query performance. These techniques were designed with usability in mind but happen to be the perfect way to model data for the Analysis Services engine in Power BI. We will begin by introducing star schemas because they are native to the Analysis Services engine and it is optimized to work with them.

The Kimball theory and implementing star schemas

Data modeling can be thought of as how to group and connect the attributes in a set of data. There are competing schools of thought as to what style of data modeling is the best and they are not always mutually exclusive. Learning about competing data modeling techniques is beyond the scope of this book.

We will be looking at **dimensional modeling**, a very popular technique that was established by the Kimball Group over 30 years ago. It is considered by many to be an excellent way to present data to business users and happens to suit Power BI's Analysis Services engine very well. It can be a better alternative than trying to include every possible required field into a single wide table that's presented to the user. We recommend that you become more familiar with Kimball techniques as they cover the entire process of developing a BI solution, starting with effective requirements gathering. The group has published many books, all of which can be found on their website: `https://www.kimballgroup.com`.

Transactional databases are optimized for efficient storage and retrieval and aim to reduce data duplication via a technique called **normalization**. This can split related data into many different tables and requires joins on common key fields to retrieve the required attributes. For example, it is common for Enterprise Resource Planning suites to contain thousands of individual tables with unintuitive table and column names.

To deal with this problem, a central concept in the world of dimensional modeling is the **star schema**. Modeling data into star schemas involves designing data structures specifically for faster analysis and reporting but where we don't have to store the data efficiently. The simplest dimensional model consists of two types of tables:

- **Fact**: These tables contain quantitative attributes and record the business event's details, such as customer order line items or answers in a survey.

- **Dimension**: These tables contain qualitative attributes that help give the metrics context and are used to group and filter the data. Date and time periods such as quarter and month are the most obvious examples.

After defining the facts and dimensions in our model, we can see how the star schema gets its name. A simple star schema has a single fact table that's related to some dimensions tables that surround it, like the points of a star. This can be seen in the following diagram:

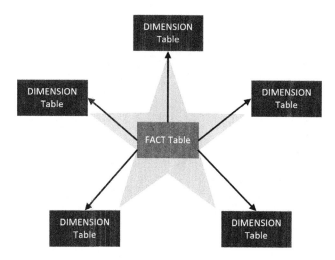

Figure 10.1 – A star schema

The preceding diagram shows a 5-pointed star simply for convenience to aid our conceptual learning. Note that there is technically no limit to how many dimensions you can include, though there are some usability considerations when there are too many. We'll look at a practical example of dimensional modeling in the next section.

Designing a basic star schema

Let's consider an example where we want to build a dimensional model to analyze employee leave bookings. We want to be able to determine the total hours they booked but also drill down to individual booking records to see how much time was booked and when the leave period starts. We need to identify the facts and dimensions and design the star schema. The Kimball group recommends a 4-step process to perform dimensional modeling. These steps are presented here, along with the results for our example scenario in parentheses:

1. Identify the business process (**Leave booking**).

2. Declare the grain (1 record per contiguous employee leave booking).

3. Identify the dimensions (**Employee**, Date).

4. Identify the facts (hours booked).

Now that we have completed the modeling process, let's look at a diagram of the star schema for this employee leave booking scenario. It contains the fact and dimensions we identified via the Kimball process. However, instead of two dimensions, you will see three related to the fact table. **Date** appears twice since we have two different dates to analyze – date booked versus start date. This is known as a **role-playing dimension**, another Kimball concept:

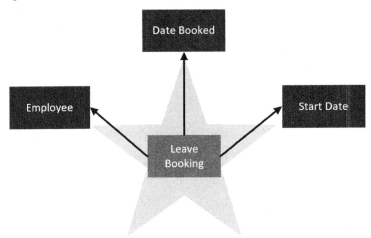

Figure 10.2 – Star schema for employee leave bookings

Steps one and two help determine our scope. The real work starts with step three, where we need to define the dimensions. With star schemas, we perform **de-normalization** and join some tables beforehand to bring the related attributes together into a single dimension table where possible. De-normalized tables can have redundant, repeated values.

Grouping values for a business entity makes for easier business analysis, and repetition isn't a problem for a column-storage engine such as Analysis Services, which is built to compress repeating data.

The concept of grouping can be seen in the following diagram, which shows normalized and de-normalized versions of the same employee data:

Table: Employee

EmployeeID	First Name	Last Name	Date Joined
1	Spider	Man	1-Dec-21
2	Super	Man	13-Apr-21
3	Wonder	Woman	12-Jun-21
4	Black	Panther	15-Jul-21

Table: Role

RoleID	RoleName
11	CEO
22	Manager
33	Analyst

Table: Employee_Role

ID	EmployeeID	RoleID
101	1	11
102	2	22
103	3	33
104	4	33

Dimension Table: Employee

DimEmployee_ID	EmployeeID	First Name	Last Name	Date Joined	RoleName
1001	1	Spider	Man	1-Dec-21	CEO
1002	2	Super	Man	13-Apr-21	Manager
1003	3	Wonder	Woman	12-Jun-21	Analyst
1004	4	Black	Panther	15-Jul-21	Analyst

Figure 10.3 – De-normalizing three tables into a single employee dimension

In the preceding diagram, we can see that the **RoleName** attribute has been duplicated across the last two roles since we have two employees who are in the **Analyst** role.

A **Date** dimension simply contains a list of contiguous dates (complete years), along with date parts such as day of the week, month name, quarter, year, and so on. This is typically generated using a database script, M query, or DAX formulas. We won't illustrate these details as they are not relevant to our example.

The final step is to model the fact table. Since we determined that we want one row per employee leave booking, we could include the following attributes in the fact table:

Fact Table: Leave Booking

Date	DimEmployee_ID	LeaveStartDate	HoursBooked
12-Jan-22	1002	12-Jun-22	24
14-Jan-22	1003	14-Feb-22	16
11-Jan-22	1001	27-Dec-22	40
12-Feb-22	1004	3-Mar-22	8
16-Mar-22	1003	1-May-22	16
24-Mar-22	1001	1-Jul-22	28

Figure 10.4 – Leave Booking fact table

> **Note**
>
> We have provided a trivial example of a business problem for dimensional modeling in this book to aid learning. Note that dimensional modeling is a unique discipline and it can be significantly more complex in some scenarios. There are different types of dimension and fact tables and even supplementary tables that can solve granularity issues. We will briefly introduce a few of these more advanced modeling topics, though we encourage you to perform deeper research to learning about these areas if needed.

Next, we will look at one advanced data modeling topic that has specific relevance to Power BI.

Dealing with many-to-many relationships

An important Kimball concept that has specific relevance to Power BI is that of **many-to-many relationships**, which we will abbreviate as **M2M**. This type of relationship is used to model a scenario where there can be duplicate values in the key columns on both sides of the relationship. For example, you may have a table of target or budget values that are set at the monthly level per department, whereas other transactions are analyzed daily. The latter requirement determines that the granularity of the date dimension should be daily. The following screenshot shows some sample source data for such a scenario. It highlights the **YearMonth** field, which we need to use to join the tables at the correct granularity, and that there are duplicate values in both tables:

Calendar (filtered to first 2 days of each month)

Date	Year	MonthName	MonthNumber	YearMonth
01-Jan-22	2022	January	1	202201
02-Jan-22	2022	January	1	202201
01-Feb-22	2022	February	2	202202
02-Feb-22	2022	February	2	202202
01-Mar-22	2022	March	3	202203
02-Mar-22	2022	March	3	202203
Total	**12132**		**12**	

Budgets

YearMonth	Department	Budget
202201	Manufacturing	$520,000
202201	Research	$50,000
202201	Sales	$250,000
202202	Manufacturing	$400,000
202202	Research	$125,000
202202	Sales	$255,000
202203	Manufacturing	$450,000
202203	Research	$375,600
202203	Sales	$260,000
Total		**$2,685,600**

Figure 10.5 – Calendar and Budgets data showing duplicates in the key column

This preceding diagram demonstrates a completely legitimate scenario that has different variations. When you try to build a relationship between columns with duplicates in Power BI, you will find that you can only create a **Many to many** type, as shown in the following screenshot:

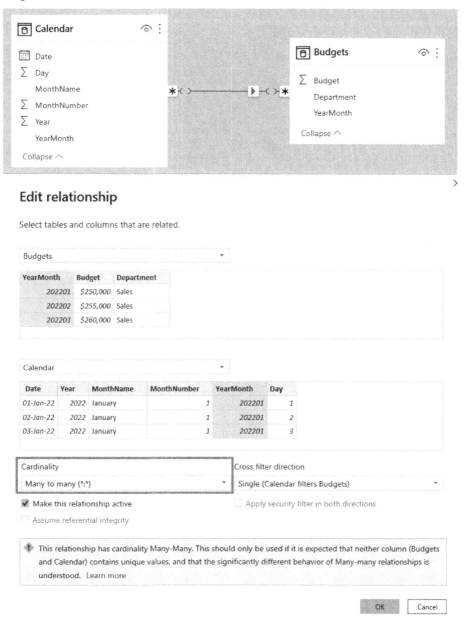

Figure 10.6 – Many-to-many relationship configuration

Once the M2M relationship has been configured, Power BI will resolve the duplication and display the correct results in visuals. For example, if you show the total **Budget** values using **Year** from the **Calendar** table, the sums will be correct, as shown in the following screenshot:

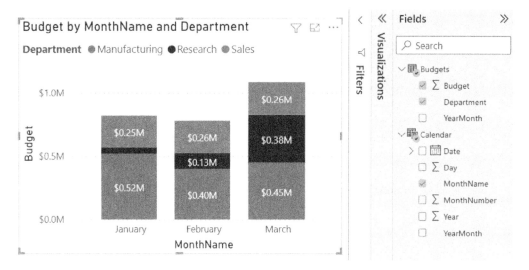

Figure 10.7 – Correct results with the M2M relationship type

Now that we have described when and how to use M2M relationships, we advise using them with care and generally with smaller datasets.

> **Important Note**
>
> The M2M relationship type should be avoided when you're dealing with large datasets, especially if there are many rows on both sides of the relationship. The performance of this relationship type is slower than the more common one-to-many relationships and can degrade more as data volumes and DAX complexity increase. Instead, we recommend employing **bridge tables** to resolve the relationship into multiple one-to-many relationships. You will also need to adjust the measures slightly. This approach will be described shortly.

You can avoid the performance penalty of using an M2M relationship by adding a new table to the dataset called a bridge table. The following screenshot shows how we can introduce a bridge table between the **Calendar** and **Budgets** tables with all the relationships being one-to-many. The bridge table simply contains pairs of keys that can connect unique rows from each table. So, we need to introduce a **BudgetKey** field to the **Budgets** table to uniquely identify each row:

Figure 10.8 – A bridge table added with only one-to-many relationships

A small change is required to ensure the bridge tables work correctly with calculations. We need to wrap any measure around a CALCULATE() statement that explicitly filters over the bridge table. In our case, we can hide the **Budget** column and replace it with a calculation, as shown here:

```
BudgetMeasure = CALCULATE(SUM(Budgets[Budget]), Budget_Bridge)
```

You can see both techniques in action in the sample Many to many.pbix file that's included with this chapter.

In our trivial example with a small number of rows, creating a bridge table would seem like an unnecessary effort, and it even introduces more data into the model. The performance benefit is likely to be negligible and using the M2M relationship type would be better for easier maintenance. However, as data volumes grow, we recommend implementing bridge tables and doing a performance comparison over typical reporting scenarios.

Next, we will learn how to reduce dataset size, which helps with the performance of refresh and report viewing.

Reducing dataset size

In *Chapter 2, Exploring Power BI Architecture and Configuration*, we learned that the import mode tables in a Power BI dataset are stored in a proprietary compressed format by Analysis Services. We should aim to keep these tables as small as possible to reduce both data refresh and query durations by having fewer data to process. There is also the initial dataset load to consider. Power BI does not keep every dataset in memory all the time for practical reasons. When a dataset has not been used recently, it must be loaded from disk into memory the next time someone needs it. This initial dataset load duration increases as the dataset's size increases.

The benefits of smaller datasets are beyond just speed. In general, fewer data to process means less CPU and memory usage, which benefits the overall environment by leaving more resources available for other processes.

The following techniques can be used to reduce dataset size:

- **Remove unused tables and columns**: If any table or column elements are not needed anywhere in the dataset or downstream reports, it is a good idea to remove them from the dataset. Sometimes, tables or attributes are used for calculations and not exposed to users directly, so these can't be removed easily.

- **Avoid high precision and high cardinality columns**: Sometimes, source data may be stored in a format that supports a much higher precision than we would ever need for our analysis. For example, a date column to the second is not required if we only ever analyze per day at the highest granularity. Similarly, the weight of a person to 2 decimal places might not be needed if we always plan to display them as a whole number. Therefore, we recommend reducing the precision in Power Query, in a pushed-down transformation, or permanently in the original data source if that's feasible and safe. Let's build on the decimal versus whole number example. Power BI stores both types as a 64-bit value that occupies 8 bytes. Initially, this won't seem like it makes a difference in terms of storage. This is true, though the dataset size reductions will be realized because we are reducing the number of unique values with lower precision (for example, all the values between 99.0 and 99.49 collapse to 99 when we reduce the precision). Fewer unique values will reduce the size of the internal dictionary.

  The same concept extends to high cardinality columns. Cardinality means the number of unique elements in a group. A high cardinality column will have few repeated values and will not compress well. Sometimes, you will already know that every value in a column is unique. This is typical of row identifiers or primary keys such as an employee ID, which are unique by design. Be aware that you may not be able to remove unique columns because they are essential for relationships or report visuals.

- **Disable auto date/time**: If you have many date columns in your dataset, a lot of space may be taken up by the hidden date tables that Power BI automatically creates. Be sure to disable this setting in Power BI Desktop, as described in *Chapter 2, Exploring Power BI Architecture and Configuration*.

- **Split datetime into date and time**: If you need to perform analysis with both date and time, consider splitting the original datetime attribute into two values – that is, date only and time only. This reduces the total number of unique date elements. If we had 10 years of data to analyze and designed a date table to the second granularity, we would have about 315 million unique datetime entries (10 years x 365 days x 24 hours x 60 minutes x 60 seconds). However, if we split this, we would only get 90,050 unique items – that is, a table of unique dates with 10 x 365 entries, and a table of unique times with 24 x 60 x 60 entries. This represents a raw row count reduction of over 99%.

- **Replace GUIDs with surrogate keys for relationships**: A **GUID** is a **Globally Unique Identifier** consisting of 32 hexadecimal characters separated by hyphens. An example of this is `123e4567-e89b-12d3-a456-426614174000`. They are stored as text in Analysis Services. Relationships across text columns are not as efficient as those across numerical columns. You can use Power Query to generate a **surrogate key** that will be substituted for the GUID in both the dimension and fact tables. This could be resource and time-intensive for large datasets, trading off refresh performance for query performance. An alternative is to work with database or data warehouse professionals to have surrogate keys provided at the source if possible. This technique does cause problems if the GUID is needed. For example, someone may want to copy the ID value to look up something in an external system. You can avoid preloading the GUID in the dataset by using a composite model and a report design that provides a drilling experience to expose just one or a small set of GUIDs on-demand via DirectQuery. We will cover composite models in more detail in *Chapter 12, High-Scale Patterns*.

- **Consider composite models or subsets for very large models**: When you have models that approach many tens or even hundreds of tables, you should consider creating subsets of smaller datasets for better performance. Try to include only facts that are highly correlated from a business perspective and that need to be analyzed by the same type of user in a single report visual, page, or analytical session. Avoid loading facts that have very few dimensions in common into the same dataset. For example, leave bookings and leave balances would likely belong to the same dataset, whereas leave bookings and website inquiries would likely not. You can also solve such problems using aggregations and composite models, which we will also discuss in *Chapter 12, High-Scale Patterns*. This tip also applies to slow DirectQuery models, where moving to composite models with aggregations can provide significant performance benefits.

- **Use the most efficient data type, and integers instead of text**: Power BI will try to choose the right data types for columns for you. If data comes from a **strongly-typed** source such as a database, it will match the source data type as closely as possible. However, with some sources, the default that's chosen may not be the most efficient, so it's worth checking. This is especially true for flat files, where whole numbers might be loaded as text. In such cases, you should manually set the data type for these columns to integers because integers use **value encoding**. This method compresses more than **dictionary encoding** and **run-length encoding**, which are used for text. Integer relationships are also faster.

- **Pre-sort integer keys**: Power BI scans values in columns as they are read, row by row. It samples rows to decide what type of compression to apply. This compression is performed on groups of rows called segments. Currently, SQL Server and Azure Analysis Services work with 8 million row segments, while Power BI Desktop and the Power BI Service work with 1 million row segments. For larger tables, it is worth loading the data into Power BI with the keys already sorted. This will reduce the range of values per segment, which is beneficial for run-length encoding.

- **Use bi-directional relationships carefully**: This type of relationship allows slicers and filter context to propagate in either direction across a relationship. If a model has many bi-directional relationships, applying a filter condition to a single part of the dataset could have a large downstream impact as all the relationships must be followed to apply the filter. Traversing all the relationships is extra work that could slow down queries. We recommend only turning on bi-directional relationships when the business scenario requires it.

- **Offload DAX calculated columns**: Calculated columns do not compress as well as physical columns. If you have calculated columns, especially with high cardinality, consider pushing the calculation down to a lower layer. You can perform this calculation in Power Query. Aim to leverage pushdown here too, using guidance from *Chapter 8, Loading, Transforming, and Refreshing Data*.

- **Set the default summarization**: Numeric columns in a Power BI dataset usually default to the Sum aggregation, and occasionally to the Count aggregation. This property can be set in the **Data** tab of Power BI Desktop. You may have integers that do not make sense to aggregate, such as a unique identifier such as an order number. If the default summarization is set to **Sum**, Power BI will try to sum this attribute in visuals. This may confuse users, but for performance, we are concerned that we are doing meaningless sums. Therefore, we advise reviewing the summarization settings, as shown in the following screenshot:

Figure 10.9 – Summarization on an identifier column set to Count instead of Sum

Next, we will look at optimizing RLS for datasets.

Avoiding pitfalls with row-level security (RLS)

RLS is a core feature of Power BI. It is the mechanism that's used to prevent users from seeing certain data in the dataset. It works by limiting the rows that a user can access in tables by applying DAX filter expressions.

There are two approaches to configuring RLS in Power BI. The simplest RLS configuration involves creating a role in the dataset, then adding members, which can be individual users or security groups. Then, DAX table filter expressions are added to the role to limit which rows members can see. A more advanced approach, sometimes referred to as **dynamic RLS**, is where you create security tables in the dataset that contain user and permission information. The latter is often used when permissions can change often, and it allows the security tables to be maintained automatically, without the Power BI dataset needing to be changed. We assume you are familiar with both approaches.

Performance issues can arise when applying filters becomes relatively expensive compared to the same query with no RLS involved. This can happen when the filter expression is not efficient and ends up using the single-threaded formula engine, which we learned about in *Chapter 6, Third-Party Utilities*. The filter may also be spawning a lot of storage engine queries.

Let's begin by providing some general guidance for RLS configuration:

- **Perform RLS filtering on dimension tables rather than fact tables**: Dimensions generally contain far fewer rows than facts, so applying the filter the dimension allows the engine to take advantage of the much lower row count and relationships to perform the filtering.

- **Avoid performing calculations in the DAX filter expression, especially string manipulation**: Operations such as conditional statements and string manipulations are formula engine bound and can become very inefficient for large datasets. Try to keep the DAX filter expressions simple and try to adjust the data model to pre-calculate any intermediate values that are needed for the filter expression. One example is **parent-child hierarchies**, where a table contains relationship information within it because each row has a parent row identifier that points to its parent in the same table. Consider the following example of a parent-child dimension for an organizational structure. It has been flattened with helper columns such as **Path** beforehand so that DAX calculations and security can be applied to the levels. This approach is typical in Power BI for handling a parent-child situation:

Dimension Table: Organization Structure

ID	ParentID	Path	Level Name	Level 1 Name	Level 2 Name	Level 2 ID	Level 3 Name	Level 3 ID
1		1	Whole Organization	Whole Organization				
2	1	1|2	Finance	Whole Organization	Finance	2		
3	1	1|3	Human Resources	Whole Organization	Human Resources	3		
4	2	1|2|4	Accounts Payable	Whole Organization	Finance	2	Accounts Payable	4
5	2	1|2|5	Accounts Receivable	Whole Organization	Finance	2	Accounts Receivable	5
6	2	1|2|6	Mergers & Acquisitions	Whole Organization	Finance	2	Mergers & Acquisitions	6
7	3	1|3|7	Recruitment	Whole Organization	Human Resources	3	Recruitment	7
8	3	1|3|8	Payroll	Whole Organization	Human Resources	3	Payroll	8

Figure 10.10 – A typical parent-child dimension configured for Power BI

Suppose we wanted to create a role to give people access to all of **Finance**. You might be tempted to configure a simple RLS expression, like so:

```
PATHCONTAINS('Organization Structure'[Path], 2)
```

This will work, but it does involve string manipulation because the function is searching for a character in the **Path** column. For better performance, the following longer expression is preferred because it only compares integers:

```
'Organization Structure'[Path] = 2
```

- **Optimize relationships**: Security filters are applied from dimensions to facts by following relationships, just like any regular filter that's used in a report or query. Therefore, you should follow the relationship best practices that were mentioned in the previous section and *Chapter 3, DirectQuery Optimization*.

- **Test RLS in realistic scenarios**: Power BI Desktop allows you to simulate roles to test RLS. You should use tools such as Desktop Performance Analyzer and DAX Studio to capture durations and engine activity with and without RLS applied. Look for differences in formula engine durations and storage engine query counts to see what the impact of the RLS filter is. It also is recommended to test a published version in the Power BI service with a realistic production data volume. This can help identify issues that may not be caught in development with smaller data volumes. Remember to establish baselines and measure the impact of individual changes, as recommended in *Chapter 7, Governing with a Performance Framework*. For a good instructional video that covers testing various forms of RLS with the tools we covered in *Chapter 3, DirectQuery Optimization*, we recommend checking out the following video, which was published by *Guy in a Cube*: `https://www.youtube.com/watch?v=nRm-yQrh-ZA`.

Next, let's look at some guidance that applies to dynamic RLS:

- **Avoid unconnected security tables and LOOKUPVALUE()**: This technique simulates relationships by using a function to search for value matches in columns across two tables. This operation involves scanning through data and is much slower than if the engine were to use a physical relationship, which we recommend instead. You may need to adjust your security table and data model to make physical relationships possible, which is worth the effort.

- **Keep security tables as small as possible**: With dynamic RLS, the filter condition is initially applied to the security tables, which then filter subsequent tables via relationships. We should model the security tables to minimize the number of rows they contain. This minimizes the number of potential matches and reduces engine filtering work. Bear in mind that a single security table is not a Power BI requirement, so you are not forced to combine many permissions and grains into a large security table. Having a few small security tables that are more **normalized** can provide better performance.

- **Avoid using bi-directional security filters**: Security filter operations are not cached when they're bi-directional, which results in lower performance. If you must use them, try to limit the security tables to less than 128,000 rows.

- **Collapse multiple security contexts into a single security table**: If you have many different RLS filters from dimensions being applied to a *single fact table*, you can build a single security table using the same principles as the Kimball **junk dimension**. This can be a complete set of every possible combination of permissions (also known as a **cross-product**) or just the actual unique permission sets that are required by users. A cross-product is very easy to generate but can result in combinations that do not make sense and can never exist.

To see this technique in practice, let's consider the following setup, where one fact table is being filtered by multiple dimensions with security applied. The arrows represent relationships and the direction of filter propagation:

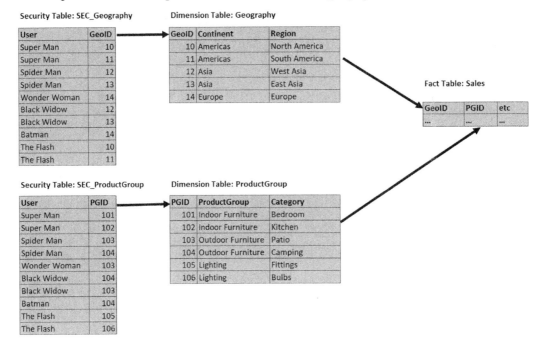

Figure 10.11 – Securing a single fact via multiple dimensions

We could reduce the amount of work that's needed to resolve security filters by combining the permissions into a single security table, as shown in the following screenshot:

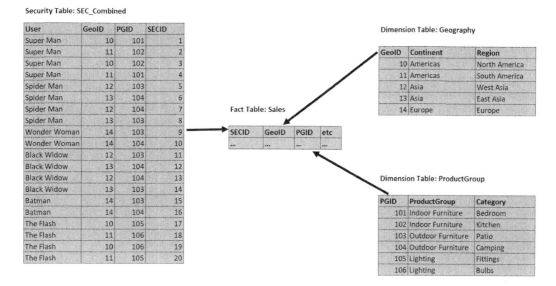

Figure 10.12 – More efficient configuration to secure a single fact

Note that our **SEC_Combined** table *does not* use a cross-product – it only contains valid combinations that exist in the source data, which will result in a smaller table. This is preferred when you have many dimensions and possible values. In our trivial example, the table contains 20 rows instead of the 30 combinations that would come from a cross-product (5 **Geography** rows x 6 **ProductGroup** rows).

You can see the effect of this change by running some report pages or queries with and without RLS applied, as described earlier. Check out RLS.pbix and RLS Combined.pbix in the sample files to see these in action. They contain the configurations from *Figure 10.10* and *Figure 10.11*, respectively, with a single fixed role to simulate the **Super Man** user.

We ran some tests in DAX Studio using a role built for **Super Man** and got the results shown in the following table. Even though we only had 25,000 rows, and the durations were trivial, you can already see a 300% difference in the total duration when RLS is applied using the combined approach. With many users, dimensions, and fact rows, this difference will be significant and noticeable in reports:

Sample File	Configuration	Formula Engine (ms)	Storage Engine (ms)	Storage Engine Queries	Total (ms)
RLS.pbix	No RLS	3	1	1	4
RLS.pbix	Super Man role	4	8	16	12
RLS Combined.pbix	No RLS	2	1	1	3
RLS Combined.pbix	Super Man role	2	1	1	3

Figure 10.13 – Performance comparison of different RLS configurations

- **Combine multiple users with the same security context**: In *Figure 10.11*, our security table contains multiple rows per user and some duplicate permission sets. For example, observe that both **Spider Man** and **Black Widow** have access to all of **Asia** and **Outdoor Furniture**. If you have many hundreds or thousands of users, security tables like this can get quite large. If users have the same permission sets, we can reduce the size significantly by performing modeling, as shown for the **Geography** dimension in the following screenshot. Observe how we have two much smaller security tables. Also, note the appropriate use of M2M and bi-directional filters by exception here – performance can improve massively with this setup when used correctly:

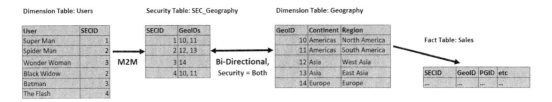

Figure 10.14 – Combining multiple users and permissions

Building specialized security tables like the one shown in the preceding screenshot can be achieved in different ways. You could build the tables externally as part of regular data warehouse loading activities, or you could leverage Power Query.

Now, let's summarize what we've learned in this chapter.

Summary

In this chapter, we learned how to speed up Power BI datasets in Import mode. We began with some theory on Kimball dimensional modeling, where we learned about star schemas, which are built from facts and dimensions. Data modeling is about grouping and relating attributes, and star schemas are one way to model data. They provide non-technical users with an intuitive way to analyze data by combining qualitative attributes into dimension tables. These dimensions are related to fact tables, which contain qualitative attributes. Power BI's Analysis Services engine works extremely well with star schemas, which are preferred. Hence, we briefly looked at the four-step dimensional modeling process and provided a practical example, including one with many-to-many relationships.

Then, we focused on reducing the size of datasets. This is important because less data means less processing, which results in better performance and more free resources for other parallel operations. We learned how to exclude any tables and columns that aren't needed for the report or calculations. We also explored techniques to help Analysis Services compress data better, such as choosing appropriate data types, reducing cardinality for columns, and preferring numbers over text strings.

Lastly, we learned how to optimize RLS. We learned that RLS works just like regular filters and that previous guidance about fast relationships also applies to RLS. The main thing to remember with RLS is to keep DAX security filter expressions as simple as possible, especially to avoid string manipulation. With dynamic RLS, we use security tables and we learned to keep the security table as small as possible. We also taught you how to use Desktop Performance Analyzer and DAX Studio to capture queries and look at performance before and after RLS is applied.

In the next chapter, we will look at DAX formulas, where we will identify common performance traps and suggest workarounds.

11
Improving DAX

In the previous chapter, we focused on Import datasets at the visual layer in Power BI, where a key point was to reduce the load on data sources by minimizing the complexity and number of queries that are issued to the Power BI dataset.

In theory, a well-designed data model should not experience performance issues easily unless there are extremely high data volumes with tens of millions of rows or more. However, it is still possible to get poor performance with good data models due to the way DAX measures are constructed.

Learning DAX basics is considered quite easy by many people. It can be approached by people without a technical data background but who are comfortable writing formulas in a tool such as Microsoft Excel. However, mastering DAX can be challenging. This is because DAX is a rich language with multiple ways to achieve the same result. Mastery requires having knowledge of row context and filter context, which determines what data is in scope at a point in the execution. In *Chapter 6, Third-Party Utilities*, we talked about the formula engine and storage engine in Analysis Services. In this chapter, we will look at examples of how DAX design patterns and being in filter context versus row context can affect how the engine behaves. We will see where time is spent in slower versus faster versions of the same calculation.

We will also identify DAX patterns that typically cause performance problems and how to rewrite them.

This chapter contains a single section presented as a collection of performance tips:

- Understanding DAX pitfalls and optimizations

Technical requirements

There is one combined sample file available for this chapter and all the sample references can be found in the `DAX Optimization.pbix` file, in the `Chapter11` folder in this book's GitHub repository: `https://github.com/PacktPublishing/Microsoft-Power-BI-Performance-Best-Practices`.

Understanding DAX pitfalls and optimizations

Before we dive into specific DAX improvements, we will briefly review the following suggested process to tune your DAX formulas.

The process for tuning DAX

In *Chapter 5*, *Desktop Performance Analyzer*, and *Chapter 6*, *Third-Party Utilities*, we provided detailed information and examples of how to use various tools to measure performance. We'll take this opportunity to remind you of which tools can help with DAX tuning and how they can be used. A recommended method to tune DAX is as follows:

1. Review the DAX expressions in the dataset. Ideally, run the **Best Practice Analyzer** (**BPA**) to identify potential DAX improvements. The BPA does cover some of the guidance provided in the next section, but it's a good idea to check all the rules manually.

2. Rank the suggestions in terms of estimated effort, from lowest to highest. Consider moving some calculations or even intermediate results to Power Query. This is usually a better place to perform row-by-row calculations.

3. In a development version of the data model, implement trivial fixes right away, but always check your measures to make sure they are still providing the same results.

4. Using the Power BI Desktop Performance Analyzer, check the performance of the report pages and visuals. Copy the queries that have been captured by the Analyzer into DAX Studio. Then use the Server Timings feature in DAX Studio to analyze load on the formula engine versus storage engine.

5. Modify your DAX expressions and confirm that performance has improved in DAX Studio – remember that DAX Studio allows you to safely overwrite measures locally without changing the actual dataset.

6. Make DAX changes in the dataset and check the report again with Performance Analyzer to ensure there are no unexpected performance degradations and that the results are still correct.

7. Test the changes in a production-like environment using realistic user scenarios and data volumes. If successful, deploy to the updates; otherwise, repeat the process to iron out any remaining issues.

Now, let's review DAX guidance.

DAX guidance

We will continue with the theme of having the Analysis Services engine do as little work as possible, with as little data as possible. Even with optimized datasets that follow good data modeling practices, inefficient DAX can make the engine unnecessarily scan rows, or perform slow logic in the formula engine. Therefore, our goals for tuning DAX are as follows:

- Reduce the work that's done by the single-threaded formula engine.

- Reduce the total number of internal queries that are generated by a DAX query.

- Avoid scanning large tables.

> **Note**
>
> In this section, we will only show the **DAX Studio** performance results for the first few tips. Please be aware that you can use DAX Studio, **Desktop Performance Analyzer**, and other tools to measure performance and tune DAX for all the cases mentioned here.

The following list represents some common design choices that lead to lower performance. We will explain why each one can be problematic and what you can do instead:

- **Use variables instead of repeating measure definitions**: Sometimes, when we are performing a calculation, we need to reuse a calculated value multiple times to get to the result. We will use an example where we have some sales figures and need to calculate the variance percentage compared to the same period in the previous year. One way to write this calculation is as follows:

```
YoY% =
(
SUM('Fact Sale'[Total Sales])
 - CALCULATE(SUM('Fact Sale'[Total Sales]),
 DATEADD('Dimension Date'[Date], -1, YEAR))
),
/
CALCULATE(SUM('Fact Sale'[Total Sales]),
 DATEADD('Dimension Date'[Date], -1, YEAR)
```

Observe that we are referencing the prior year's sales value twice – once to calculate the numerator and again to calculate the denominator. This makes the engine duplicate some effort and might not take full advantage of caching in Analysis Services. A better way of doing this would be to use a variable. Note that we have not handled error cases and fully optimized this yet:

```
YoY% VAR =
VAR __PREV_YEAR =
CALCULATE(
SUM('Fact Sale'[Total Sales]),
DATEADD('Dimension Date'[Date], -1, YEAR))
RETURN
(SUM('Fact Sale'[Total Sales]) - __PREV_YEAR) /__PREV_
YEAR
```

The difference here is that we have introduced the VAR statement to define a variable called __PREV_YEAR, which will hold the value of last year's sales. This value can be reused anywhere in the formula simply by name, without incurring recalculation.

You can see this in action in the sample file, which contains both versions of the measure. The `Without Variable` and `With Variable` report pages contain a table visual, like this:

Calendar Year Month	2014 Total Sales	YoY%	2015 Total Sales	YoY%	2016 Total Sales	YoY%
January						
1	239,249	Infinity	200,959	-16.0%	232,040	15.5%
2	230,158	602.9%	260,229	13.1%	106,474	-59.1%
3	129,815	-29.6%	150,456	15.9%	174,732	16.1%
4	219,301	40.6%	51,394	-76.6%		-100.0%
5	78,483	-36.7%		-100.0%	266,416	Infinity
6		-100.0%	273,002	Infinity	264,426	-3.1%
7	192,654	Infinity	164,946	-14.4%	310,255	88.1%
8	171,123	-40.9%	142,349	-16.8%	289,464	103.3%
9	123,393	23.2%	200,223	62.3%	227,649	13.7%
10	84,998	-47.7%	160,666	89.0%	148,332	-7.7%
11	260,385	33.4%	59,860	-77.0%		-100.0%

Figure 11.1 – Table visual showing a year-on-year % growth measure

We captured the query trace information in DAX Studio to see how these perform. The results can be seen in the following screenshot:

Total	SE CPU	Line	Subclass	Duration	CPU	Par.	Rows	KB	Query
72 ms	16 ms x1.5	2	Scan	6	16	x2.7	1,069	13	SELECT 'Dimension Date'[Calendar Year], 'LocalDateTabl
		4	Scan	0	0		1,464	12	SELECT 'Dimension Date'[Date] FROM 'Dimension Date'
FE	SE	6	Scan	1	0		1,461	6	SELECT 'Dimension Date'[Date], Dimension Date'[Calen
61 ms	11 ms	8	Scan	4	0		1,464	23	SELECT 'Dimension Date'[Date], SUM ('Fact Sale'[Total S
84.7%	15.3%	10	Scan	0	0		1,464	23	SELECT 'Dimension Date'[Date], SUM ('Fact Sale'[Total S
SE Queries	**SE Cache**								**Variable NOT used in YoY% measure**
5	1 20.0%								

Total	SE CPU	Line	Subclass	Duration	CPU	Par.	Rows	KB	Query
58 ms	0 ms x0.0	2	Scan	6	0		1,069	13	SELECT 'Dimension Date'[Calendar Year], 'LocalDateTable
		4	Scan	1	0		1,464	12	SELECT 'Dimension Date'[Date] FROM 'Dimension Date';
FE	SE	6	Scan	1	0		1,461	6	SELECT 'Dimension Date'[Date], 'Dimension Date'[Calend
47 ms	11 ms	8	Scan	3	0		1,464	23	SELECT 'Dimension Date'[Date], SUM ('Fact Sale'[Total Sa
81.0%	19.0%								
SE Queries	**SE Cache**								**Variable was used in YoY% measure**
4	0 0.0%								

Figure 11.2 – DAX Studio showing less work and duration with a variable

In the preceding screenshot, the first query without the variable was a bit slower. We can see it executed one extra storage engine query, which does appear to have hit a cache in our simple example. We can also see more time being spent in the formula engine than with the version with a variable. In our example, where the fact table contains about 220,000 rows, this difference would be unnoticeable. This can become significant with higher volumes and more sophisticated calculations, especially if a base measure is used in other measures that are all displayed at the same time.

> **Note**
>
> Using variables is probably the single most important tip for DAX performance. There are so many examples of calculations that need to use calculated values multiple times to achieve the desired result. You will also find that Power BI automatically uses this and other recommended practices in areas where it generates code for you, such as **Quick Measures**.

- **Use DIVIDE instead of the division operator**: When we divide numbers, we sometimes need to avoid errors by checking for blank or zero values in the denominator. This results in conditional logic statements, which add extra work for the formula engine. Let's continue with the example from *Figure 11.1*. Instead of year-on-year growth, we now want to calculate a profit margin. We want to avoid report errors by handling blank and zero values:

```
Profit IF =
IF(
    OR(
        ISBLANK([Sales]),[Sales] == 0
    ),
    BLANK(),
    [Profit]/[Sales]
)
```

An improved version would use the DIVIDE function, as follows:

```
Profit DIVIDE =
DIVIDE([Profit], [Sales])
```

This function has several advantages. It automatically handles zero and blank values at the storage engine layer, which is parallel and faster. It has an optional third parameter that allows you to specify an alternative value to use if the denominator is zero or blank. It is also a much shorter measure that is easier to understand and maintain.

When we take a look at the performance numbers from DAX Studio, we can see stark differences. The first version is nearly three times slower than the optimized version, as shown in the following screenshot:

Total	SE CPU	Line	Subclass	Duration	CPU	Par.	Rows	KB	Query
55 ms	31 ms	2	Scan	7	0		1,069	13	SELECT 'Dimension Date'[Calendar Y
	x1.1	4	Scan	20	31	x1.6	1,069	21	SELECT 'Dimension Date'[Calendar Y
FE	**SE**	6	Scan	1	0		7	1	SELECT 'Dimension Date'[Calendar Y
26 ms	29 ms	8	Scan	1	0		7,650	60	SELECT 'LocalDateTable'[MonthNo],
47.3%	52.7%								

This version uses / and conditionals

SE Queries	**SE Cache**
4	0
	0.0%

Total	SE CPU	Line	Subclass	Duration	CPU	Par.	Rows	KB	Query
20 ms	16 ms	2	Scan	7	16	x2.3	1,069	21	SELECT 'Dimension Date'[Calendar Y
	x2.3								
FE	**SE**								
13 ms	7 ms								
65.0%	35.0%								

This version uses DIVIDE()

SE Queries	**SE Cache**
1	0
	0.0%

Figure 11.3 – DAX Studio showing less work done by DIVIDE

The preceding screenshot also shows us that the slower version issued more internal queries and spent about four times longer in the storage engine. It also spent about twice as much time in the formula engine. Once again, this is just a single query for one visual. This difference can be compounded for a typical report page that runs many queries. You can experiment with this using the Profit IF and Profit DIVIDE pages in the sample file.

- **For numerical measures, avoid converting blank results into zero or some text value**: Sometimes, for usability reasons, people write measures with conditional statements to check for a blank result and replace it with zero. This is more common in financial reporting, where people need to see every dimensional value (for example, Cost Code or SKU), regardless of whether any activity occurred. Let's look at an example. We have a simple measure called Sales in our sample file that sums the 'Fact Sale'[Total Including Tax] column. We have adjusted it to return zero instead of blanks, as follows:

```
SalesNoBlank =
    VAR SumSales =
SUM('Fact Sale'[Total Including Tax])
RETURN
    IF(ISBLANK(SumSales), 0, SumSales)
```

Then, we constructed a matrix visual that shows sales by product barcode for both versions of the measure. The results are shown in the following screenshot. At the top, we can see the values for 2016, which implies there are no sales for these product bar codes in other years. At the bottom, we can see 2013 onwards, which we can scroll through:

STANDARD SUM MEASURE:

Year	8302039293647	8302039293929	8792838293234	8792838293236	8792838293289	8792838293728	8792838293820	8792838293987	Total
2016	143,550.00	161,164.08	148,975.20	170,418.60	147,620.88	144,686.52	190,056.24	140,172.12	1,246,643.64
January	22,968.00	32,503.68	22,120.56	40,178.16	31,149.36	32,729.40	33,632.28	24,829.20	240,110.64
February	20,288.40	24,829.20	25,957.80	28,892.16	26,183.52	15,574.68	38,372.40	22,572.00	202,670.16
March	36,748.80	41,306.76	30,246.48	34,760.88	32,052.24	29,343.60	32,729.40	31,375.08	268,563.24
April	29,475.60	36,340.92	28,215.00	34,760.88	27,989.28	41,758.20	34,760.88	31,826.52	265,127.28
May	34,069.20	26,183.52	42,435.36	31,826.52	30,246.48	25,280.64	50,561.28	29,569.32	270,172.32
Total	143,550.00	161,164.08	148,975.20	170,418.60	147,620.88	144,686.52	190,056.24	140,172.12	1,246,643.64

MODIFIED MEASURE TO REPLACE BLANKS WITH ZERO:

Year	8302039293647	8302039293929	8792838293234	8792838293236	8792838293289	8792838293728	8792838293820	8792838293987	Total
2013	0.00	0.00	0.00	0.00	0.00	0.00	0.00	0.00	0.00
January	0.00	0.00	0.00	0.00	0.00	0.00	0.00	0.00	0.00
February	0.00	0.00	0.00	0.00	0.00	0.00	0.00	0.00	0.00
March	0.00	0.00	0.00	0.00	0.00	0.00	0.00	0.00	0.00
April	0.00	0.00	0.00	0.00	0.00	0.00	0.00	0.00	0.00
May	0.00	0.00	0.00	0.00	0.00	0.00	0.00	0.00	0.00
June	0.00	0.00	0.00	0.00	0.00	0.00	0.00	0.00	0.00
July	0.00	0.00	0.00	0.00	0.00	0.00	0.00	0.00	0.00
August	0.00	0.00	0.00	0.00	0.00	0.00	0.00	0.00	0.00
Total	143,550.00	161,164.08	148,975.20	170,418.60	147,620.88	144,686.52	190,056.24	140,172.12	1,246,643.64

Figure 11.4 – The same totals but many more rows when replacing blanks

Both results shown in the preceding screenshot are technically correct. However, there is a performance penalty for replacing blanks. If we think about a dimensional model, in theory, we could record a fact for every possible combination of dimensions. In practical terms, for our Sales example, in theory, we could sell things every single day, for every product, for every employee, in every location, and so on. However, there will nearly always be some combinations that are not realistic or simply don't have activities against them. Analysis Services is highly optimized to take advantage of empty dimensional intersections and doesn't return rows for combinations where all the measures are blank. We measured the query that was produced by the visuals in the preceding screenshot. You can see the performance difference in DAX Studio in the following screenshot:

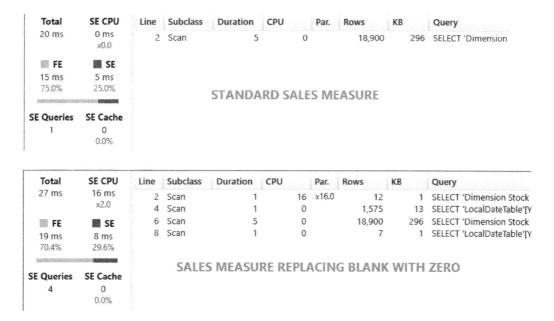

Figure 11.5 – Slower performance when replacing blanks

The preceding screenshot shows a longer total duration, more queries executed, and significantly more time spent in the formula engine. You can see these on the `MeasureWithBlank` and `MeasureNoBlank` report pages in the sample file.

Consider not replacing blanks in your measure but solving this problem on a per-visual basis. You can do this by selecting a visual and using the **Fields** pane in Power BI Desktop to enable **Show items with no data** for specific attributes of a dimension, as shown in the following screenshot. This change will still produce a less optimal query, but not one that's quite as slow as using measures:

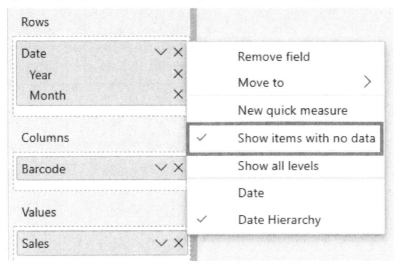

Figure 11.6 – Show items with no data

Another advantage of the visual-based approach is that you are not forced to take a performance hit everywhere the measure is used. You can balance performance with usability selectively.

If you still need to implement blank handling centrally, you could consider making the measures more complex to only substitute a blank for the correct scope of data. We recommended checking out the detailed article from SQLBI on this topic, which shows a combination of DAX and data modeling techniques to use, depending on your scenario: `https://www.sqlbi.com/articles/how-to-return-0-instead-of-blank-in-dax`.

A final point here is to avoid replacing blanks in numerical data with text values such as *No data*. While this can be helpful for users, it can be even slower than substituting zero because we are forcing the measure to become a string. This can also create problems downstream if the measure is used in other calculations.

- **Use SELECTEDVALUE instead of VALUES**: Sometimes, a calculation is only relevant when a single item from a dimension is in scope. For example, you may use a slicer as a parameter table to allow users to dynamically change measures, such as scaling by some factor. One pattern to access the single value in scope is to use HASONEVALUE to check for only one value, and then use the VALUES DAX function. If we had a parameter table called Scale, our measure would look like this:

```
Sales by Scale =
DIVIDE (
    [Sales Amount],
    IF( HASONEVALUE ( Scale[Scale] ), VALUES (
Scale[Scale] ), 1 )
)
```

Instead, we suggest that you use SELECTEDVALUE, which performs both steps internally. It returns blank if there are no items or multiple items in scope and allows you to specify an alternate value if there are zero or multiple items in scope. A better version is as follows:

```
Sales by Scale =
DIVIDE (
    [Sales],
    SELECTEDVALUE ( 'Scale'[Scale], 1 )
)
```

You can see this technique in use in the sample file on the SELECTEDVALUE report page.

- **Use IFERROR and ISERROR appropriately**: These are helpful functions that a data modeler can use to catch calculation errors. They can be wrapped around a measure to provide alternatives if there are calculation errors. However, they should be used with care because they increase the number of storage engine scans required and can force row-by-row operations in the engine. We recommend dealing with data errors at the source or in the ETL stages to avoid performing error checking in DAX. This may not always be feasible, so depending on the situation, you should try to use other techniques, such as the following:

  - The FIND or SEARCH functions to search for and substitute values for failed matches

  - The DIVIDE or SELECTEDVALUE functions to handle zeros and blanks

- **Use SUMMARIZE only for text columns**: This is the original function that's included in DAX to perform grouping. While it allows any column type, we advise not using numerical columns for performance reasons. Instead, use SUMMARIZECOLUMNS, which is newer and more optimized. There are many examples and use cases here, so we recommend checking out the following article by SQLBI, which provides much deeper coverage: https://www.sqlbi.com/articles/introducing-summarizecolumns.

- **Avoid FILTER in functions that accept filter conditions**: Functions such as CALCULATE and CALCULATETABLE accept a filter parameter that is used to adjust the context of the calculation. The FILTER function returns a table, which is not efficient when it's used as a filter condition in other functions. Instead, try to convert the FILTER statement into a **Boolean** expression. Consider the following measure:

```
Wingtip Sales FILTER =
CALCULATE(
    [Sales],
    FILTER('Dimension Customer', 'Dimension
Customer'[Buying Group] == "Wingtip Toys")
)
```

It is better to replace the table expression with a Boolean expression, as follows:

```
Wingtip Sales =
CALCULATE(
    [Sales],
    'Dimension Customer'[Buying Group] == "Wingtip Toys")
)
```

The FILTER function can force row-by-row operations in the engine, whereas the improved Boolean version will use more efficient filtering on the column stores.

- **Use COUNTROWS instead of COUNT**: We often write measures to count the number of rows in a table within a context. Two choices will provide the same result, but only if there are no blank values. The COUNT function accepts a column reference, whereas the COUNTROWS function accepts a table reference. When you need to count rows and do not care about blanks, the latter will perform better.

- **Use ISBLANK instead of = BLANK to check for empty values**: They achieve the same result, but ISBLANK is faster.

- **Optimize virtual relationships with TREATAS**: There are times when we need to filter a table based on column values from another table but cannot create a physical relationship in the dataset. It may be that multiple columns are needed to form a unique key, or that the relationship is many-to-many. You can solve this using FILTER and CONTAINS, or INTERSECT. However, TREATAS will perform better and is recommended.

Look at the TREATAS report page in our sample file. The following screenshot shows an example where we added a new table to hold rewards groupings for customers based on their **Buying Group** and **Postal Code**. We want to filter sales using a new **Reward Group** column. We will not be able to build a single relationship with more than one key field:

Reward Group	Buying Group	Postal Code
Wingtip Premium	Wingtip Toys	90031
Wingtip Select	Wingtip Toys	90005
Tailspin Premium	Tailspin Toys	90031
Tailspin Select	Tailspin Toys	90011
Wingtip Premium	Wingtip Toys	90041
Wingtip Select	Wingtip Toys	90043
Tailspin Premium	Tailspin Toys	90041
Tailspin Select	Tailspin Toys	90045

Customer Key	WWI Customer ID	Customer	Bill To Customer	Category	Buying Group	Primary Contact	Postal Code
162	162	Tailspin Toys (Glen Park, NY)	Tailspin Toys (Head Office)	Novelty Shop	Tailspin Toys	Nu Bach	90026
170	170	Tailspin Toys (Eastchester, NY)	Tailspin Toys (Head Office)	Novelty Shop	Tailspin Toys	Daniella Barbosa	90031
341	540	Wingtip Toys (Weld, ME)	Wingtip Toys (Head Office)	Novelty Shop	Wingtip Toys	Åšani Nair	90031
300	499	Wingtip Toys (East Fultonham, OH)	Wingtip Toys (Head Office)	Novelty Shop	Wingtip Toys	Masa Buecek	90032
311	510	Wingtip Toys (Grabill, IN)	Wingtip Toys (Head Office)	Novelty Shop	Wingtip Toys	Manish Ghosh	90032
247	446	Wingtip Toys (Saint Landry, LA)	Wingtip Toys (Head Office)	Novelty Shop	Wingtip Toys	Chetana Kamath	90033

Figure 11.7 – The new Reward Group table cannot be connected to the Customer table

We can write a measure to handle this using CONTAINS, as follows:

```
RG Sales CONTAINS =
CALCULATE (
    [Sales],
    FILTER (
        ALL('Dimension Customer'[Buying Group]),
        CONTAINS (
            VALUES (RewardsGroup[Buying Group]),
            RewardsGroup[Buying Group],
            'Dimension Customer'[Buying Group]
        )
    ),
    FILTER (
```

```
        ALL('Dimension Customer'[Postal Code]),
        CONTAINS (
            VALUES(RewardsGroup[Postal Code]),
            RewardsGroup[Postal Code],
            'Dimension Customer'[Postal Code]
        )
    )
)
```

This is quite long for a simple piece of logic, and it does not perform that well. A better version that uses TREATAS would look like this:

```
RG Sales TREATAS =
CALCULATE (
    [Sales],
    TREATAS (
SUMMARIZE(RewardsGroup, RewardsGroup[Buying Group],
RewardsGroup[Postal Code]),
    'Dimension Customer'[Buying Group],
    'Dimension Customer'[Postal Code]
    )
)
```

We haven't shown the INTERSECT version here, but note that it will be a little easier to write and can provide better performance. However, the TREATAS version is much shorter and easier to read and maintain. It will also perform better. Here, we visualized a simple table, as shown in the following screenshot, and managed to get nearly a 25% speed improvement with TREATAS. We also reduced the number of storage engine queries from 11 to 8:

Reward Group	First Characters	RG Sales CONTAINS
Tailspin Premium	"The Gu" red sh	90,417.60
Tailspin Premium	10 mm Anti stat	28,922.50
Tailspin Premium	10 mm Double si	49,162.50
Tailspin Premium	20 mm Anti stat	61,548.00

Figure 11.8 – The visual that was used to test CONTAINS versus TREATAS performance

Now that we have learned about DAX optimizations, let's summarize what we've learned in this chapter.

Summary

In this chapter, we learned that DAX tuning is important because inefficient formulas can impact performance, even with well-designed datasets. This is because the DAX pattern directly influences how Analysis Services retrieves data and calculates query results.

We looked at a process for DAX tuning using tools that were introduced earlier in this book. First, we suggested using the Best Practice Analyzer and manual reviews to identify DAX improvements and then prioritize the changes to handle trivial fixes. Then, we suggested using Desktop Performance Analyzer to capture the queries that have been generated by visuals and running them in DAX Studio to understand their behavior. It is important to look at the total duration, number of internal queries, and time spent in the formula engine versus the storage engine. Once the changes have been prototyped and verified in DAX Studio, they can be made in the dataset; reports should be checked in production scenarios for performance gains.

Next, we looked at a range of common DAX pitfalls and alternative designs that can improve performance. We learned that, in general, we are trying to avoid formula engine work and wish to reduce the number of storage engine queries. Whenever possible, we explained why a performance penalty is incurred. We also provided examples of visual treatments and DAX Studio results for common optimizations to help you learn where to look, and what to look for.

Considering what we've learned so far, there may still be issues where the sheer volume of data can cause problems where additional modeling and architectural approaches need to be used to provide acceptable performance. Therefore, in the next chapter, we will look at techniques that can help us manage big data that reaches the terabyte scale.

12
High-Scale Patterns

In the previous chapter, we learned how to optimize DAX expressions. Having reached this point, we have rounded up all the advice on optimizing different layers of a Power BI solution, from the dataset layer to report design. In this chapter, we will take a step back and revisit architectural concepts and related features that help deal with very high data volumes.

The amount of data that organizations collect and need to analyze is increasing all the time. With the advent of the **Internet of Things** (**IoT**) and predictive analytics, certain industries, such as energy and resources, are collecting more data than ever. It is common for a modern mine or gas plant to have tens of thousands of sensors, each generating many data points at granularities much higher than a second.

Even with Power BI's data compression technology, it isn't always possible to load and store massive amounts of data in an Import mode model in a reasonable amount of time. This problem is worse when you must support hundreds or thousands of users in parallel. This chapter will cover the options you have for dealing with such issues by leveraging composite data models and aggregations, Power BI Premium, and Azure technologies. The concepts in this chapter are complementary and can be combined in the same solution as appropriate.

In this chapter, we will cover the following topics:

- Scaling with Power BI Premium and Azure Analysis Services
- Scaling with composite models and aggregations
- Scaling with Azure Synapse and Data Lake

Technical requirements

There is a combined sample file available for this chapter. All the sample references can be found in the `Composite and Aggs.pbix` file, in the `Chapter12` folder in this book's GitHub repository: `https://github.com/PacktPublishing/Microsoft-Power-BI-Performance-Best-Practices`. Since this example uses DirectQuery to access a SQL server database, we have included the `AdventureWorksLT2016.bak` SQL backup. Please restore that database to a SQL server and update the connection in Power BI Desktop to run the sample successfully.

Scaling with Power BI Premium and Azure Analysis Services

Power BI users with Pro licenses can create workspaces in the Shared or Premium capacity. Shared capacity is available by default to any organization using Power BI. Shared capacity is managed entirely by Microsoft, which load balance multiple tenants over thousands of physical machines around the world. To provide a consistent and fair experience for everyone, there are certain limits in Shared capacity. One that affects data volumes is the 1 GB size limit of a compressed dataset. Power BI Desktop will allow you to create datasets that are only limited by the amount of memory on the computer, but you will not be allowed to upload a dataset that's larger than 1 GB to Shared capacity. Similarly, if a dataset hosted in Shared capacity grows to over 1 GB, it will result in refresh errors. Note that this limit refers to the compressed data size, so the actual source data can be many times larger.

Leveraging Power BI Premium for data scale

One way to resolve the Shared dataset size limit issue is to leverage dedicated capacity via Power BI Premium. Premium capacity must be purchased separately, and the computing resources are dedicated to the organization. Customers can purchase Premium capacity of different sizes, ranging from P1 (8 cores and 25 GB of RAM) to P5 (128 cores and 400 GB of RAM). Also, note that Microsoft offers Power BI Embedded capacities. While these are licensed, purchased, and billed differently from the Premium capacities, the technology is the same and any advice given here applies to both Premium and Embedded.

Premium capacity offers a range of unique features, higher limits, and some enhancements that help with performance and scale. We will cover Premium optimization in detail in *Chapter 13, Optimizing Premium and Embedded Capacities*. For now, the important point is that the dataset limit in Premium is raised to 10 GB. However, this is just the limit of the initial dataset that is uploaded to the Premium capacity.

> **Tip**
>
> If your dataset will grow beyond 1 GB in size, you should consider using Power BI Premium. Power BI Premium will allow you to upload a dataset up to a maximum size of 10 GB that can grow to 12 GB after being refreshed. However, if you choose the large dataset format, the dataset will have no size limit. The available capacity memory is the only limiting factor. You can even provision multiple Premium capacities of different sizes and spread your load accordingly. Always plan to have free memory on the capacity to handle temporary storage for queries, which can include uncompressed data. Lastly, the large dataset format can also speed up write operations that are performed via the XMLA endpoint.

The following screenshot shows the **Large dataset storage format** setting on a published dataset. It is part of the **Dataset settings** page and can be accessed from a Power BI workspace. You can enable this to remove the dataset's size limit:

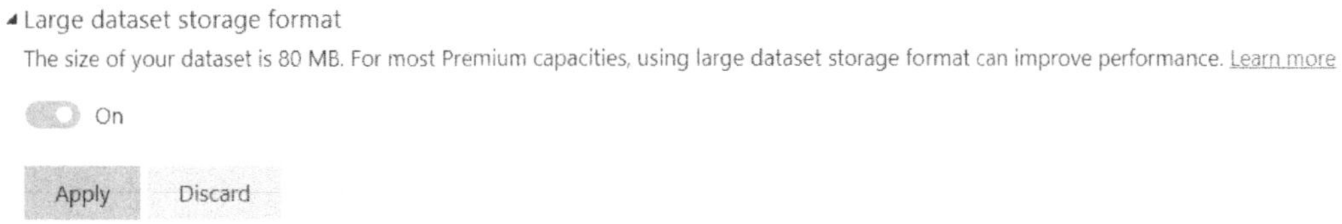

◢ Large dataset storage format

The size of your dataset is 80 MB. For most Premium capacities, using large dataset storage format can improve performance. Learn more

◖◗ On

Apply   Discard

Figure 12.1 – Large dataset storage format option in Dataset settings

Be aware that you can set the large dataset storage format to be the default on a Premium capacity. Administrators can set a limit on the maximum dataset size to prevent users from consuming significant amounts of a capacity.

With the large dataset format, Premium is an excellent choice to handle data scale. It can also support more users simply by having more computing resources available on the platform that can handle more concurrent queries and, therefore, users. The ability to provision multiple capacities also provides user-scale benefits since you can avoid having very popular datasets in the same capacity.

However, you may still have a scenario where you have extreme data volumes with many concurrent users that are pushing a Premium capacity to its limits. Next, we will learn how to deal with this problem with Azure Analysis Services.

Leveraging Azure Analysis Services for data and user scale

Azure Analysis Services (**AAS**) is a **Platform-as-a-Service** (**PaaS**) offering. It is part of the broader suite of data services offered by Microsoft in the Azure cloud. A range of SKUs are available, with processing power stated in **Query Processing Units** (**QPU**).

AAS can be considered as the cloud alternative to SQL Server Analysis Services. For organizations that already use SQL Server Analysis Services and want to migrate to the cloud, AAS is the best option and offers the most direct migration path. AAS is billed on a *pay-as-you-go* basis, can be paused and scaled on demand, and offers comprehensive support for Power BI Pro developer tools such as Microsoft Visual Studio with version control and the ability to perform **Continuous Integration/Continuous Development** (**CI/CD**). Like SQL Server Analysis Services, AAS is the data engine only, so it only supports hosting datasets and the mashup engine. You would still need to use a client tool such as Power BI Desktop or a portal such as *PowerBI.com* to host reports that read from AAS. AAS can be considered a subset of Premium, though this is not completely true today. This is because there are differences, such as dynamic memory management, which is only offered in Premium, and **Query Scale Out** (**QSO**), which is only available in AAS (Standard tier). QSO is a great way of handling high user concurrency with minimal maintenance, so it is a pity to not have it available in Premium today. However, it is encouraging to note that Microsoft has stated their intention to have Premium become a true superset of AAS.

Using Query Scale Out to achieve higher user concurrency

Power BI Premium and AAS have the same dataset size limits, so you can host the same data volumes on either. However, QSO is a unique capability of AAS that allows it to handle many more concurrent users by spreading the query read load across multiple redundant copies of the data. You simply configure the service to create additional read replicas (up to a maximum of 7 additional replicas). When client connections are made, they are load-balanced across query replicas. Note that not every region and SKU supports 7 replicas, so please consult the documentation for information on availability by region at `https://docs.microsoft.com/azure/analysis-services/analysis-services-overview`. Also, please note that replicas do incur costs, so you should consider this aspect when you review your performance gains.

Another useful performance-related feature of AAS is its ability to separate the query and processing servers when we use QSO. This maximizes the performance of both processing and query operations. The separation means that at refresh time, one of the replicas will be dedicated to the refresh and no new client connections will be assigned to it. New connections will be assigned to query replicas only so that they can handle reads while the processing replica can handle writes.

Configuring replicas can be done via the Azure portal or scripted via PowerShell. The following screenshot shows an example where we are allowed to create one additional replica:

Figure 12.2 – AAS server with 1 replica highlighting the query pool separation setting

Note that creating replicas does not allow you to host larger datasets than if you were not using QSO. It simply creates additional identical copies with the same server SKU.

Lastly, let's talk about how to determine the right time to scale out. You can observe AAS metrics in the Azure portal to look at QPU over time. If you find that you regularly reach the maximum QPU of your service and that those time frames are correlated with performance issues, it is time to consider QSO. The following screenshot shows the QPU metric for an S0-sized AAS server that has a QPU limit of 40. We can see that we are not hitting that limit right now:

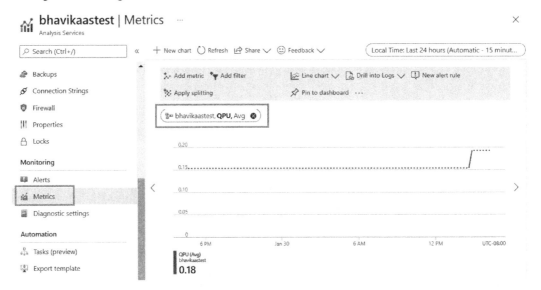

Figure 12.3 – Metrics in the Azure portal showing QPU over time

Next, we'll learn how partitions can improve refresh performance.

Using partitions with AAS and Premium

AAS has supported partitioned tables for many years. Partitions simply divide a table into smaller parts that can be managed independently. Typically, partitioning is done by date and is applied to fact tables. For example, you could have 5 years of data split into 60 monthly partitions. In this case, you could process individual partitions separately and even perform entirely different operations on them, such as clearing data from one while loading data into another.

From a performance perspective, partitions can speed up data refresh operations in two ways:

- Firstly, you can only process new and updated data by leaving historical partitions untouched and avoiding a full refresh.

- Secondly, you can get better refresh performance since partitions can be processed in parallel.

Maximum parallelism assumes that there is sufficient CPU power and memory available in AAS and that the data source can support the load. AAS automatically utilizes parallel processing for two or more partitions and there are no associated configuration settings for it.

> **Tip**
> Power BI Premium (with a large dataset storage format) and AAS use a segment size of 8 million rows. Segments are the internal structures that are used to split columns into manageable chunks, and compression is applied at the segment level. Therefore, we recommend employing a strategy where partitions have at least 8 million rows when fully populated. This will help AAS get the best compression and avoid doing extra maintenance work on many small partitions. Over-partitioning can slow down a dataset refresh and result in slightly larger datasets.

Tables defined in a Power BI dataset have a single partition by default. You cannot directly control partitioning in Power BI Desktop. However, note that when you configure incremental refreshes, partitions are automatically created and managed based on your time granularity and data freshness settings.

So, when we're using AAS or Power BI Premium, we need to define partitions manually using other tools. Partitions can be defined at design time in Visual Studio using the **Partition Manager** screen. Post-deployment, they can be managed using SQL Server Management Studio by running **Tabular Model Scripting Language (TMSL)**. You can also manage them programmatically via the **Tabular Object Model (TOM)**.

You can control parallelism at refresh time by using the TMSL parameter called **MaxParallelism**, which limits the total number of parallel operations, regardless of the data source. Some sample code for this was provided in the first section of *Chapter 8, Loading, Transforming, and Refreshing Data*.

Earlier in this section, we described a simple approach that used monthly partitions. A more advanced approach could be to have yearly or monthly historical partitions with daily active partitions. This provides you with a lot more flexibility to update recent facts and minimize re-processing if refresh failures occur since you can re-process at the single-day granularity. However, this advanced strategy requires extra maintenance since partitions would need to be merged. For example, at the end of each month, you may merge all the daily partitions into a monthly one. Performing this type of maintenance manually can become tedious. Therefore, it is recommended that you automate this process with the help of some tracking tables to manage date ranges and partitions. A detailed automated partition management sample has been published by Microsoft that we recommend: `https://github.com/microsoft/Analysis-Services/blob/master/AsPartitionProcessing/Automated%20Partition%20Management%20for%20Analysis%20Services%20Tabular%20Models.pdf`.

The final performance-related point is about **synchronization mode** for query replicas. When datasets are updated, the replicas that are used for QSO also need to be updated to give all the users the latest data. By default, these replicas are rehydrated in full (not incrementally) and in stages. Assuming there are at least three replicas, they are detached and attached two at a time, which can disconnect some clients. This behavior is determined by a server property called **ReplicaSyncMode**. It is an advanced property that you can set using SQL Server Management Studio, as shown in the following screenshot. This setting can be changed to make synchronization occur in parallel. Parallel synchronization updates in-memory caches incrementally and can significantly reduce synchronization time. It also provides the benefit of not dropping any connections because replicas are always kept online:

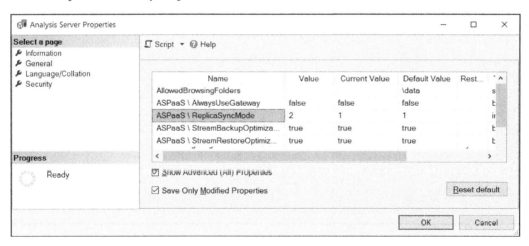

Figure 12.4 – Analysis Server Properties showing that ReplicaSyncMode has been updated

The following settings for **ReplicaSyncMode** are allowed:

- 1: Full rehydration performed in stages. This is the default.
- 2: Parallel synchronization.

> **Note**
>
> When using parallel synchronization, additional memory may be consumed by query replicas because they stay online and are still available for queries. The synchronization operation behaves like a regular data refresh, which could require double the dataset memory for a full refresh, as discussed in *Chapter 2, Exploring Power BI Architecture and Configuration.*

In the next section, we'll learn how to take advantage of composite models in Power BI to address big data and slow DirectQuery problems.

Scaling with composite models and aggregations

So far, we have discussed how Import mode offers the best possible speed for Power BI datasets. However, sometimes, high data volumes and their associated refresh limitations may lead you to select DirectQuery mode instead. At this point, you may want to review the *Choosing between Import and DirectQuery mode* section on choosing a storage mode in *Chapter 2, Exploring Power BI Architecture and Configuration*, to remind yourself about the differences and rationale for choosing one over the other.

We also discussed how the Analysis Services engine is designed to aggregate data efficiently because BI solutions typically aggregate data most of the time. When we use DirectQuery, we want to push these aggregations down to the source where possible to avoid Power BI having to bring all the data over to compute them. With very large tables containing tens of millions to billions of rows, these aggregations can be costly and time-consuming, even when the source has been optimized. This is where the composite models and aggregations features become relevant.

Leveraging composite models

So far, we have talked about the Import and DirectQuery modes separately. This may have implied that you must choose only one mode, but this is not the case. A composite model (also known as Mixed mode) is a feature of Analysis Services that lets you combine DirectQuery and Import data sources in the same dataset. This opens up interesting possibilities. You could enhance a DirectQuery source with infrequently changing Import data that is held elsewhere. You can even combine different DirectQuery sources. Regardless of the requirement, you are advised to follow all the recommended guidelines we have provided for Import and DirectQuery to date. There are some additional performance concepts and considerations for composite models that we will introduce in the remainder of this chapter.

Analysis Services maintains storage mode at the table level. This allows us to mix storage modes within a dataset. The bottom-right corner of Power BI Desktop gives us an indication of the type of model. An Import mode model will not show any status, but DirectQuery and Composite will show some text, as shown in the following screenshot:

Figure 12.5 – Power BI Desktop indicating the DirectQuery or Mixed (composite) storage mode

There are different ways to achieve Mixed mode in Power BI Desktop. You could add a new table in Import mode to an existing DirectQuery model, or vice versa. Another way is to directly change the storage mode in the **Model** view of Power BI Desktop, as shown here:

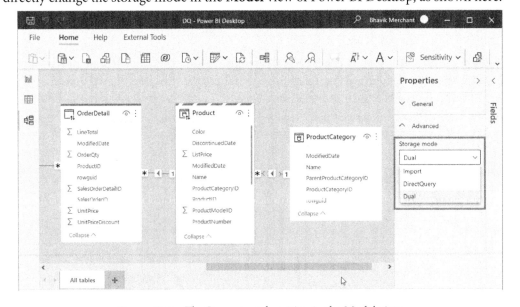

Figure 12.6 – The Storage mode setting in the Model view

There are interesting things to note in the preceding screenshot. The **Storage mode** dropdown offers the **Import**, **DirectQuery**, and **Dual** storage modes. In the model diagram view, the table header's colors and icons indicate what type of storage mode is used. With Dual mode, depending on the query's scope and granularity, Analysis Services will decide whether to use the in-memory cache or use the latest data from the data source. Let's look at these table storage modes and learn when to use them:

- **DirectQuery**: This is the blue header bar with the DirectQuery icon (for example, **OrderDetail**). Choose this mode for tables that contain very large data volumes, or where you need to fetch the latest results all the time. Power BI will never import this data during a data refresh. Typically, these would be fact tables.

- **Import**: This is the plain white header bar with the **Import** icon (for example, **ProductCategory**). Choose this mode for smaller or very compressible tables that need to be fast and don't change as frequently as the DirectQuery source. When you choose Import storage mode, you mustn't plan to use this table to filter or group fact tables.

- **Dual**: This is the banded blue and white header bar with the **DirectQuery** icon (for example, **Product**). Choose this mode for tables that act as dimensions that are used to filter or group data in the fact table – that is, DirectQuery. This means there are scenarios where the table will be queried together with fact tables at the source.

Now, let's explore how these storage modes are used by the engine in different scenarios. This will help you design and define the storage modes appropriately. This is important because it determines the type of relationship that's used, which directly impacts performance. The following are some possible query scenarios:

- **Query uses Import or Dual table(s) only**: This populates slicers or filters, typically on dimension tables. Such queries achieve the best performance by using the local in-memory cache.

- **Query uses Dual or DirectQuery table(s) from the same source**: This occurs when the query needs to relate Dual mode dimension tables to DirectQuery fact tables. It will issue one or more native queries to the DirectQuery source and can achieve relatively good performance if the source is optimized, as discussed in *Chapter 3, DirectQuery Optimization*. One-to-one or one-to-many relationships within the same data source are evaluated as regular relationships that perform better. A regular relationship is where the column on the "one" side contains unique values.

- **Any other query**: Any query that needs to resolve relationships across different data sources falls into this category. This happens when a Dual or Import mode table from source A needs to join a DirectQuery table from source B. Here, the engine uses **limited relationships**, which are slower. Many-to-many relationships and relationships across different data sources are limited.

Let's order relationships from best to worst performance:

- One-to-many relationships within the same source (fastest)
- Many-to-many relationships that use a bridge table and at least one bi-directional relationship
- Many-to-many relationships
- Cross-source group relationships (slowest)

Next, we will introduce aggregations and how they relate to composite models.

Leveraging aggregations

Most analytical scenarios involve aggregating data in some way. It is common to look at historical trends, exceptions, and outliers at a summary level, and then drill down to more detail as required. Let's look at an example of a logistics company tracking thousands of daily shipments to watch for delays. They are unlikely to start this analysis at the individual package level. They would more likely have some performance indicators grouped by transportation type or region. If they see unsatisfactory numbers at the summary level, they may drill down to more and more detail to narrow down the root cause. In *Chapter 9, Report and Dashboard Design*, we recommended designing reporting experiences like this to provide better performance and usability.

You may follow the recommended design principles and still have performance issues with very large DirectQuery datasets. Even with great optimizations, there is still a physical limit as to how fast you can process data with fixed computing resources. This is where the aggregations capability of Power BI can help. An aggregation table is a summary of another fact table but one that's always stored in Import mode in memory. As such, aggregation tables must be reloaded during data refresh.

We will build on the example shown in *Figure 12.6* to illustrate this. We want to add aggregations to the **OrderDetail** table to avoid generating an external DirectQuery. Suppose our requirements have determined that many reports aggregate total sales at the product level. We can achieve better performance by adding an aggregation table. We will add a table in Import mode called **Agg_SalesByProduct** that's defined by the following SQL expression:

```
SELECT
ProductID,
sum(sod.LineTotal) as TotalSales,
sum(sod.OrderQty) as TotalQuantity
FROM
  [SalesLT].[SalesOrderDetail] sod
GROUP BY ProductID
```

Once the aggregation table exists, we need to tell Power BI how to use it. Right-click the **OrderDetail** table in the model view, select the **Manage aggregations** option, and configure the aggregations, as shown in the following screenshot:

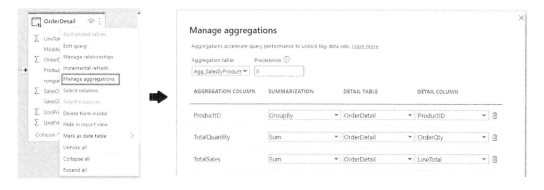

Figure 12.7 – Configuring the aggregations for OrderDetail

There are a few things to note in the previous screenshot. First, we had to tell Power BI which table we wanted to use as an aggregate for **OrderDetail**. We also had to map the columns and identify what type of summarization was used. There is also the option to select **precedence** because you can have multiple aggregation tables at different granularities. Precedence will determine which table is used first when the result can be served by more than one aggregation table. Once the aggregations have been configured, the final step is to create the relationship between the aggregation table and the **Product** dimension, as shown in the following screenshot:

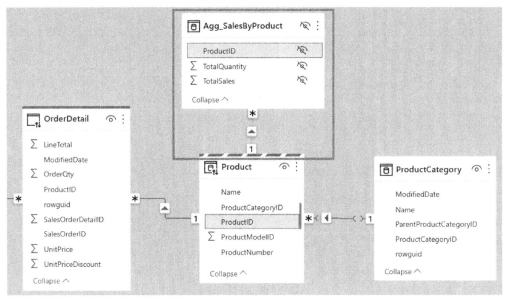

Figure 12.8 – The Import mode Agg_SalesByProduct table related to the Dual mode Product table

In the preceding screenshot, notice that the aggregation table and its columns are all hidden in the Power BI dataset. Power BI will do this by default since we do not want to confuse users. We can hide aggregation tables and rely on the engine to pick the correct tables internally.

> **Note**
>
> The example shown in the preceding screenshot demonstrates aggregations based on relationships. We are relying on a relationship so that the values from the **Product** table could filter **OrderDetails**. When we added the aggregation table, we needed to create this relationship.
>
> In typical big data systems based on **Hadoop** data is often stored in wide denormalized tables to avoid expensive joins at query time. We can still use aggregations in Power BI for such a scenario, but we wouldn't need to create any relationships.

Next, we'll learn how to identify when and which aggregations are used with DAX Studio. We will begin by constructing three table visuals showing different sales groupings. You can see these in the sample file on the `Aggs Comparison` report page:

A: Grouping by Product table		
Color	LineTotal	OrderQty
	6,265.00	249
Black	207,283.02	463
Blue	155,210.77	333
Multi	2,940.96	143
Red	10,286.22	44
Silver	109,834.94	292
Silver/Black	2,996.50	84
White	345.21	66
Yellow	213,527.55	413
Total	708,690.15	2087

B: Grouping by ProductCategory table		
CategoryName	LineTotal	OrderQty
Vests	4,309.90	121
Touring Frames	19,066.26	39
Touring Bikes	220,655.38	252
Tires and Tubes	27.48	20
Socks	345.21	66
Shorts	3,299.80	80
Saddles	1,010.30	39
Road Frames	24,346.58	60
Road Bikes	183,130.30	222
Pedals	2,996.50	84
Mountain Frames	54,949.60	128
Total	708,690.15	2087

C: Grouping by ProductCategory and Customer tables			
CategoryName	CompanyName	LineTotal	OrderQty
Bike Racks	Action Bicycle Specialists	432.00	6
Bike Racks	Bulk Discount Store	216.00	3
Bike Racks	Channel Outlet	216.00	3
Bike Racks	Discount Tours	72.00	1
Bike Racks	Eastside Department Store	144.00	2
Bike Racks	Many Bikes Store	288.00	4
Bike Racks	Professional Sales and Service	216.00	3
Bike Racks	Riding Cycles	720.00	10
Bottles and Cages	Action Bicycle Specialists	31.20	11
Bottles and Cages	Bulk Discount Store	23.95	8
Bottles and Cages	Eastside Department Store	29.94	10
Total		708,690.15	2087

Figure 12.9 – Different sales groupings to test aggregations

The visual titles in the preceding screenshot refer to the tables in the sample, which are shown in *Figure 12.8*. We constructed the visuals in *Figure 12.9* at different granularities, using different grouping tables, to see how the queries behave. We used DAX Studio to capture the output and found the following:

- **A: Grouping by Product table**: The query was completely satisfied through Import tables. Only one storage engine query was needed. Note how DAX Studio provides information on the **RewriteAttempted** event subclass, which means the engine recognized that aggregations were present and tried to use them. You can click on the event to get the detail on the right-hand side, confirming which aggregation table was used:

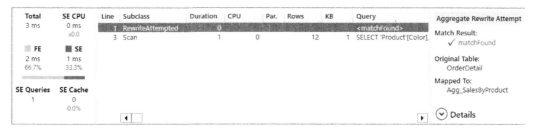

Figure 12.10 – Query performance information for visual A

- **B: Grouping by ProductCategory table**: Again, the query was completely satisfied through Import tables. What is great here is that even though **ProductCategory** is not directly related to the aggregation table, the engine does use it, leveraging the **Product** table as a bridge. This has allowed us to avoid an external query for a scenario that we did not originally plan for:

Total	SE CPU	Line	Subclass	Duration	CPU	Par.	Rows	KB	Query	Aggregate Rewrite Attempt
4 ms	0 ms x0.0	1	RewriteAttempted	0					<matchFound>	**Match Result:** ✓ matchFound
		3	Scan	0	0		40	1	SELECT 'Product'[Produc	
▇ FE	▇ SE	5	Scan	1	0		1,936	16	SELECT 'ProductCategor	**Original Table:** OrderDetail
3 ms	1 ms	6	RewriteAttempted	0					<matchFound>	
75.0%	25.0%	8	Scan	0	0		1	1	SELECT SUM ('Agg_Sale	**Mapped To:** Agg_SalesByProduct
SE Queries	**SE Cache**									
3	0 0.0%									⌄ Details

Figure 12.11 – Query performance information for visual B

- **C: Grouping by Product and Customer table**: This time, the query tried to use aggregation for a customer but was unable to since we did not define our aggregation at the customer granularity level. The engine did use an external query, which is proven by the **SQL** event subclass. However, it was still able to use the aggregation table later:

Total	SE CPU	Line	Subclass	Duration	CPU	Par.	Rows	KB	Query	Aggregate Rewrite Attempt
505 ms	47 ms x0.1	2	Scan	1	0		847	4	SELECT 'Customer'[Cust	**Match Result:** ✗ attemptFailed
		3	RewriteAttempted	0					<attemptFailed>	
▇ FE	▇ SE	4	SQL	457	47	x0.1			SELECT TOP (1000001)	**Original Table:** OrderDetail
47 ms	458 ms	6	Scan	0	0		1,936	16	SELECT 'ProductCategor	
9.3%	90.7%	7	RewriteAttempted	0					<matchFound>	**Mapped To:**
		9	Scan	0	0		1	1	SELECT SUM ('Agg_Sale	
SE Queries	**SE Cache**									
4	0 0.0%									⌄ Details

Figure 12.12 – Query performance information for visual C

The previous examples demonstrate how aggregations are used, but we have not compared the same query with and without aggregations yet. To test this, we can simply delete the aggregation table and profile the same visuals in DAX Studio, with the following total query durations:

	No Aggregations	With Aggregations	Comments
Visual A	80 ms	3 ms	Aggregations much faster.
Visual B	155 ms	5 ms	Aggregations much faster.
Visual C	340 ms	500 ms	Aggregations were a bit slower due to multiple source overhead with small data volumes.

Figure 12.13 – Performance comparison of different visual groupings with aggregations

In our example, designing and managing aggregations would be simple. In the real world, it can be difficult to predict the complexity, volume, and frequency of the queries that will be generated. This makes it hard to design aggregations beforehand. Microsoft has considered this problem and has released automatic aggregations as an enhancement to user-defined aggregations. With automatic aggregations, the system uses machine learning to maintain aggregations automatically based on user behavior. This can greatly simplify aggregation management if you can use it.

> **Note**
>
> Automatic aggregations are currently only available to the Power BI Premium and Embedded capacities. The feature is in preview and subject to change, so we won't provide further details. Check out the relevant documentation to learn more: `https://docs.microsoft.com/power-bi/admin/aggregations-auto`.

Finally, let's touch on Azure Synapse and Data Lake. These are first-party technologies from Microsoft that you may wish to consider for external data storage in big data scenarios that need DirectQuery.

Scaling with Azure Synapse and Azure Data Lake

Many data analytics platforms are based on a **symmetric multi-processing** (**SMP**) design. This involves a single computer system with one instance of an operating system that has multiple processors that work with shared memory, input, and output devices. This is just like any desktop computer or laptop we use today and extends to many server technologies too. An alternative paradigm is **massively parallel processing** (**MPP**). This involves a grid or cluster of computers, each with a processor, operating system, and memory. Each machine is referred to as a **node**.

In practical terms, consider computing a sum across 100 billion rows of data. With SMP, a single computer would need to do all the work. With MPP, you could logically allocate 10 groups of 10 billion rows each to a dedicated computer, have each machine calculate the sum of its group in parallel, and then add up the sums. If we wanted the results faster, we could spread the load further with more parallelism, such as by having 50 machines handle about 2 billion rows each. Even with communications and synchronization overhead, the latter approach will be much faster.

Big data systems such as Hadoop, Apache Spark, and Azure Synapse use the MPP architecture because parallel operations can process data much faster. MPP also gives us the ability to both scale up (bigger machines) and scale out (more machines). With SMP, only the former is possible until you reach a physical limit regarding how large a machine you can provision.

The increasing rate of data ingestion from modern global applications such as IoT systems creates an upstream problem when we think about data analysis. BI applications typically use cleaned and modeled data, which requires modeling and transformation beforehand. This works fine for typical business applications. However, with big data, such as a stream of sensor data or web app user tracking, it is impractical to store raw data in a traditional database due to the sheer volume. Hence, many big data systems use files (specially optimized, such as Parquet) that store denormalized tables. They perform **Extract-Load-Transform (ELT)** instead of the typical **Extract-Transform-Load (ETL)** as we can do in Power Query. With ELT, raw data is shaped on the fly in parallel.

Now, let's relate these concepts to the data warehouse architecture and the Azure offerings.

The modern data warehouse architecture

We can combine traditional ETL style analytics with ELT and big data analytics using a hybrid data warehouse architecture based on a data lake. A data lake can be described as a landing area for raw data. Data in the lake is not typically accessed directly by business users.

Once data is in the lake, it can be used in different ways, depending on the purpose. For example, data scientists may want to analyze raw data and create subsets for machine learning models. On the other hand, business analytics team members might regularly transform and load some data into structured storage systems such as SQL Server. The following diagram shows a highly simplified view of Azure components that could make up a modern data warehouse:

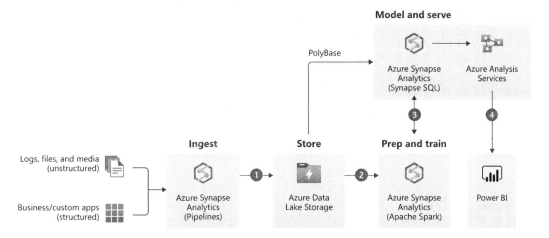

Figure 12.14 – A modern data warehouse architecture (image credit: Microsoft)

The numbered steps in the preceding diagram indicate typical activities:

1. Store all types of raw data in Azure Data Lake Storage using Azure Synapse Analytics pipelines.

2. Leverage Synapse Analytics to clean up data.

3. Store clean, structured data in Synapse SQL and enrich it in Azure Analysis Services.

4. Build reporting experiences over Synapse and Azure Analysis Services using Power BI.

> **Note**
>
> The steps in the preceding diagram are ordered, and the diagram only shows connections between some components. This represents production-style data paths and is only to aid learning. In a modern enterprise, it is realistic to skip some steps or connect different technologies, depending on the scenario and user's skill level. For example, a data engineer may connect Power BI directly to ADLS to explore data format and quality. Other Azure services complement this architecture, which haven't been shown.

Now, let's take a closer look at some technologies that help with data scaling.

Azure Data Lake Storage

Azure Data Lake Storage (ADLS) is a modern data store that's designed for big data scenarios. It provides limitless storage and is compatible with non-proprietary technologies such as **Hadoop Distributed File System (HDFS)**, which is a core requirement for many Hadoop-based systems. Note that the current version is referred to by Microsoft as ADLS Gen2, indicating that we are in the second generation offering. While the original data lake technology is still available, we recommend using Gen2 as it offers better performance and functionality. Platforms such as Synapse will only work on Gen2. Synapse services are optimized to work with data in parallel over ADLS.

Azure Synapse analytics

Azure Synapse is an analytics platform that contains different services that address the special needs of different stages of data analytics. It was previously called SQL Server Data Warehouse, and at the time, the focus was to provide a distributed version of SQL Server to handle multi-terabyte and larger data volumes. Since then, it has been rebranded and grown into a complete suite that offers the following services and capabilities:

- **Synapse Studio**: A web-based environment that serves multiple personas. People can ingest, transform, explore, and visualize data here.

- **Power BI integration**: You can link Power BI workspaces to your Synapse workspace in Synapse Studio. Then, you can analyze data hosted in Synapse services using Power BI within Synapse Studio.

- **Notebook integration**: Synapse Studio supports Python notebooks for interactive data exploration and documentation.

- **Serverless and dedicated SQL pools**: These offer structured SQL Server storage in the cloud. A serverless pool needs little configuration and management – you do not need to provision a server, the service auto-scales, and you pay per query. A dedicated pool must be configured beforehand and is billed constantly over time. Dedicated pools can be paused and scaled up or down. These options provide a balance between costs and management overhead.

- **Serverless and dedicated Spark pools**: Apache Spark is a very popular open source big data platform. It is an in-memory technology and offers a SQL interface over data. It also offers integrated data science capabilities. Synapse integrates with Spark pools directly, allowing analysts to run Spark Jobs from Synapse Studio.

- **Data flows**: These provide visually designed data transformation logic to clean and shape data using the power of processing pools.

- **Data pipelines**: Allows users to orchestrate and monitor data transformation jobs.

There are many options and variations within the modern data warehouse architecture. Unfortunately, it is beyond the scope of this book to cover these. Microsoft offers multiple reference architectures to deal with analytics problems, ranging from business data warehousing to near-real-time predictive analytics on streaming data. Therefore, we recommend checking out the Microsoft Azure Architecture site to learn about which Azure services can be used for varying analytics needs: `https://docs.microsoft.com/azure/architecture/browse/?azure_categories=analytics`.

Now that we have provided an introduction to the Azure technologies we can use to deal with data at a high scale, let's summarize what we've learned in this chapter.

Summary

In this chapter, we learned how to deal with exceptionally large volumes of data. The first use case was where we had Power BI datasets growing beyond the 1 GB storage limit that's available to Power BI Pro users in the Shared capacity. In such cases, we recommended considering Power BI Premium. The dataset limit in Premium is 10 GB. With the large dataset storage format enabled, we learned that datasets could grow well beyond this size. Technically, we can use all the available memory on the capacity, which is 400 GB on a Premium P5 capacity. Larger Premium capacities also have higher concurrency limits, which can give us better refresh and query performance.

Then, we looked at a case where the scale problem comes from concurrent users and learned why this can put pressure on memory and CPU resources. We introduced AAS as a solution to this problem due to its ability to leverage QSO. We also recommended using partitions on Premium and AAS to speed up refreshes on large tables. We advised you to carefully consider the features and roadmap of Premium versus AAS as there are currently differences.

After that, we looked at improving DirectQuery performance with composite models, a feature that lets you combine Import and DirectQuery sources into the same Power BI dataset. We saw how Power BI controls storage mode at the table level and that we can configure individual tables as Import, DirectQuery, or Dual. The Dual mode tables will Import data and store it in local memory and allow DirectQuery when needed. We showed you when to use these storage modes and how Analysis Services will choose the best option, depending on the scenario.

Next, we looked at aggregations, a complementary feature to composite models. Microsoft designed aggregations around the premise that data from large fact tables is often summarized. Even with good optimizations in a DirectQuery source, summaries over tens of millions to billions of rows can still take time. The problem is worse when we have high user concurrency. An aggregation table in Power BI allows us to define grouped subsets of fact tables, which Analysis Services can use as an alternative to a slow down DirectQuery. You can achieve huge performance gains when aggregate tables are in Import mode.

Finally, we looked at other technologies from Microsoft that can deal with big data problems. We learned that it is not practical to ingest and transform certain types of data due to their sheer speed and volume. Hence, big data systems tend to use the MPP architecture and rely on ELT paradigms to shape data on demand for different purposes. In the modern data warehouse, all raw data is stored in a central data lake first. Different technologies sit over the lake and perform exploration, ETL, or ELT as suits the use case. We introduced Azure Data Lake Storage and Azure Synapse Analytics as the primary technologies you can use to implement a modern data warehouse.

In the next chapter, we will focus on the Power BI Premium and Embedded capacities. Here, Microsoft provides you with settings and controls where there are additional performance considerations.

Further reading

Note that just like Power BI, every area of Synapse benefits from specific performance tuning guidance. The following are some references to the relevant performance guidance material:

- *Serverless SQL pool best practices*: https://docs.microsoft.com/azure/synapse-analytics/sql/best-practices-serverless-sql-pool

- *Dedicated SQL pool best practices*: https://docs.microsoft.com/azure/synapse-analytics/sql/best-practices-dedicated-sql-pool

- *Azure Advisor recommendations for dedicated SQL pools*: https://docs.microsoft.com/azure/synapse-analytics/sql-data-warehouse/sql-data-warehouse-concept-recommendations

- *Materialized view optimization*: https://docs.microsoft.com/azure/synapse-analytics/sql/develop-materialized-view-performance-tuning

- *Clustered index optimization*: https://docs.microsoft.com/azure/synapse-analytics/sql-data-warehouse/performance-tuning-ordered-cci

- *Result set cache optimization*: https://docs.microsoft.com/azure/synapse-analytics/sql-data-warehouse/performance-tuning-result-set-caching

- *Optimizing Synapse query performance tutorial*: https://docs.microsoft.com/learn/modules/optimize-data-warehouse-query-performance-azure-synapse-analytics

- *Tuning Synapse data flows*: https://docs.microsoft.com/azure/data-factory/concepts-data-flow-performance?context=/azure/synapse-analytics/context/context

Part 5: Optimizing Premium and Embedded Capacities

In this part, you will become familiar with Power BI Premium settings and resource limits, and will gain a deep understanding of workload prioritization and memory management in Power BI Premium/Embedded. You will learn how to implement embedding efficiently, along with how to size and load test capacities.

This part comprises the following chapters:

- *Chapter 13, Optimizing Premium and Embedded Capacities*
- *Chapter 14, Embedding in Applications*

13
Optimizing Premium and Embedded Capacities

In the previous chapter, we looked at ways to deal with high data and user scale. The first option we provided was to leverage Power BI Premium because it has higher dataset size limits than Power BI's shared capacity.

In this chapter, we will take a much closer look at the **Premium** (**P** and **EM**) and **Embedded** (**A**) capacities. Even though they are purchased and billed differently, with a couple of minor exceptions, they offer the same services on similar hardware and benefit from the same optimization guidance. Therefore, we will continue to refer to just the Premium capacity for the remainder of this chapter and will call out Embedded only if there is a material difference. We will treat the **Premium Per User** (**PPU**) licensing model the same way.

We will learn how there is more to differentiate Premium than just the increased dataset limits. This is because the Premium capacity offers unique services and advanced features that are not available in the shared capacity. However, the caveat is that these extra capabilities come with additional management responsibilities that fall upon the capacity administrators. Hence, we will review the available services and settings, such as Autoscale, and discuss how they can affect performance.

Then, we will learn how to determine an adequate capacity size and plan for future growth. One important technique is load testing to help determine the limits and bottlenecks of your data and usage patterns. We will also learn how to use the Premium Capacity Metrics App provided by Microsoft to identify areas of concern, perform root cause analysis, and determine the best corrective actions.

Microsoft released Premium Gen2 (that is, the second generation) to general availability in October 2021. This release improved areas of the service. We will cover the significant new Gen2 capability, which is its ability to automatically scale a capacity using additional CPU cores that are held in reserve. Note that while the first generation of Premium is still being used in production by customers, Gen2 is the default and Microsoft announced that they would automatically migrate customers to the new service starting March 2022. Therefore, we will not cover the first generation in this book.

In this chapter, we will cover the following topics:

- Understanding Premium services, resource usage, and Autoscale
- Capacity planning, monitoring, and optimization

Understanding Premium services, resource usage, and Autoscale

Power BI Premium provides reserved capacity for your organization. This isolates you from the noisy-neighbor problem that you may experience in the shared capacity. Let's start by briefly reviewing the capabilities of the Premium capacities that differentiate it by providing greater performance and scale:

- **Ability to Autoscale**: This is a new capability that was introduced in Gen2 that allows administrators to assign spare CPU cores to be used in periods of excessive load (not available for PPU).

- **Higher Storage and Dataset Size Limits**: 100 TB of total storage and a 400 GB dataset size (100 GB in PPU).

- **More Frequent Dataset Refresh**: 48 times per day via the UI and potentially more via scripting through the XMLA endpoint.

- **Greater Refresh Parallelism**: You can have more refreshes running at the same time, ranging from 5 (Embedded A1) to 640 (Premium P5/Embedded A8).

- **Advanced Dataflows Features**: Premium dataflows have performance enhancements, such as the enhanced compute engine.

- **On-Demand Load with Large Dataset Storage Formats**: Premium capacities do not keep every dataset in memory all the time. Datasets that are unused for a period are evicted to free up memory. Premium capacities can speed up the initial load in memory when using the large dataset format that we described in *Chapter 10, Data Modeling and Row-Level Security*. This on-demand load can speed up the initial load experience by loading the data pages that are required to satisfy a query. Without this feature, the entire dataset needs to be loaded into memory first, which can take a while for very large models in the tens of GB. For datasets that are bigger than 5 GB, you can see up to a 35% increase in report load times. The benefit is greater with very large models in the 50 GB+ range.

Other capabilities in Premium are not directly related to performance. We'll list them here for awareness. Note that the final three items are not available for PPU:

- **Availability of Paginated Reports**: Highly formatted reports based on SQL Server Reporting Services that are optimized for printing and broad distribution.

- **XMLA Endpoint**: API access to allow automation and custom deployment/refresh configurations.

- **Application Life Cycle Management** (ALM): You can use deployment pipelines, manage development, and evaluate app versions.

- **Advanced AI Features**: Text analytics, image detection, and automated machined learning become available.

- **Multi-region deployments**: You can deploy Premium capacities in different regions to help with data sovereignty requirements.

- **Bring Your Own Key** (BYOK): You can apply your encryption key to secure data.

Now, let's explore how Premium capacities manage resources and what to expect as demand and load increase.

Premium capacity behavior and resource usage

When an organization purchases Premium capacity, they are allocated **virtual cores** (**v-cores**) and a certain amount of RAM. All the workloads running on that capacity share these resources. For example, a paginated report can be executing queries and processing data at the same time as a dataset refresh operation is occurring.

With the first release of Premium, customers needed to pay close attention to the available memory and concurrent refresh operations. They needed to understand how capacities prioritized different types of operations, namely the following:

- **Interactive Operations** (fast running):

  - **Dataset workload**: Queries, report views, and XMLA Read are considered

  - **Dataflow workload**: Any execution is considered

  - **Paginated report workload**: Report renders are considered

- **Background Operations** (longer running):

  - **Dataset workload**: Scheduled refresh, on-demand refresh, and background queries after a refresh are considered

  - **Dataflow workload**: Scheduled refreshes are considered

  - **Paginated report workload**: Data-driven subscriptions are considered

  - **AI workloads**: Function evaluations are considered

  - API calls to export the report to a file

These terms are still relevant for Premium Gen2. However, Microsoft has changed the way limits apply in Gen2, so we will describe these changes here.

> **Important Note**
>
> In the original release of Premium, the total amount of memory that could be allocated to the capacity was shared by all the workloads and could never be exceeded. For example, with a P1, all concurrent activity on the capacity could not consume more than 25 GB of memory.
>
> With Gen2, the utilization model was changed so that heavy background operations would not penalize users by consuming all the available resources. The capacity memory limit now applies per dataset, not across all workloads. This means that for a P1, you can have multiple active datasets consuming up to 25 GB of memory. Note that the available CPU cores may still be a limiting factor because of limited threads not being available, which means they can't be assigned to refresh mashup containers. This is where Autoscale can help, which we will discuss later in this chapter.

Microsoft achieved increased scale and parallelism with Gen2 by having more capacity behind the scenes than what can be purchased by customers. For example, a P1 capacity may be running on a physical machine that is more like a P3 in size. Microsoft runs groups of these large nodes, which are dedicated to specific Premium workloads. This allows them to load balance by spreading work as evenly as possible. The Microsoft documentation states that the system only runs a workload on a node where sufficient memory is available.

Let's begin by looking at the settings we can adjust to control scale and performance. The following screenshot shows the **Capacity Settings** area of the Power BI Admin Portal for a Gen2 capacity. The **Workloads** section contains settings relevant to performance:

Figure 13.1 – Premium settings relevant to performance tuning

The settings you can adjust to manage these performance and scale issues are shown in the following list. You can set specific limits here to safeguard against issues in dataset design or from ad hoc reports that are generating complex, expensive queries:

- **Query Memory Limit (%)**: This is the maximum percentage of memory that a single can use to execute a query. The default value is 0, which results in a default capacity size-specific limit being applied.

- **Query Timeout (seconds)**: The number of seconds a query is allowed to execute before being considered timed out. The default value represents 1 hour and 0 disables the timeout.

- **Max Intermediate Row Count**: For DirectQuery, this limits the number of rows that are returned by a query, which can help reduce the load on source systems.

- **Max Result Row Count**: Maximum number of rows that can be returned by a DAX query.

- **Max Offline Dataset Size (GB)**: Determines how large an offline dataset can be (size on disk).

- **Minimum refresh interval** (for **Automatic Page Refresh** with a fixed interval): How often a report with automatic page refresh can issue queries to fetch new data. This can prevent developers from setting up refresh cadences more frequently than it is necessary.

- **Minimum execution interval** (for **Automatic Page Refresh** with change detection): This is like the previous point but applies to the frequency of checking the change detection measure.

Next, we will learn how capacities evaluate load and what happens when the capacity gets busy.

Understanding how capacities evaluate load

Premium Gen2 capacities evaluate load every 30 seconds, with each bucket referred to as an evaluation cycle. We will use practical examples to explain how the load calculations work in each cycle and what happens when the capacity threshold is reached.

Power BI evaluates capacity utilization using **CPU time**, which is typically measured in CPU seconds. If a single CPU core is completely utilized for 1 second, that is 1 CPU second. However, this is different from the actual duration when it's measured from start to finish. Taking our example one step further, if we know that an operation took 1 CPU second, this does not necessarily mean that the start to finish duration was 1 second. It could mean that a single CPU core was 100% utilized for 1 second or that the operation used less than 100% of the CPU over more than 1 second.

We will use a P1 capacity for our examples. This capacity comes with four backend cores and four frontend cores. The backend cores are used for core Power BI functions such as query processing, dataset refresh, and R server processing, while the frontend cores are responsible for the user experience aspects such as the web service, content management, permission management, and scheduling. Capacity load is evaluated against the backend cores only.

Knowing that Power BI evaluates the total load every 30 seconds, we can work out the maximum CPU time that's available to us over this during the evaluation cycle of a P1. This is 30 seconds x 4 cores = 120 CPU seconds. So, for a P1 capacity, every 30 seconds, the system will determine whether the workloads are consuming more or less than 120 CPU seconds. As a reminder, with Gen2, it is possible by design for a P1 capacity to temporarily consume more than 120 CPU seconds since spare capacity is available. What happens at this point of CPU saturation depends on your capacity configuration.

Before we describe this in more detail, it is useful to know how CPU load is aggregated since interactive and background operations are treated differently. Interactive operations are counted within the evaluation cycle in which they ran. CPU usage for background activity is smoothed over a rolling 24-hour period, which is also evaluated regularly in the same 30-second buckets. The system smooths background operations by spreading the last 24 rolling hours of background CPU time evenly over all the evaluation cycles. There are 2,880 evaluation cycles in 24 hours.

Let's illustrate this with a simple but realistic example. Suppose we have a P1 capacity that has just been provisioned. Two scheduled refreshes named A and B have been configured and will complete by 1 A.M. and 4 A.M., respectively. Suppose that the former refresh will take 14,400 CPU seconds (5 per evaluation cycle), while the latter will take 5,760 CPU seconds (2 per evaluation cycle). Finally, suppose that users start running reports hosted on the capacity around 9 A.M. and they do not hit the capacity threshold. The following diagram shows how load evaluation works for this scenario and how the available capacity changes over time. We have marked four different evaluation cycles to explain how the operations contribute to the load score. The example scenario we've described covers a period that's smaller than 24 hours. Let's visualize this behavior and load:

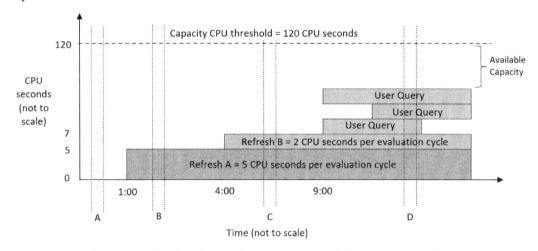

Figure 13.2 – Load evaluation for a P1 capacity at different times (A to D)

> **Note**
>
> In *Figure 13.2* and *Figure 13.5*, since the background refresh activity is spread out over 2,880 evaluation cycles, it is correct to show the load that's been incurred by those operations being constant over time once they have been completed. For the interactive operations shown in green, the CPU load will vary over time for each operation. However, for simplicity, we have illustrated interactive operations as if they generate constant load.

Let's walk through the four evaluation cycles to understand how the capacity load is calculated at each of these points:

1. **Evaluation Cycle A**: At this point, the capacity is brand new and completely unused. There is no prior background activity to consider in this evaluation cycle.

2. **Evaluation Cycle B**: This occurs after refresh A has completed but before refresh B has started. The background load for refresh A is 14,400 CPU seconds divided into 30-second buckets, which gives 5 CPU seconds per evaluation cycle. Since there are no other activities, the total load during this cycle is 5 CPU seconds.

3. **Evaluation cycle C**: This occurs after refresh B has been completed. The background load for refresh B is 5,760, which smooths to 2 CPU seconds per evaluation cycle. This time, the background activities from refresh A and B are both considered because they are both within 24 hours of the current evaluation cycle. Even though both refreshes are already complete at this point, their smoothed activity carries forward, so the total load on the capacity is 7 CPU seconds.

4. **Evaluation Cycle D**: Now, we have both the background activity and interactive activity occurring at the same time. The total load on the capacity is the background contribution of 7 CPU seconds, plus the actual work that's been done by the queries in that cycle. The number is not important for this example. The main point is that the total activity in the evaluation cycle is less than 120 CPU seconds.

Next, we will explore what happens if we reach an **overload** situation. This term is used to describe a capacity that needs more CPU resources than what's been allocated.

Managing capacity overload and Autoscale

For a P1 capacity, overload means that the total load (including smoothed background activity) is exceeding 120 CPU seconds during an evaluation cycle. When this state is reached, unless Autoscale is enabled, the system starts to perform **throttling**, also called **interactive request delay** mode. The system will remain in delay mode while each new evaluation cycle exceeds the available capacity. In delay mode, the system will artificially delay interactive requests. The amount of delay is dynamic and increases as a function of the capacity load.

This delay mode is new with Gen2. Previously, it was possible to overload a capacity to the point where it became completely unresponsive. With Gen2, this behavior has been changed to prevent this from happening. Delaying new interactive requests when overloaded may seem like it would make the problem worse, but this is not the case. For users who experience delayed requests, the experience will be slower than if the capacity was not overloaded. However, they are still much more likely to have their requests completed successfully. This is because delaying operations gives the capacity time to finish ones that are already in progress, preventing them from being overloaded to the point where new interactive actions fail.

The following diagram illustrates how request delays work. Observe that in **cycle A**, we needed more capacity than was allocated, indicated by the queries stacking up higher than the 120-second capacity threshold. Therefore, in **cycle B**, any new interactive requests are delayed, which protects the capacity and reduces the degradation of the user experience:

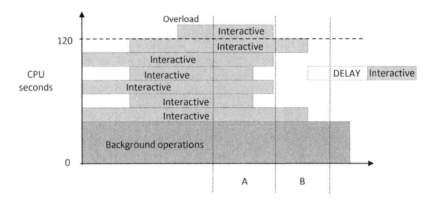

Figure 13.3 – Interactive operations in cycle B delayed due to the overload in cycle A

If you often experience overload, you should consider scaling up to a larger capacity. However, a larger capacity represents a significant cost increase, which may be hard to justify when the scale issues are transient and unpredictable. You could also manually scale out by spreading workspaces around multiple capacities so that a single capacity does not experience a disproportionately high load. If you only have one capacity available to you, distributing load in this way is not an option.

We will investigate overload more when we cover monitoring and optimization in the next section. First, let's look at another way to mitigate peak load.

Handling peak loads with Autoscale

An efficient way to manage excessive load in Premium capacities without incurring upfront costs is to use the Autoscale capability that was introduced with Gen2.

> **Important Note**
>
> Autoscale is not available for Power BI Embedded (A SKU) capacities in the same way it is for Premium. For Embedded, you must use a combination of metrics and APIs or PowerShell to manually check resource metrics and issue the appropriate scale up or down commands. See the following link for more information: `https://docs.microsoft.com/en-us/power-bi/developer/embedded/power-bi-embedded-generation-2#autoscaling-in-embedded-gen2`.

Autoscale in Premium works by linking an Azure subscription to a Premium capacity and allowing it to use extra v-cores when an overload occurs. Power BI will assign one v-core at a time up to the maximum allowed, as configured by the administrator. V-cores are assigned for 24 hours at a time and are only charged when they're assigned during these 24-hour overload periods. The following screenshot shows the **Autoscale settings** pane, which can be found in the **Capacity Settings** area of the admin portal:

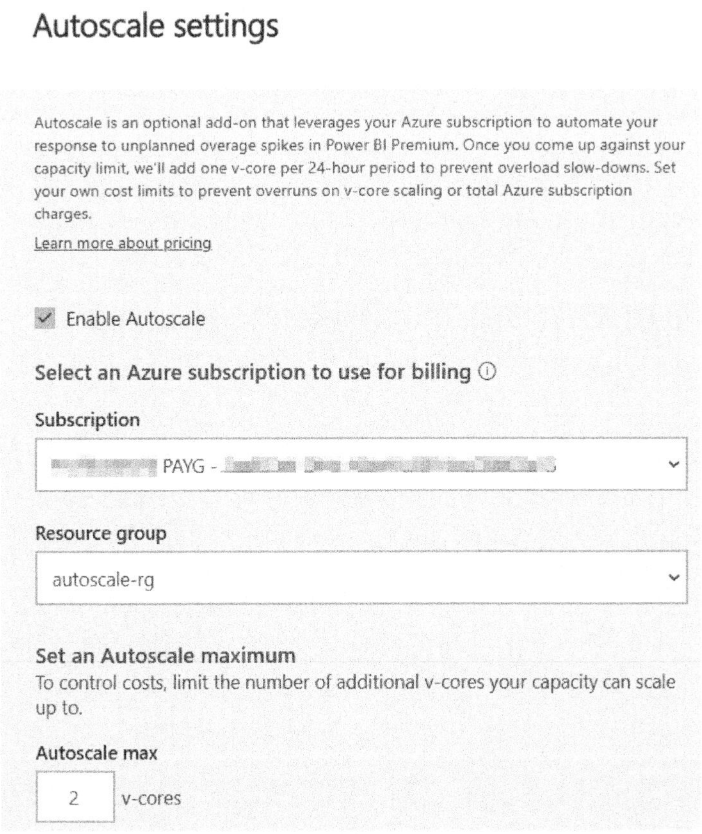

Autoscale settings

Autoscale is an optional add-on that leverages your Azure subscription to automate your response to unplanned overage spikes in Power BI Premium. Once you come up against your capacity limit, we'll add one v-core per 24-hour period to prevent overload slow-downs. Set your own cost limits to prevent overruns on v-core scaling or total Azure subscription charges.

Learn more about pricing

☑ Enable Autoscale

Select an Azure subscription to use for billing ⓘ

Subscription

| PAYG - ▾ |

Resource group

| autoscale-rg ▾ |

Set an Autoscale maximum
To control costs, limit the number of additional v-cores your capacity can scale up to.

Autoscale max

| 2 | v-cores |

Figure 13.4 – Autoscale settings to link an Azure subscription and assign v-cores

The following diagram shows how the overload scenario we described in *Figure 13.3* would change if Autoscale was enabled. We can see that a v-core was assigned in the next evaluation after an overload occurred, which increased the capacity threshold. It is also important to note that the interactive operation that occurred after the overload was not delayed:

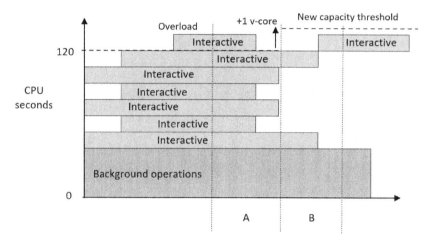

Figure 13.5 – Autoscale assigns an additional core and avoids delays

Now that we have learned how capacities evaluate load and can be scaled, let's learn how to plan for the right capacity size and keep it running efficiently.

Capacity planning, monitoring, and optimization

A natural question that occurs when organizations consider purchasing Premium or Embedded capacity is what size to provision. We know that there are different services available in Premium and we can safely assume that workload intensity and distribution vary between organizations. This can make it difficult to predict the correct size based on simple metrics such as total users. Capacity usage naturally increases over time too, so even if you have the right size to begin with, there may come a point where you need to scale. Therefore, in the next few sections, you will learn about the initial sizing and then how to monitor and scale when necessary.

Determining the initial capacity size

Earlier in this chapter, we mentioned that Power BI capacities are available in varied sizes through different licensing models. We will assume that you will choose the appropriate **Stock-Keeping Unit** (**SKU** – that is, the unique product type) based on your organizational needs. We would like to provide a reminder here that feature-based dependencies may force you to use a certain minimum size if you are considering the A series of SKUs from Azure, or the P and EM series available via Office. For example, paginated reports are not available on the A1-A3 or EM1-EM3 capacities, and AI is not available on EM1 or A1.

It is useful to have these capacity limits in mind when you start planning. At the time of writing, these capacities and limits are as follows

Capacity SKUs	Total v-cores	Backend v-cores	Frontend v-cores	RAM (GB)	DirectQuery/ Live connections per second	Max memory per query (GB)	Model Refresh Parallelism
EM1/A1	1	0.5	0.5	3	3.75	1	5
EM2/A2	2	1	1	5	7.5	2	10
EM3/A3	4	2	2	10	15	2	20
P1/A4	8	4	4	25	30	6	40
P2/A5	16	8	8	50	60	6	80
P3/A6	32	16	16	100	120	10	160
P4/A73	64	32	32	200	240	10	320
P5/A83	128	64	64	400	480	10	640

Figure 13.6 – Available SKUs and limits for reserved capacities

Now, let's look at what to consider when sizing a capacity. We will consider all of these in the next section on load testing:

- **Size of Individual Datasets**: Focus on larger, more complex datasets that will have heavier usage. You can prototype datasets in Power BI Desktop and use DAX Studio and VertiPaq Analyzer to estimate the compressibility of data to predict the dataset's size. Ensure that the capacity you choose has enough room to host the largest dataset.

- **Number and Complexity of Queries**: Think about how a large number of users might be viewing different reports at the same time. Consider centralized organizational reports, and then consider adding a percentage on top for self-service content. You can estimate this percentage from how broadly the organization wishes to support self-service content. You can determine the number and complexity of queries from typical report actions using Desktop Performance Analyzer and DAX Studio.

- **Number and Complexity of Data Refreshes**: Estimate the maximum number of datasets you may need to refresh at the same time at various stages of your initiative. Choose a capacity that has an appropriate refresh parallelism limit. Also, bear in mind that a dataset's total memory footprint is the sum of what's used by its tables and data structures, executing queries, and background data refreshes. If this exceeds the capacity limit, the refresh will fail.

- **Load from Other Services**: Bear in mind that dataflows, AI, paginated reports, and potentially other services in the future all use capacity resources. If you plan to use these services, build them into your test plan.

- **Periodic Distribution of Load**: Capacity load will vary at different times of the day in line with work hours. There may also be predictable times of extra activity, such as month-end or holiday sales such as Black Friday in the USA. We suggest that you compare regular peak activity to these unique events. If the unique events need far more resources compared to normal peak times, it would be better to rely on Autoscale than to provision a larger capacity upfront.

With a little effort, it is possible to get well-informed estimates from the considerations mentioned in the previous list. The next step of capacity planning is to perform some testing with some of your content to evaluate the scalability of your solutions and observe how the capacity behaves. We will explore this next.

Validating capacity size with load testing

Once you have a proposed capacity size, you should perform testing to gauge how the capacity responds to different situations. Microsoft has provided two sets of PowerShell scripts to help simulate load in different scenarios. These tools take advantage of REST APIs that are only available in the Premium capacity. You can configure the tool to execute reports that are hosted in a reserved capacity under certain conditions. We should try to host datasets and reports that represent realistic use cases so that the tool can generate actionable data. This activity will be captured by the system and will be visible in the Capacity Metrics App, which we will describe later in this section. We will use this app to investigate resource usage, overload, and Autoscale.

First, let's review the testing tools provided by Microsoft. Both suites are available in subfolders at the same location on GitHub: `https://github.com/microsoft/PowerBI-Tools-For-Capacities`. These are described as follows:

- **LoadTestingPowerShellTool**: This tool is simple. It aims to simulate a lot of users opening the same reports at the same time. This represents a worst-case scenario that is unlikely to occur, but it provides value by showing just how much load the capacity can manage for a given report in a short amount of time. The script will ask how many reports you want to run; then, it will ask you to authenticate with the user you want to test for each report and which filter values to cycle through. When the configuration is complete, it will open a new browser window for each report and continuously execute it, looping over the filter values you supply.

- **RealisticLoadTestTool**: This is a more sophisticated script that requires additional setup. It is designed to simulate a realistic set of user actions, such as changing slicers and filters. It also allows time to be taken between actions to simulate users interpreting information before interacting with the report again. This script will also begin to ask you how many reports you want to test and which users to use. At this point, it will simply generate a configuration file called `PBIReport.json` in a new subfolder named with the current date and time. Then, you need to edit that file to customize the configuration. This time, you can load specific pages or bookmarks, control how many times the session restarts, specify filter or slicer combinations with multiple selections, and add "think time" in seconds between the actions. The following sample file is a modified version of one that's been included with the tool and clearly illustrates these configurations:

```
reportParameters={

"reportUrl":"https://app.powerbi.com/
reportEmbed?reportId=36621bde-4614-40df-8e08-
79481d767bcb",

"pageName": "ReportSectiond1b63329887eb2e20791",

"bookmarkList": [""],

"sessionRestart":100,

"filters": [

{

"filterTable":"DimSalesTerritory",

"filterColumn":"SalesTerritoryCountry",

"isSlicer":true,

"filtersList":[

"United States",

  ["France","Germany"]
```

```
    ]
  },
  {
"filterTable":"DimDate",
"filterColumn":"Quarter",
"isSlicer":false,
"filtersList":["Q1","Q2","Q3","Q4"]
  }
  ],
&"thinkTimeSeconds":1
  };
```

Note that the scripts have prerequisites:

- PowerShell must be executed with elevated privileges ("Run as administrator").

- You need to set your execution policy to allow the unsigned testing scripts to be run by running Set-ExecutionPolicy Unrestricted.

- Power BI commandlet modules must be installed by running Install-Module MicrosoftPowerBIMgmt.

However, these scripts have limitations and caveats that you should be aware of:

- The scripts work by launching a basic HTML web page in Google Chrome, which contains code to embed the Power BI reports you want to specify for testing. If you want to use a different browser, you must modify the PowerShell script to reference that browser with the appropriate command-line arguments.

- If you have spaces and long folder names in the path that contains the scripts, the browser may launch with incorrect parameters and not load any reports.

- The LoadTestingPowerShellTool version only works with a start and end number to govern the range of numerical filters. If you enter text-based filters, the script will execute but the browser may not load the report.

- The script saves a user token from Azure Active Directory, which it uses to simulate users. Access tokens expire in 60 minutes. Reports will run for 60 minutes once initiated and stop with an error once the access token expires.

- Since the browser instances run on the machine where the script is executed, all the client-side load will be borne by that machine. Take care with how many reports you run in parallel. The recommendation is to match the number of cores on your computer. Hence, with an 8-core machine, you can safely run 8 reports in parallel. More may be possible, but you should check your local CPU usage so that you don't overload the client machine. This presents a major challenge for load testing because it limits the number of users you can simulate. Unfortunately, there is no easy way to solve this problem. You need to run the tests on machines with more cores available and multiple machines in parallel. One option is to provision virtual machines in the cloud just for testing. Microsoft Visual Studio and Azure DevOps include built-in web load testing frameworks that can automate aspects of load testing, though these are now deprecated in favor of Azure Load Testing. More information is available here: `https://docs.microsoft.com/en-us/azure/load-testing/overview-what-is-azure-load-testing`.

Now, let's review the suggested practices for performing such tests. When you're preparing content for load testing, we recommend doing the following:

- Test some datasets that are near the maximum size allowed by the capacity.

- Test a range of reports with different complexities. We suggest low, medium, and high based on the number of visuals and the duration of queries. There is no absolute number here; it will vary by organization. Your tests should involve different combinations of sequential and parallel report runs.

- Create different users with different RLS permissions and run the tests under their context.

- Schedule or run on-demand refreshes during tests. The tool does not support this, so you can do this as usual in the Power BI web portal. This will generate background activity that can be reviewed in the metrics app. It's a good idea to run refreshes individually when the capacity is not loaded, then in parallel with other refreshes and report activity. You can compare the parallel results to the single run best case to see if a busier capacity can still complete refreshes in a reasonable time.

- Remember to consider load from other services, such as dataflows and paginated reports. While the tool does not support this, you can run dataflow refreshes or data-driven paginated report subscriptions in the Power BI web portal or use APIs during testing.

Next, we will introduce the capacity metrics app and learn how to use it to identify and diagnose capacity load issues.

Monitoring capacity resource usage and overload

Power BI allows a capacity administrator to configure customized notifications for each capacity. These are available in the capacity settings and allow you to set thresholds that will trigger email alerts. We recommend configuring the items shown in the following screenshot to be proactively notified when problematic conditions are met:

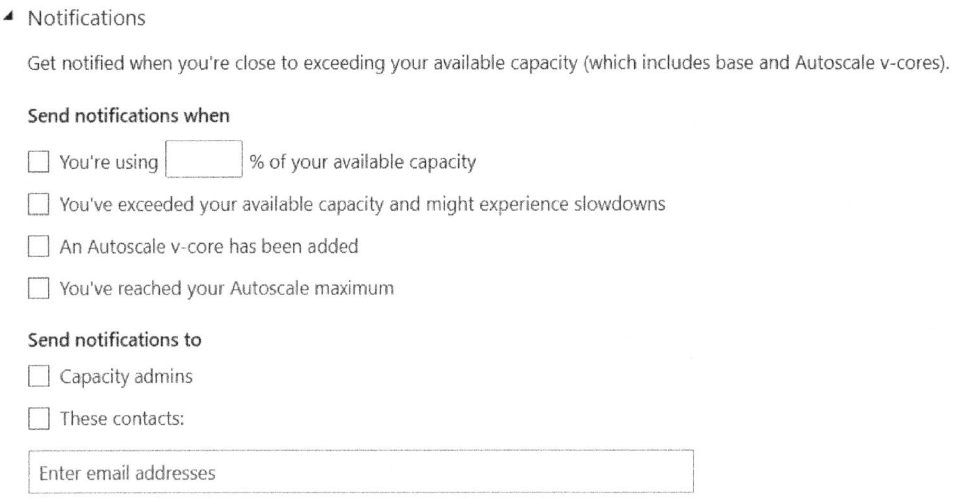

◢ Notifications

Get notified when you're close to exceeding your available capacity (which includes base and Autoscale v-cores).

Send notifications when

☐ You're using [   ] % of your available capacity

☐ You've exceeded your available capacity and might experience slowdowns

☐ An Autoscale v-core has been added

☐ You've reached your Autoscale maximum

Send notifications to

☐ Capacity admins

☐ These contacts:

[Enter email addresses   ]

Figure 13.7 – Capacity notification settings

We suggest configuring the first notification so that it's around 85%. This will help you identify load peaks before they become a problem. This gives you time to plan for an increased capacity scale or identify content that could be optimized to reduce load. The rest of the checkboxes in the preceding screenshot are self-explanatory.

All your planning is not worth much if you cannot examine the effect that organic growth, design choices, and user behavior have on the capacity. You will need a way to determine load issues at a high level, then investigate deeper at varying levels of granularity. Microsoft provides a template app called **Premium Capacity Utilization and Metrics** that can help with this. It is not built into the service and must be manually installed from the AppSource portal. You can access it directly here, though note that you must be a capacity admin to install it: `https://appsource.microsoft.com/en-us/product/power-bi/pbi_pcmm.pbipremiumcapacitymonitoringreport`.

Currently, the app contains 14 days of near-real-time data and allows you to drill down to the artifact and operation levels. An obvious example of an artifact is a dataset, and the operations that are performed on it could be data refreshes or queries.

The official documentation describes each page and visual of the report sequentially and in detail. We will not repeat this, but we will illustrate how to use the report to investigate a few scenarios. We performed our testing on a one-core EM1. This size was selected because it is small enough to be overloaded from a single eight-core client machine. After uploading some datasets, we performed the following tests over a few hours:

1. Between 5 A.M. and 5:30 A.M., we opened and interacted with reports manually.

2. Between 7 A.M. and 7:45 A.M., we ran continuous load tests on the capacity *without* Autoscale. The testing tool was configured to load 12 parallel browsers. Two of those browsers ran a report with an expensive query that takes about 15 seconds to complete under ideal conditions. We also performed some manual refreshes in the background. We noticed that, over time, the reports started taking longer and longer to load.

3. At around 10 A.M., we added one Autoscale core and generated some more load.

4. At around 10:30 A.M., we increased the Autoscale limit to 4 and generated a more intense load by executing 16 browsers in parallel, with four complex reports. Data refreshes were also performed manually.

5. Before 11 A.M., we decreased the level of activity by stopping the browsers that were running complex reports.

Now, let's look at the capacity metrics report to trace the activity. We want to see if we can identify where we experienced load, interactive delay mode, and how Autoscale worked.

The following screenshot shows the overview page of the metrics app. We have highlighted some interesting areas here, all of which have been numbered and will be described shortly:

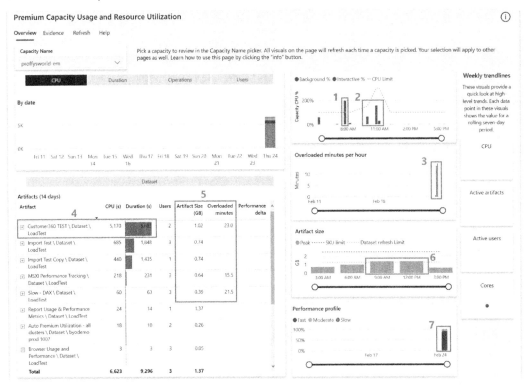

Figure 13.8 – The Overview page of Capacity Metrics

Before we review the numbered items in the preceding screenshot, we would like to provide some initial guidance about our example:

- We only provisioned the capacity before testing to limit costs. Thus, we only have data for a day, which explains why the CPU chart at the top left is mostly empty. This is broken down by artifact, and it is worth noting that we do see one artifact that seems to use a lot of the CPU in proportion to others. This chart can be switched using the buttons above it, to show different metrics.

- The weekly trend sparklines on the right-hand side of the report are empty for the same reason as mentioned previously.

- Since we do not have historical activity, no **Performance Delta** is available. This is a relative score with negative values, which means that the performance of the artifact is degrading over time and should be investigated via the **Artifact Detail** page shown in *Figure 13.12*. Rows with negative performance delta scores will be shaded in orange to make them more obvious.

- The report has a **Help** link in the top navigation area, which will open a detailed guidance page in the same report. Help pages have been included for each report page.

- The report has also implemented visual help tooltips, so you can hover over the question mark icon near the top right of the visual to get contextual help. This can be seen in the following screenshot, which is the help for the **Artifacts (14 days)** visual at the bottom left of the report:

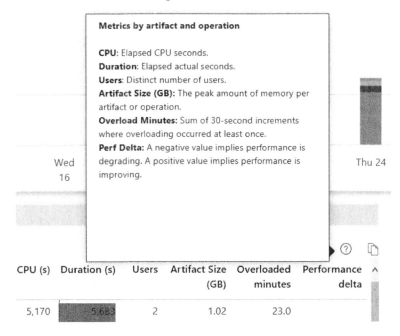

Figure 13.9 – Example of a visual help tooltip

Now let's review the numbered items shown in *Figure 13.8*. We will explore each of these areas in more detail:

1. In the CPU capacity trend chart, we can see that we exceeded our 100% capacity threshold (dotted line) after 7 A.M, which corresponds to the extra load we generated. This could explain the gradual slowdown in report performance we observed.

2. These two clumps of activity represent the lessened load and the extra high load we generated after scaling to one and then four extra v-cores.

3. Here, it looks like we had 2 hours recently where we experienced an overload. We can click these bars to cross filter the table on the left to see which artifacts were being used during that hour.

4. This visual provides useful information as we can see the impact each artifact has on resources and users. Here, we can see that one dataset, called **Customer360 TEST**, is taking up the majority of the CPU. You can drill into the operations here for more context.

5. You should regularly review the **Artifact Size** and **Overloaded Minutes** metrics. This gives you a snapshot of the largest artifacts and which ones are experiencing the most overload. In our case, with the EM1 capacity, the maximum memory that's available to a dataset is 3 GB, so we know that the dataset can be hosted successfully. We may need to perform some actions when the size approaches the capacity limit. Remember that the memory footprint of a dataset includes the refreshes and memory that's been used by queries. If the dataset is approaching the capacity limit, we may not be leaving enough memory available to avoid overloads.

6. This visual shows the peak memory that's used across all the dataset artifacts in 3-hour periods. Here, we can see that we hit our parallel refresh limit for two of those periods. In such cases, we should investigate which refreshes occurred and if there were overlaps that delayed any refreshes enough to impact business.

7. This visual groups operations into **Fast (< 100 ms)**, **Moderate (100 ms to 2 s)**, and **Slow (>2 s)**. We would like to see as little slow activity as possible, and the trend should be constant or decreasing. If it is increasing, you should explore the data to see if specific artifacts are contributing to the trend or if natural content growth and users are the culprits.

Now that we have gained initial insights, let's explore the data in more detail to determine which artifacts and operations contributed to the visualizations that were highlighted in *Figure 13.8*.

Investigating overload

The first thing we can do is get more granularity from the top two charts on the **overview** page. We drilled down on February 24 in the left CPU visual, which breaks this into an hourly view. It also automatically drills into the right visual to show CPU usage at 30-second granularity, which aligns with the evaluation cycles we discussed earlier.

The results are shown in the following figure. Note that we rearranged the charts here for better visibility. We hovered over one of the tall bars going beyond 100% between 7 A.M. and 8 A.M. while we had only one core assigned to show you how much extra capacity was needed in that cycle. You can also see where we increased capacity by one core and then four cores, taking the total available up to 150%. Finally, you can see how the extra load we generated at the end of the tests required more than 150% for a short period:

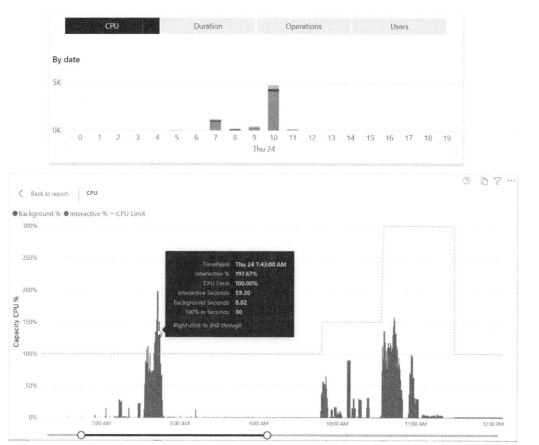

Figure 13.10 – Drilling down to 30-second granularity and highlighting the overload

> **Important Note**
>
> You would expect adding one core to an EM1 capacity would double the available CPU power to 200%. However, you will notice that adding an extra core takes us to 150% while adding four extra cores takes us to 300%. This is because Autoscale cores are split equally between backend and frontend processing. When you add one core to an EM1, you are adding only 50% more *backend* CPU power, which is where all the capacity metrics are derived.

Next, we clicked on the bar highlighted in the preceding figure to cross-filter the report and see which artifacts contributed to the activity in that overloaded window. We expanded the artifact view to show the operations for the two most expensive items, as shown in the following screenshot:

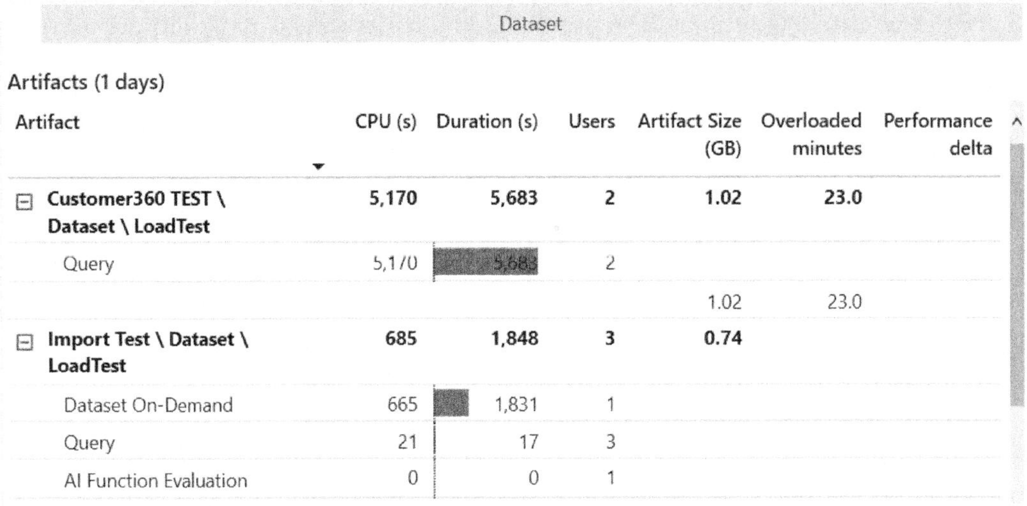

Dataset						

Artifacts (1 days)

Artifact	CPU (s)	Duration (s)	Users	Artifact Size (GB)	Overloaded minutes	Performance delta
⊟ **Customer360 TEST \ Dataset \ LoadTest**	5,170	5,683	2	1.02	23.0	
Query	5,170	5,68	2			
				1.02	23.0	
⊟ **Import Test \ Dataset \ LoadTest**	685	1,848	3	0.74		
Dataset On-Demand	665	1,831	1			
Query	21	17	3			
AI Function Evaluation	0	0	1			

Figure 13.11 – Artifact and operation details

From the path structure shown on the left, we can see that both artifacts are datasets in the **LoadTest** workspace. We can see that the first dataset only served queries and experienced an overload. The second had other operations too and had a much lower CPU impact.

Next, we right-clicked the **Customer360 TEST** dataset and drilled to a page called **Artifact Detail**, as shown in the following screenshot. This page helps you spot unusual spikes in activity and trends in activity. Spikes should be investigated using other drills, which we will introduce shortly.

The following screenshot shows us hourly breakdowns for this dataset by different metrics and operations. You should check if there is any correlation in increased activity at any hour. The goal is to work out whether the increase was due to more users than usual, other activity on the capacity in that period, or another change, such as more data or updated reports/datasets:

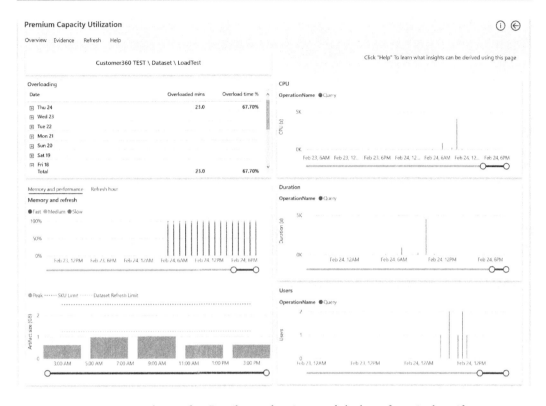

Figure 13.12 – The Artifact Detail page showing trends by hour for a single artifact

Now, let's go ahead and investigate our busy periods in more detail. To do this, we will return to the overview, right-click the 7:43 A.M. spike in the **Capacity CPU %** chart, and select the **TimePoint Detail** drill, as shown in the following screenshot:

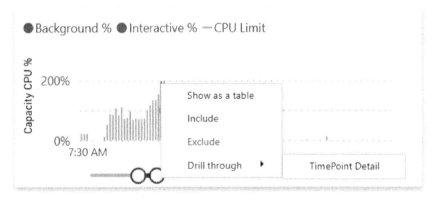

Figure 13.13 – Drilling to the Timepoint Detail page

The **TimePoint Detail** page reveals useful granular information, as shown in the following screenshot. It displays about an hour of capacity activity with the selected time point in the middle, shown as a vertical red bar. Observe that **Interactive Operations** are separated from **Background Operations**. The interactive operations are scoped to the hour, while the background operations are from the previous 24 hours since they all contribute to load. The **% of Capacity** metric tells us what proportion of the total capacity was used by the operation. We can also see how long it took and if any interactive delay was added, listed as **Throttling (s)** in the report.

At this point in our analysis, we would expect some collaboration between capacity admins and content owners to determine if the throttling is impacting users and to what extent. If users are impacted and we saw that the background operations contributed a lot, we could look at the scheduling refreshes at different times to lessen the total smoothed background activity and reduce the chance of an overload occurring. In our case, the background activity is minimal, so we could consider content optimization and/or scaling:

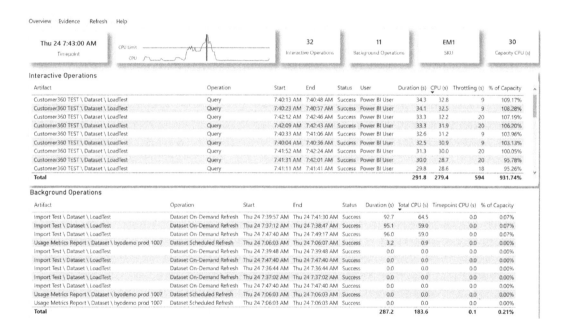

Figure 13.14 – Timepoint Detail for the 7:43 A.M. evaluation cycle

Next, we will investigate the **Evidence** page, as shown in the following screenshot. This page is scoped to overloaded artifacts and only shows data if an overload has occurred. This page offers an **Overloading score** per artifact. You will notice in our example that the top three artifacts all experienced overloaded minutes in the same range of around 15 to 23 minutes. However, notice that the **Overloading** score for **Customer360 TEST** is about 200,000 compared to only a few hundred for the other two. The absolute value of the score is meaningless. It is computed by considering how frequently the artifact contributed to overloads and how severe the load was. You should tackle the artifacts with the highest relative score first. In our case, since we saw so much query activity on this dataset and cannot change the background load, we could consider moving the dataset to a different capacity or scaling up:

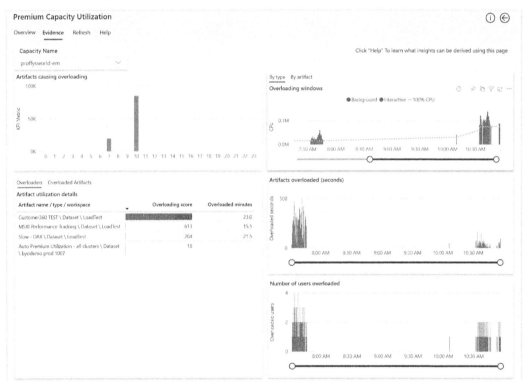

Figure 13.15 – The Evidence page focusing on the artifacts involved in the overload

The only remaining page to consider is the **Refresh** page, as shown in the following screenshot. It can be reached by drilling from an artifact in a visual, or by accessing it directly from the navigation links. In the latter case, it will cover all artifacts, which is what we will show in the example that follows. You can use this page to understand refresh load by day or hour by artifact.

We suggest using the **Duration (s)** and **Ratio** metrics from the table to work out the best candidates for further investigation. You want to optimize the longest-running refreshes that have the highest ratio, which is the CPU used divided by the duration. Optimizing here can mean improving the performance of the M queries and/or changing schedules or capacities:

Figure 13.16 – The Refresh page showing trends and individual details of each refresh

We will conclude this section by looking at the 10:00 A.M period onwards when we had one and then four Autoscale cores available. Even with Autoscale, we did experience some overload initially. This can be seen in the following screenshot, where it's represented by the second bar in the **Overloaded minutes per hour** visual. We will use the **Timepoint Detail** page to make some observations on capacity behavior and tie it back to the tests we performed

The following screenshot includes a tooltip that shows that we had about **153%** usage in the **10:44:00 AM** cycle. Here, we can see that some queries did experience throttling but notice how the numbers are all around 8 or 9 seconds. Compare this to *Figure 13.14*, where we had delays of 20 seconds for the same dataset. Let's explain what is happening here. Before 10.44 A.M., we can see an increase in activity. As we reached the total 150% CPU that's available with the extra core, the system injected some delays while it was allocating more cores. This is because the available cores are not used until they need to help with overloads:

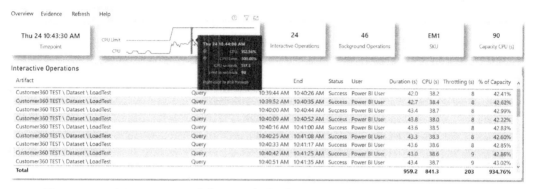

Figure 13.17 – Timepoint Detail showing the load pattern with one Autoscale v-core active

Now, we will look at a slightly later period. We will focus on the **10:56:30 AM** time point in the following screenshot. Observe that the same queries are no longer throttled. Even though the generated load was less than 100% here, we would not expect any throttling:

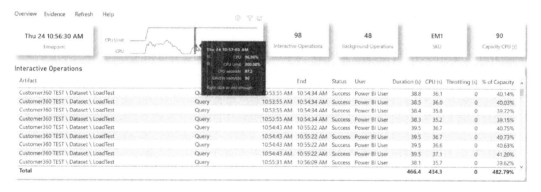

Figure 13.18 – Timepoint Detail showing the load pattern with four Autoscale v-cores active

We are almost ready to review what we've investigated and the actions to take when using the capacity metrics app.

Important Note

The actions that we will describe here assume that the architecture, datasets, RLS, data transformations, and reports have already been optimized. All too often, people choose to increase capacity to solve performance issues. This incurs cost and should not be the first choice unless you are confident that your content cannot be improved much. It is reasonable to scale temporarily to unblock users while working on performance improvements in parallel. Another argument against always scaling first is that it does not promote recommended design practices and performance governance.

If you suspect that you need to optimize content, we recommend focusing on the most popular datasets and reports that have the worst performance relative to others in the capacity. This reduces the CPU and memory load and frees up more capacity. Also, improve the longest-running refreshes that have a high proportion of background CPU usage. The guidance that was provided in the previous chapters can help you here.

Let's summarize this section with some guidance on the steps you should take when you see overloads in a report:

1. Begin by identifying the largest artifacts that contribute to overloading, with an emphasis on those that are used by a higher proportion of users.

2. Look at the trends for the artifacts to see if this problem is isolated or periodic. Also, check if there is a visible increase in activity, users, or overloaded minutes over time. Gradual uptrends are an indication of organic growth, which could lead to a decision to scale up or out.

3. Investigate the periods of high load to see what other activity is occurring on the capacity. You may be able to identify interactive usage peaks in the same periods across different datasets. You could move some busy artifacts to a capacity with more available resources or choose to increase the capacity's size or enable Autoscale.

> **Note**
>
> Embedded A SKUs are PaaS services that are purchased and billed through Azure. They support native integration with Azure Log Analytics. This integration is an alternate source of capacity activity and provides near-real-time traces and metrics, such as those available from Log Analytics for Azure Analysis Services. The Embedded Gen2 version has been modernized and contains more data points, but there is no associated reporting, and you will bear the Azure costs and maintenance effort. You can find out more about setting this up here: `https://docs.microsoft.com/power-bi/ developer/embedded/monitor-power-bi-embedded-reference`.

Now, let's summarize what we've learned in this chapter.

Summary

In this chapter, we have come closer to the end of our journey of performance optimization in Power BI. We focused on reserved capacities that are available as Power BI Premium and Embedded offerings. We learned that you could purchase and license the offerings differently, but that they share most functionality across SKUs. This means that the same performance optimization guidance applies to capacities consistently.

We introduced Power BI Premium and covered the unique features it offers that help with performance and scaling large datasets. Then, we introduced Gen2, which is the latest and now default offering from Microsoft. Since Gen2 is *Generally Available*, we did not cover the previous generation due to huge improvements in design and reduced maintenance. After that, we took a brief look at capacity settings such as query timeouts and refresh intervals, which you can use to prevent expensive operations from severely affecting the capacity.

Then, we discussed how Gen2 has a different model for evaluating capacity load and how the memory limits have changed to provide better scalability, especially with data refresh. This included learning how a capacity can delay requests in an overloaded state.

For overload situations, we suggested that Autoscale would be a great option to avoid capacity resource starvation, while not having to pay for extra capacity upfront. You learned how the capacity gauges load in 30-second evaluation cycles. These cycles look at the sum of activity from all the operations in that period to determine if an overload has occurred. An overload occurs when the CPU time that's required by the operations in the 30-second window is more than the allocated v-cores can support.

Next, we looked at capacity planning and showed you how to determine the initial capacity size using estimates regarding the dataset's size, refresh frequency, and other metrics. We introduced the load testing suites based on PowerShell that Microsoft publishes, including limitations and caveats. We showed how to use these tools to simulate continuous maximum load with many reports being open at once. We also described how to use the testing tool to simulate more realistic scenarios involving slicers, filters, page changes, and bookmark usage.

We concluded this chapter by learning about monitoring capacities. First, we introduced the alerting settings you can use to notify administrators when the capacity reaches the resource thresholds, Autoscale cores are assigned, or when they reach the maximum. Then, we described how to provision a small EM1 capacity to perform load testing and how to generate the load over a few hours. We introduced the Premium Capacity Metrics and Utilization app and showed how it can be used to identify high-level capacity overload issues and which artifacts and operations contributed. We also showed how to interact and drill to get a lot of useful information about artifact behavior and the impact of overloads.

After that, we suggested how to approach capacity scaling and optimization and stressed that underperforming solutions should be carefully reviewed and optimized for performance instead of always relying on scaling up or out. Forcing this governance is the point of this book, and it can improve your solution's quality in general. However, something that's more important for some organizations is that it can also save you money by only scaling when necessary. The main point was to look for patterns such as trends and periodicity and work out what else was happening on the capacity in that period to figure out which workload, artifact, and operations contributed most.

In the next and final chapter of this book, we will learn how to optimize the process of embedding Power BI content in custom web applications.

14
Embedding in Applications

In the previous chapter, we had a close look at reserved capacities in Power BI, which are sold under the Power BI Premium and Embedded product lines. We learned about the additional features they offer, focusing on those that help with scalability and performance. We also learned how capacities manage resource usage and overload, as well as how to monitor, optimize, and scale.

In this chapter, we will learn how to optimize for embedding, a capability that extends the reach of Power BI. This allows developers to use Power BI APIs to embed reports, dashboards, or tiles into their custom applications. There are many possible uses of this, with popular choices being serving analytical content within company intranets, public-facing websites, or even commercial applications.

Embedding is technically possible with any Power BI capacity, so you don't need to buy Premium or Embedded to try it. However, for this to work properly at scale, you need to purchase reserved capacity to get around the limits of shared capacities, such as a limited number of embed tokens. Hence, the material in this chapter is relevant to the Premium and Embedded capacities. We will not cover Publish to Web, which is intended for mass distribution and behaves differently.

We will discuss what embedding involves, why there are special considerations, and how to make sure that Power BI content is loaded into the external application as quickly as possible. We will also learn how to monitor Embedded content to identify areas that are slowing you down.

In this chapter, we will cover the following topics:

- Improving Embedded performance
- Measuring Embedded performance

Improving Embedded performance

Embedding content in external applications gives organizations more flexibility in how they deploy and consume Power BI. There are different deployment, cost, and licensing considerations that will affect which type of capacity you purchase. Microsoft effectively provides reserved capacity offerings that are catered primarily to externally sharing content versus internally sharing content. However, the Embedded functionality and mechanisms that are used to surface and optimize the content are the same. Hence, the advice that will be provided in this chapter can be considered as generally applicable. If you would like to learn more about embedding licensing and distribution models and which capacity type is best for you, please check out the following documentation: `https://docs.microsoft.com/power-bi/developer/embedded/embedded-faq`.

Embedding content using APIs is an alternate way to expose content where you don't use Power BI's web frontend. This can be seen in the following diagram:

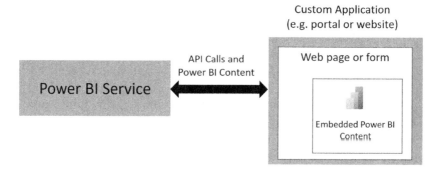

Figure 14.1 – Embedding Power BI content in other applications

In this configuration, users are interacting with the external application and not directly on `powerbi.com`. Once the content has been initialized within the external application, performance is not affected by that application, unless it is also competing for CPU on the client.

> **Note**
>
> When you're embedding content, you should optimize it the same way as you would any other Power BI content. Follow all the guidance we have provided around data modeling, loading, report design, and so on. It is also important to perform capacity planning and sizing using the methods described in the previous chapter.
>
> However, there are additional considerations regarding how the application is configured with Power BI and how it interacts with Power BI Service. Next, we will learn why embedding is different and how we can speed it up.

When we embed Power BI content in another application, we are adding another layer of processing and latency. When we view a report on the Power BI website, under most conditions, the Power BI application is already bootstrapped. This means that the core application code and dependencies have already been loaded. However, when we load Power BI on-demand within our applications, this may not be the case. There may also be some overhead and latency between your application and the Power BI services. This includes time taken by your application before it even calls Power BI, where users can see other content already. This has the effect of exaggerating the delayed experience of loading Power BI content. Therefore, the advice we will give focuses on minimizing the embedding overhead.

The following list provides guidance and rationale for optimizing Embedded scenarios:

- **Consider Application Location and Architecture**: The bi-directional arrow shown in the preceding diagram represents communications and data transfer between Power BI and your custom application. You should minimize communication latency by placing the custom applications as close to the Power BI home region as possible. This includes ensuring the number of network hops is minimized and sufficient bandwidth is available between Power BI and the custom app. Do keep in mind that visuals are executed on the client side, so if you have users in different geographic locations, some may have a different performance experience for the same content.

- **Keep SDK Packages and Tools up to Date**: The Power BI team regularly updates both client tools and services, as frequently as monthly. These updates often contain new features, but they do contain performance improvements as well. When you deploy an application with Embedded content, it's easy to continue updating the content without looking at the embedding mechanisms. To avoid missing out on embedding improvements, we recommend using the latest **SDK**, API versions, and authoring tools, such as Power BI Desktop. The SDK can be found at `https://www.nuget.org/packages/Microsoft.PowerBI.Api`, while the client libraries for embedding can be found at `https://docs.microsoft.com/javascript/api/overview/powerbi`.

- **Preload Dependencies**: The Power BI Embedded API provides a method called `powerbi.preload` that allows you to load core Power BI dependencies on demand. This is useful when you have a custom application that does not display Power BI content immediately to users. If you know your users are likely to eventually reach Power BI content, you can improve the first load experience. You can do this by calling `powerbi.preload` when you initialize the application, but before your users reach areas that display Power BI content. This will load JavaScript files, CSS stylesheets, and any other artifacts and cache them locally. When the application needs to show Power BI content, it can avoid fetching the dependencies first. Additional information about preloading can be found here: `https://docs.microsoft.com/javascript/api/overview/powerbi/preload`.

> **Note**
>
> Use preload only when the Power BI content is on a different page of the application. It is best to bootstrap the iFrame when possible, as described in the next point.

- **Bootstrap the iFrame**: Embedding uses an HTML construct called an **iFrame** to host Power BI's content. An iFrame is used to embed one HTML document within another and is typically used to expose external content that's served from a different web location or server. For example, you could use it to embed the Google search home page into a section of your website.

When you embed content using `powerbi.embed`, you need a report identifier, an embed URL, and an access token. Not all of these are immediately available, depending on the application's design and user journey. When you call the `powerbi.embed` method, the iFrame is prepared and initialized before the content loads. However, it is possible to perform this initialization earlier using `powerbi.bootstrap(element, config)`. You must provide it with an HTML element and an Embedded configuration object as parameters. When all the required parameters are ready, you can call `powerbi.embed`, passing in the same HTML element that has been already initialized. This is a great way to prepare for Power BI content to be displayed in the background while the user is doing something else in the application. Depending on the application's architecture and configuration, this can save some precious seconds, making a big difference to the user experience.

- **Use Embed Parameters Effectively**: The second parameter in `powerbi.embed(element, config)` allows you to set options that control what features are enabled in the Embedded content. The properties of the configuration object that affect performance are as follows:

  - **EmbedURL**: This property is the URL of the content you are embedding and is assigned to the `src` attribute of the iFrame. Avoid generating this URL yourself. You can obtain the best URL from the service using the Get reports, Get dashboards, or Get tiles APIs.

  - **Permissions**: This property determines which operations you grant the person viewing the content. Use the `Read` permission if the user does not need to create content or copy or edit the report. This avoids initializing UI components that are not needed. Similarly, only set the minimum permission level that's needed if they require editing rights.

  - **Slicers, filters, and bookmarks**: These are separate properties in the configuration that allow you to set the context for the content. By design, Power BI tries to cache visuals to speed up report content while queries are executed in the background. This cached result considers the report's context set by slicers, plus more. However, if you are embedding and supplying this context via the code, the cache is not used. Therefore, if you have a default starting context for an Embedded report, you should publish the report with that context already set. Then, you can call the `embed` method without context to take advantage of the cache.

- **Change Reports Efficiently**: A custom application allows you to build interesting functionality, such as a custom navigation UI that controls which Power BI reports a user sees. A user could simply click a button or a link to replace the current report, without reloading the page. If you implement something like this, ensure that you reuse the iFrame. When you call `powerbi.embed`, use a different configuration but pass it the same HTML element.

- **Use a Custom UI to Reduce Slicer Complexity**: You can reduce the complexity of reports by removing slicer visuals from the report canvas and setting them in the Embedded report configuration object described earlier in this list. This lets you capture a lot of different slicer and filter selections and pass them all at once while you're loading the initial Embedded report.

- **Throttle the Custom Application to Prevent Misuse**: Users can double-click custom report links or navigate between reports in the custom app very quickly, causing many calls to be issued to Power BI's backend. You can limit this kind of behavior in your application by setting a short duration within which to ignore a user action that occurs too soon after the last one. A good rule of thumb here is about 100 ms.

- **Handling Multiple Visuals**: Many reports contain more than just visuals. You can embed a page containing multiple visuals as it was designed within a single iFrame. However, you may need to combine embed multiple reports or even individual tiles in your custom application, interspersed with other content. If you Embedded each one separately, each would need an iFrame. Initializing an iFrame is relatively expensive, so you should try to have as few as possible. Here are some options:

  - **Consolidate reports**: If possible, consolidate data and visuals from separate datasets and reports. This will allow you to embed the content in one iFrame.

  - **Use a dashboard to combine disparate content**: A Power BI dashboard is designed to contain report tiles from different reports and datasets that have no technical relationship with one another. If you need to embed tiles from different reports into your application, consider putting them in a dashboard and embedding it instead of all the individual tiles. This reduces the load to a single iFrame. You can also embed individual tiles from dashboards instead of reports. These are more efficient than report tiles and will load faster. Consider this option when you do not want all the tiles appearing together in your application and you don't want to use multiple iFrames.

- **Use a Custom Layout**: The Embedded config has a `layoutType` property that can be set to `customLayout`. The latter allows you to define a page's size and visual layout, which will override the defaults. It even allows you to hide visuals you don't want to see. It is also useful to rearrange visuals so that they can be viewed on mobile devices. More information on setting a custom layout can be found here: `https://docs.microsoft.com/javascript/api/overview/powerbi/custom-layout`.

Now that we know how to optimize embedding scenarios, let's learn how to gauge embedding performance.

Measuring Embedded performance

When you embed Power BI content in your applications, it is recommended that you measure the embedding activity to understand the performance profile. The methods we have described in this book can help you measure and resolve the performance of the Power BI artifacts themselves, but they do not tell you what is happening in your application and if there is any inefficiency when it is communicating with Power BI and loading content. For example, the Embedded Power BI report may execute queries and render visuals within 2 seconds, but the user experiences a longer total wait time due to the embedding overhead. Before we learn how to measure the embedding overhead, we will introduce a recommended practice.

> **Important Note**
>
> When you're performance tuning your Embedded content, it is very important to obtain a baseline of performance *without* embedding. This will help you set the appropriate range for the best case in performance, as well as help you identify any issues unrelated to embedding. You can optimize their datasets, DAX, and so on, independently and in parallel to the embedding optimization. Just be sure to optimize the embedding code in your web application using the same Power BI content all the time. This way, you can ensure that any improvements are from the embedding changes, and not from Power BI content changes.

When you embed Power BI content, the system generates events to help you track and optimize embedding behavior. To learn more about capturing Embedded events, please see the following documentation: `https://docs.microsoft.com/javascript/api/overview/powerbi/handle-events`.

Next, we will describe the relevant events and how they can help with performance tuning:

- **Loaded**: This event fires when a Power BI report or dashboard has been initialized. Loading is complete when the Power BI logo shown in the following screenshot is no longer shown:

Loading your report...

Figure 14.2 – The Power BI logo and progress bar that's shown when a report has been initialized

- **Rendered**: This event is raised after the report visuals have completed any work and displayed their results on the screen.

- **VisualRendered**: This event is fired for every visual. It is not enabled by default and needs to be enabled by setting `visualRenderedEvents` to true in the embedding's configuration. This allows you to track the speed of each visual, as well as rank the visuals and focus on the slowest ones. This information can also be gained from Desktop Performance Analyzer and is a good way to compare the performance of content that's deployed to production versus in development.

Now, let's learn how to use events to understand where delays are occurring. We suggest using a combination of the Power BI events we described in the previous list, plus the events that you manually generate in the custom application. This will give you a complete picture of all activities. The following diagram shows a timeline representation of a user action in a custom application. In this example, we assume that a user has clicked a button in the custom web application (not a Power BI report), which makes the calls to load a Power BI report that contains two visuals:

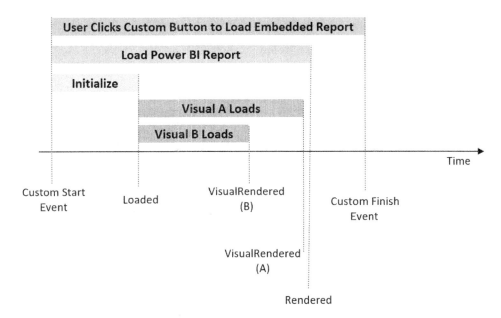

Figure 14.3 – Timeline of embedded activity and event generation

The preceding diagram shows a **Custom Start Event** and a **Custom Finish Event**. These represent the entire user action from the time they clicked the custom button to the time the custom web app finished its work. There may be other work besides loading the Power report, which is why we have included a gap between the **Rendered** event and **Custom Finish Event**.

Once you have captured these events, you can subtract the timestamps to work out the duration of any component. Then, you can compare this to the results of the service, as well as in Performance Analyzer, to see if there is a substantial difference.

Now, let's summarize what we've learned in this chapter.

Summary

In this chapter, we concluded our Power BI optimization journey by learning how to embed content efficiently. We learned that reserved capacities that are sold under the Premium and Embedded product lines allow developers to embed content in external applications. This allows them to build their own user experience that's been enhanced by analytical content from Power BI. When they do this, they avoid using the Power BI user interface, and users access reports through the custom application. We learned that it is important to plan for and optimize Embedded capacities and the content they host per all the guidance provided earlier in this book.

Then, we learned that embedding involves communication between Power BI Service and the custom application via APIs. The Embedded SDK allows developers to authenticate against Power BI, load the Power BI base application code, and then place reports, dashboards, or tiles inside the custom application. This adds some overhead, which can be very noticeable if there is significant latency between the application and Power BI. However, we have highlighted that you can – and should – optimize your Power BI content separately to the embedding mechanisms. Ideally, this should have already been done so that you can focus on performance tuning.

We also learned that it is important to use the latest tools and SDKs when embedding to take advantage of the performance improvements that have been made by Microsoft. We also introduced the API methods that are provided by Microsoft that can be used to load or initialize Power components ahead of time. This reduces the initial load time for Power BI content by having dependent assets such as JavaScript and CSS files loaded before the user needs to view Power BI content. We also looked at configuration settings such as minimal permissions, which can speed up content by only loading the necessary UI components.

After that, we learned that when a custom application needs to load Embedded Power content, it does so in an iFrame. We discussed how every separate piece of Embedded content uses an iFrame and that it is important to minimize how many iFrames are used to reduce initialization overhead. Here, we suggested consolidating content into fewer reports or using dashboards and individual tilers, which can load faster.

Finally, we learned how to measure the performance of Embedded code. We introduced the concept of events and suggested that you use both custom events and the ones provided by Microsoft to build up a full picture. This allows you to understand the duration of the entire operation from the user's perspective and break out report initialization, overall rendering, and the duration of individual visuals.

Final Thoughts

Congratulations! You have completed your Power BI optimization journey and should be ready to tailor and apply what you've learned to your work. We will close with a reminder that performance management should be a discipline that is ingrained into every stage of your development life cycle. You can achieve great results and maintain good designs with a bit of planning and strong collaboration between stakeholders with different roles and skillsets.

Index

T

Table object 139
Tabular Editor
  about 101
  Advanced Scripting
      functionality 102, 104
  Best Practice Analyzer (BPA) 102
  download link 101
Tabular Model Scripting
    Language (TMSL) 217
Tabular Object Model (TOM) 217
throttling 245
TMSL script 134
tolerable wait time (TWT) 5
tooltip 166

U

Universally Unique Identifier (UUID) 43
unused columns
  identifying 100
usage metrics dataset
  dimensions 57
  model measures 57
  report load times 58
  report page views 58
  report rank 58
  report views 58
  workspace reports 58
  workspace views 58
usage metrics report customization
  about 55
  granular performance data, viewing 61
  performance metrics, collecting
      from multiple workspaces 66
  raw data, accessing via Analyze
      in Excel 60, 61

raw data, accessing via editable copy 56
raw data, accessing with custom
    usage metrics report 59
report performance metrics,
    analyzing 62-65
usage metrics, filtering 55
user principal names (UPNs) 58
user scale
  Azure Analysis Services
      (AAS), leveraging 214

V

value encoding 186
VertiPaq Analyzer
  about 107
  model size, analyzing 107-109
virtual cores (v-cores) 239
virtual machine (VM) 22, 85
virtual private networks (VPNs) 85
visual-related design patterns 162-167
visuals
  associated queries 164, 165
  controlling 161

W

What You See is What You Get
    (WYSIWYG) 160
Working Set 134

X

XMLA endpoint
  about 134
  using, for Analysis Services
      server traces 67
xVelocity 16

Packt.com

Subscribe to our online digital library for full access to over 7,000 books and videos, as well as industry leading tools to help you plan your personal development and advance your career. For more information, please visit our website.

Why subscribe?

- Spend less time learning and more time coding with practical eBooks and Videos from over 4,000 industry professionals

- Improve your learning with Skill Plans built especially for you

- Get a free eBook or video every month

- Fully searchable for easy access to vital information

- Copy and paste, print, and bookmark content

Did you know that Packt offers eBook versions of every book published, with PDF and ePub files available? You can upgrade to the eBook version at packt.com and as a print book customer, you are entitled to a discount on the eBook copy. Get in touch with us at customercare@packtpub.com for more details.

At www.packt.com, you can also read a collection of free technical articles, sign up for a range of free newsletters, and receive exclusive discounts and offers on Packt books and eBooks.

Other Books You May Enjoy

If you enjoyed this book, you may be interested in these other books by Packt:

Extending Power BI with Python and RFrank

Luca Zavarella

ISBN: 978-1-80107-820-7

- Discover best practices for using Python and R in Power BI products
- Use Python and R to perform complex data manipulations in Power BI
- Apply data anonymization and data pseudonymization in Power BI
- Log data and load large datasets in Power BI using Python and R
- Enrich your Power BI dashboards using external APIs and machine learning models
- Extract insights from your data using linear optimization and other algorithms
- Handle outliers and missing values for multivariate and time-series data
- Create any visualization, as complex as you want, using R scripts

Learn Power BI - Second Edition

Greg Deckler

ISBN: 978-1-80181-195-8

- Get up and running quickly with Power BI
- Understand and plan your business intelligence projects
- Connect to and transform data using Power Query
- Create data models optimized for analysis and reporting
- Perform simple and complex DAX calculations to enhance analysis
- Discover business insights and create professional reports
- Collaborate via Power BI dashboards, apps, goals, and scorecards
- Deploy and govern Power BI, including using deployment pipelines

Packt is searching for authors like you

If you're interested in becoming an author for Packt, please visit `authors.packtpub.com` and apply today. We have worked with thousands of developers and tech professionals, just like you, to help them share their insight with the global tech community. You can make a general application, apply for a specific hot topic that we are recruiting an author for, or submit your own idea.

Share Your Thoughts

Now you've finished *Microsoft Power BI Performance Best Practices*, we'd love to hear your thoughts! Scan the QR code below to go straight to the Amazon review page for this book and share your feedback or leave a review on the site that you purchased it from.

`https://packt.link/r/1-801-07644-8`

Your review is important to us and the tech community and will help us make sure we're delivering excellent quality content.